C-1683 CAREER EXAMINATION SERIES

This is your
PASSBOOK for...

Management Assistant

Test Preparation Study Guide
Questions & Answers

NLC

NATIONAL LEARNING CORPORATION®

COPYRIGHT NOTICE

This book is SOLELY intended for, is sold ONLY to, and its use is RESTRICTED to individual, bona fide applicants or candidates who qualify by virtue of having seriously filed applications for appropriate license, certificate, professional and/or promotional advancement, higher school matriculation, scholarship, or other legitimate requirements of education and/or governmental authorities.

This book is NOT intended for use, class instruction, tutoring, training, duplication, copying, reprinting, excerption, or adaptation, etc., by:

1) Other publishers
2) Proprietors and/or Instructors of "Coaching" and/or Preparatory Courses
3) Personnel and/or Training Divisions of commercial, industrial, and governmental organizations
4) Schools, colleges, or universities and/or their departments and staffs, including teachers and other personnel
5) Testing Agencies or Bureaus
6) Study groups which seek by the purchase of a single volume to copy and/or duplicate and/or adapt this material for use by the group as a whole without having purchased individual volumes for each of the members of the group
7) Et al.

Such persons would be in violation of appropriate Federal and State statutes.

PROVISION OF LICENSING AGREEMENTS – Recognized educational, commercial, industrial, and governmental institutions and organizations, and others legitimately engaged in educational pursuits, including training, testing, and measurement activities, may address request for a licensing agreement to the copyright owners, who will determine whether, and under what conditions, including fees and charges, the materials in this book may be used them. In other words, a licensing facility exists for the legitimate use of the material in this book on other than an individual basis. However, it is asseverated and affirmed here that the material in this book CANNOT be used without the receipt of the express permission of such a licensing agreement from the Publishers. Inquiries re licensing should be addressed to the company, attention rights and permissions department.

All rights reserved, including the right of reproduction in whole or in part, in any form or by any means, electronic or mechanical, including photocopying, recording, or by any information storage and retrieval system, without permission in writing from the Publisher.

Copyright © 2024 by
National Learning Corporation

212 Michael Drive, Syosset, NY 11791
(516) 921-8888 • www.passbooks.com
E-mail: info@passbooks.com

PUBLISHED IN THE UNITED STATES OF AMERICA

PASSBOOK® SERIES

THE *PASSBOOK® SERIES* has been created to prepare applicants and candidates for the ultimate academic battlefield – the examination room.

At some time in our lives, each and every one of us may be required to take an examination – for validation, matriculation, admission, qualification, registration, certification, or licensure.

Based on the assumption that every applicant or candidate has met the basic formal educational standards, has taken the required number of courses, and read the necessary texts, the *PASSBOOK® SERIES* furnishes the one special preparation which may assure passing with confidence, instead of failing with insecurity. Examination questions – together with answers – are furnished as the basic vehicle for study so that the mysteries of the examination and its compounding difficulties may be eliminated or diminished by a sure method.

This book is meant to help you pass your examination provided that you qualify and are serious in your objective.

The entire field is reviewed through the huge store of content information which is succinctly presented through a provocative and challenging approach – the question-and-answer method.

A climate of success is established by furnishing the correct answers at the end of each test.

You soon learn to recognize types of questions, forms of questions, and patterns of questioning. You may even begin to anticipate expected outcomes.

You perceive that many questions are repeated or adapted so that you can gain acute insights, which may enable you to score many sure points.

You learn how to confront new questions, or types of questions, and to attack them confidently and work out the correct answers.

You note objectives and emphases, and recognize pitfalls and dangers, so that you may make positive educational adjustments.

Moreover, you are kept fully informed in relation to new concepts, methods, practices, and directions in the field.

You discover that you are actually taking the examination all the time: you are preparing for the examination by "taking" an examination, not by reading extraneous and/or supererogatory textbooks.

In short, this PASSBOOK®, used directedly, should be an important factor in helping you to pass your test.

MANAGEMENT ASSISTANT

DUTIES

A Management Assistant is an entry-level professional position which can lead to a career in personnel administration, budget and fiscal analysis, or general management. Typical duties relate to departmental and citywide administrative problems, data collection and report writing, program coordination activities, and assisting the coordination of management or administrative activities of an assigned unit or work area; performs other related duties.

SCOPE OF THE EXAMINATION

The examination will consist of a qualifying multiple-choice written test, an advisory essay, and an interview. The qualifying multiple-choice written test is designed to assess quantitative and verbal reasoning, analytical ability, reading comprehension; and other necessary skills, knowledge and abilities.

HOW TO TAKE A TEST

I. YOU MUST PASS AN EXAMINATION

A. *WHAT EVERY CANDIDATE SHOULD KNOW*

Examination applicants often ask us for help in preparing for the written test. What can I study in advance? What kinds of questions will be asked? How will the test be given? How will the papers be graded?

As an applicant for a civil service examination, you may be wondering about some of these things. Our purpose here is to suggest effective methods of advance study and to describe civil service examinations.

Your chances for success on this examination can be increased if you know how to prepare. Those "pre-examination jitters" can be reduced if you know what to expect. You can even experience an adventure in good citizenship if you know why civil service exams are given.

B. *WHY ARE CIVIL SERVICE EXAMINATIONS GIVEN?*

Civil service examinations are important to you in two ways. As a citizen, you want public jobs filled by employees who know how to do their work. As a job seeker, you want a fair chance to compete for that job on an equal footing with other candidates. The best-known means of accomplishing this two-fold goal is the competitive examination.

Exams are widely publicized throughout the nation. They may be administered for jobs in federal, state, city, municipal, town or village governments or agencies.

Any citizen may apply, with some limitations, such as the age or residence of applicants. Your experience and education may be reviewed to see whether you meet the requirements for the particular examination. When these requirements exist, they are reasonable and applied consistently to all applicants. Thus, a competitive examination may cause you some uneasiness now, but it is your privilege and safeguard.

C. *HOW ARE CIVIL SERVICE EXAMS DEVELOPED?*

Examinations are carefully written by trained technicians who are specialists in the field known as "psychological measurement," in consultation with recognized authorities in the field of work that the test will cover. These experts recommend the subject matter areas or skills to be tested; only those knowledges or skills important to your success on the job are included. The most reliable books and source materials available are used as references. Together, the experts and technicians judge the difficulty level of the questions.

Test technicians know how to phrase questions so that the problem is clearly stated. Their ethics do not permit "trick" or "catch" questions. Questions may have been tried out on sample groups, or subjected to statistical analysis, to determine their usefulness.

Written tests are often used in combination with performance tests, ratings of training and experience, and oral interviews. All of these measures combine to form the best-known means of finding the right person for the right job.

II. HOW TO PASS THE WRITTEN TEST

A. NATURE OF THE EXAMINATION

To prepare intelligently for civil service examinations, you should know how they differ from school examinations you have taken. In school you were assigned certain definite pages to read or subjects to cover. The examination questions were quite detailed and usually emphasized memory. Civil service exams, on the other hand, try to discover your present ability to perform the duties of a position, plus your potentiality to learn these duties. In other words, a civil service exam attempts to predict how successful you will be. Questions cover such a broad area that they cannot be as minute and detailed as school exam questions.

In the public service similar kinds of work, or positions, are grouped together in one "class." This process is known as *position-classification*. All the positions in a class are paid according to the salary range for that class. One class title covers all of these positions, and they are all tested by the same examination.

B. FOUR BASIC STEPS

1) Study the announcement

How, then, can you know what subjects to study? Our best answer is: "Learn as much as possible about the class of positions for which you've applied." The exam will test the knowledge, skills and abilities needed to do the work.

Your most valuable source of information about the position you want is the official exam announcement. This announcement lists the training and experience qualifications. Check these standards and apply only if you come reasonably close to meeting them.

The brief description of the position in the examination announcement offers some clues to the subjects which will be tested. Think about the job itself. Review the duties in your mind. Can you perform them, or are there some in which you are rusty? Fill in the blank spots in your preparation.

Many jurisdictions preview the written test in the exam announcement by including a section called "Knowledge and Abilities Required," "Scope of the Examination," or some similar heading. Here you will find out specifically what fields will be tested.

2) Review your own background

Once you learn in general what the position is all about, and what you need to know to do the work, ask yourself which subjects you already know fairly well and which need improvement. You may wonder whether to concentrate on improving your strong areas or on building some background in your fields of weakness. When the announcement has specified "some knowledge" or "considerable knowledge," or has used adjectives like "beginning principles of…" or "advanced … methods," you can get a clue as to the number and difficulty of questions to be asked in any given field. More questions, and hence broader coverage, would be included for those subjects which are more important in the work. Now weigh your strengths and weaknesses against the job requirements and prepare accordingly.

3) Determine the level of the position

Another way to tell how intensively you should prepare is to understand the level of the job for which you are applying. Is it the entering level? In other words, is this the position in which beginners in a field of work are hired? Or is it an intermediate or advanced level? Sometimes this is indicated by such words as "Junior" or "Senior" in the class title. Other jurisdictions use Roman numerals to designate the level – Clerk I, Clerk II, for example. The word "Supervisor" sometimes appears in the title. If the level is not indicated by the title, check the description of duties. Will you be working under very close supervision, or will you have responsibility for independent decisions in this work?

4) Choose appropriate study materials

Now that you know the subjects to be examined and the relative amount of each subject to be covered, you can choose suitable study materials. For beginning level jobs, or even advanced ones, if you have a pronounced weakness in some aspect of your training, read a modern, standard textbook in that field. Be sure it is up to date and has general coverage. Such books are normally available at your library, and the librarian will be glad to help you locate one. For entry-level positions, questions of appropriate difficulty are chosen – neither highly advanced questions, nor those too simple. Such questions require careful thought but not advanced training.

If the position for which you are applying is technical or advanced, you will read more advanced, specialized material. If you are already familiar with the basic principles of your field, elementary textbooks would waste your time. Concentrate on advanced textbooks and technical periodicals. Think through the concepts and review difficult problems in your field.

These are all general sources. You can get more ideas on your own initiative, following these leads. For example, training manuals and publications of the government agency which employs workers in your field can be useful, particularly for technical and professional positions. A letter or visit to the government department involved may result in more specific study suggestions, and certainly will provide you with a more definite idea of the exact nature of the position you are seeking.

III. KINDS OF TESTS

Tests are used for purposes other than measuring knowledge and ability to perform specified duties. For some positions, it is equally important to test ability to make adjustments to new situations or to profit from training. In others, basic mental abilities not dependent on information are essential. Questions which test these things may not appear as pertinent to the duties of the position as those which test for knowledge and information. Yet they are often highly important parts of a fair examination. For very general questions, it is almost impossible to help you direct your study efforts. What we can do is to point out some of the more common of these general abilities needed in public service positions and describe some typical questions.

1) General information

Broad, general information has been found useful for predicting job success in some kinds of work. This is tested in a variety of ways, from vocabulary lists to questions about current events. Basic background in some field of work, such as sociology or economics, may be sampled in a group of questions. Often these are principles which have become familiar to most persons through exposure rather than through formal training. It is difficult to advise you how to study for these questions; being alert to the world around you is our best suggestion.

2) Verbal ability

An example of an ability needed in many positions is verbal or language ability. Verbal ability is, in brief, the ability to use and understand words. Vocabulary and grammar tests are typical measures of this ability. Reading comprehension or paragraph interpretation questions are common in many kinds of civil service tests. You are given a paragraph of written material and asked to find its central meaning.

3) Numerical ability

Number skills can be tested by the familiar arithmetic problem, by checking paired lists of numbers to see which are alike and which are different, or by interpreting charts and graphs. In the latter test, a graph may be printed in the test booklet which you are asked to use as the basis for answering questions.

4) Observation

A popular test for law-enforcement positions is the observation test. A picture is shown to you for several minutes, then taken away. Questions about the picture test your ability to observe both details and larger elements.

5) Following directions

In many positions in the public service, the employee must be able to carry out written instructions dependably and accurately. You may be given a chart with several columns, each column listing a variety of information. The questions require you to carry out directions involving the information given in the chart.

6) Skills and aptitudes

Performance tests effectively measure some manual skills and aptitudes. When the skill is one in which you are trained, such as typing or shorthand, you can practice. These tests are often very much like those given in business school or high school courses. For many of the other skills and aptitudes, however, no short-time preparation can be made. Skills and abilities natural to you or that you have developed throughout your lifetime are being tested.

Many of the general questions just described provide all the data needed to answer the questions and ask you to use your reasoning ability to find the answers. Your best preparation for these tests, as well as for tests of facts and ideas, is to be at your physical and mental best. You, no doubt, have your own methods of getting into an exam-taking mood and keeping "in shape." The next section lists some ideas on this subject.

IV. KINDS OF QUESTIONS

Only rarely is the "essay" question, which you answer in narrative form, used in civil service tests. Civil service tests are usually of the short-answer type. Full instructions for answering these questions will be given to you at the examination. But in case this is your first experience with short-answer questions and separate answer sheets, here is what you need to know:

1) Multiple-choice Questions

Most popular of the short-answer questions is the "multiple choice" or "best answer" question. It can be used, for example, to test for factual knowledge, ability to solve problems or judgment in meeting situations found at work.

A multiple-choice question is normally one of three types—
- It can begin with an incomplete statement followed by several possible endings. You are to find the one ending which *best* completes the statement, although some of the others may not be entirely wrong.
- It can also be a complete statement in the form of a question which is answered by choosing one of the statements listed.

- It can be in the form of a problem – again you select the best answer.

Here is an example of a multiple-choice question with a discussion which should give you some clues as to the method for choosing the right answer:

When an employee has a complaint about his assignment, the action which will *best* help him overcome his difficulty is to
- A. discuss his difficulty with his coworkers
- B. take the problem to the head of the organization
- C. take the problem to the person who gave him the assignment
- D. say nothing to anyone about his complaint

In answering this question, you should study each of the choices to find which is best. Consider choice "A" – Certainly an employee may discuss his complaint with fellow employees, but no change or improvement can result, and the complaint remains unresolved. Choice "B" is a poor choice since the head of the organization probably does not know what assignment you have been given, and taking your problem to him is known as "going over the head" of the supervisor. The supervisor, or person who made the assignment, is the person who can clarify it or correct any injustice. Choice "C" is, therefore, correct. To say nothing, as in choice "D," is unwise. Supervisors have and interest in knowing the problems employees are facing, and the employee is seeking a solution to his problem.

2) True/False Questions

The "true/false" or "right/wrong" form of question is sometimes used. Here a complete statement is given. Your job is to decide whether the statement is right or wrong.

SAMPLE: A roaming cell-phone call to a nearby city costs less than a non-roaming call to a distant city.

This statement is wrong, or false, since roaming calls are more expensive.

This is not a complete list of all possible question forms, although most of the others are variations of these common types. You will always get complete directions for answering questions. Be sure you understand *how* to mark your answers – ask questions until you do.

V. RECORDING YOUR ANSWERS

Computer terminals are used more and more today for many different kinds of exams.

For an examination with very few applicants, you may be told to record your answers in the test booklet itself. Separate answer sheets are much more common. If this separate answer sheet is to be scored by machine – and this is often the case – it is highly important that you mark your answers correctly in order to get credit.

An electronic scoring machine is often used in civil service offices because of the speed with which papers can be scored. Machine-scored answer sheets must be marked with a pencil, which will be given to you. This pencil has a high graphite content which responds to the electronic scoring machine. As a matter of fact, stray dots may register as answers, so do not let your pencil rest on the answer sheet while you are pondering the correct answer. Also, if your pencil lead breaks or is otherwise defective, ask for another.

Since the answer sheet will be dropped in a slot in the scoring machine, be careful not to bend the corners or get the paper crumpled.

The answer sheet normally has five vertical columns of numbers, with 30 numbers to a column. These numbers correspond to the question numbers in your test booklet. After each number, going across the page are four or five pairs of dotted lines. These short dotted lines have small letters or numbers above them. The first two pairs may also have a "T" or "F" above the letters. This indicates that the first two pairs only are to be used if the questions are of the true-false type. If the questions are multiple choice, disregard the "T" and "F" and pay attention only to the small letters or numbers.

Answer your questions in the manner of the sample that follows:

32. The largest city in the United States is
    A. Washington, D.C.
    B. New York City
    C. Chicago
    D. Detroit
    E. San Francisco

1) Choose the answer you think is best. (New York City is the largest, so "B" is correct.)
2) Find the row of dotted lines numbered the same as the question you are answering. (Find row number 32)
3) Find the pair of dotted lines corresponding to the answer. (Find the pair of lines under the mark "B.")
4) Make a solid black mark between the dotted lines.

VI. BEFORE THE TEST

Common sense will help you find procedures to follow to get ready for an examination. Too many of us, however, overlook these sensible measures. Indeed, nervousness and fatigue have been found to be the most serious reasons why applicants fail to do their best on civil service tests. Here is a list of reminders:

- Begin your preparation early – Don't wait until the last minute to go scurrying around for books and materials or to find out what the position is all about.
- Prepare continuously – An hour a night for a week is better than an all-night cram session. This has been definitely established. What is more, a night a week for a month will return better dividends than crowding your study into a shorter period of time.
- Locate the place of the exam – You have been sent a notice telling you when and where to report for the examination. If the location is in a different town or otherwise unfamiliar to you, it would be well to inquire the best route and learn something about the building.
- Relax the night before the test – Allow your mind to rest. Do not study at all that night. Plan some mild recreation or diversion; then go to bed early and get a good night's sleep.
- Get up early enough to make a leisurely trip to the place for the test – This way unforeseen events, traffic snarls, unfamiliar buildings, etc. will not upset you.
- Dress comfortably – A written test is not a fashion show. You will be known by number and not by name, so wear something comfortable.

- Leave excess paraphernalia at home – Shopping bags and odd bundles will get in your way. You need bring only the items mentioned in the official notice you received; usually everything you need is provided. Do not bring reference books to the exam. They will only confuse those last minutes and be taken away from you when in the test room.
- Arrive somewhat ahead of time – If because of transportation schedules you must get there very early, bring a newspaper or magazine to take your mind off yourself while waiting.
- Locate the examination room – When you have found the proper room, you will be directed to the seat or part of the room where you will sit. Sometimes you are given a sheet of instructions to read while you are waiting. Do not fill out any forms until you are told to do so; just read them and be prepared.
- Relax and prepare to listen to the instructions
- If you have any physical problem that may keep you from doing your best, be sure to tell the test administrator. If you are sick or in poor health, you really cannot do your best on the exam. You can come back and take the test some other time.

VII. AT THE TEST

The day of the test is here and you have the test booklet in your hand. The temptation to get going is very strong. Caution! There is more to success than knowing the right answers. You must know how to identify your papers and understand variations in the type of short-answer question used in this particular examination. Follow these suggestions for maximum results from your efforts:

1) Cooperate with the monitor

The test administrator has a duty to create a situation in which you can be as much at ease as possible. He will give instructions, tell you when to begin, check to see that you are marking your answer sheet correctly, and so on. He is not there to guard you, although he will see that your competitors do not take unfair advantage. He wants to help you do your best.

2) Listen to all instructions

Don't jump the gun! Wait until you understand all directions. In most civil service tests you get more time than you need to answer the questions. So don't be in a hurry. Read each word of instructions until you clearly understand the meaning. Study the examples, listen to all announcements and follow directions. Ask questions if you do not understand what to do.

3) Identify your papers

Civil service exams are usually identified by number only. You will be assigned a number; you must not put your name on your test papers. Be sure to copy your number correctly. Since more than one exam may be given, copy your exact examination title.

4) Plan your time

Unless you are told that a test is a "speed" or "rate of work" test, speed itself is usually not important. Time enough to answer all the questions will be provided, but this does not mean that you have all day. An overall time limit has been set. Divide the total time (in minutes) by the number of questions to determine the approximate time you have for each question.

5) Do not linger over difficult questions

If you come across a difficult question, mark it with a paper clip (useful to have along) and come back to it when you have been through the booklet. One caution if you do this – be sure to skip a number on your answer sheet as well. Check often to be sure that you have not lost your place and that you are marking in the row numbered the same as the question you are answering.

6) Read the questions

Be sure you know what the question asks! Many capable people are unsuccessful because they failed to *read* the questions correctly.

7) Answer all questions

Unless you have been instructed that a penalty will be deducted for incorrect answers, it is better to guess than to omit a question.

8) Speed tests

It is often better NOT to guess on speed tests. It has been found that on timed tests people are tempted to spend the last few seconds before time is called in marking answers at random – without even reading them – in the hope of picking up a few extra points. To discourage this practice, the instructions may warn you that your score will be "corrected" for guessing. That is, a penalty will be applied. The incorrect answers will be deducted from the correct ones, or some other penalty formula will be used.

9) Review your answers

If you finish before time is called, go back to the questions you guessed or omitted to give them further thought. Review other answers if you have time.

10) Return your test materials

If you are ready to leave before others have finished or time is called, take ALL your materials to the monitor and leave quietly. Never take any test material with you. The monitor can discover whose papers are not complete, and taking a test booklet may be grounds for disqualification.

VIII. EXAMINATION TECHNIQUES

1) Read the general instructions carefully. These are usually printed on the first page of the exam booklet. As a rule, these instructions refer to the timing of the examination; the fact that you should not start work until the signal and must stop work at a signal, etc. If there are any *special* instructions, such as a choice of questions to be answered, make sure that you note this instruction carefully.

2) When you are ready to start work on the examination, that is as soon as the signal has been given, read the instructions to each question booklet, underline any key words or phrases, such as *least, best, outline, describe* and the like. In this way you will tend to answer as requested rather than discover on reviewing your paper that you *listed without describing*, that you selected the *worst* choice rather than the *best* choice, etc.

3) If the examination is of the objective or multiple-choice type – that is, each question will also give a series of possible answers: A, B, C or D, and you are called upon to select the best answer and write the letter next to that answer on your answer paper – it is advisable to start answering each question in turn. There may be anywhere from 50 to 100 such questions in the three or four hours allotted and you can see how much time would be taken if you read through all the questions before beginning to answer any. Furthermore, if you come across a question or group of questions which you know would be difficult to answer, it would undoubtedly affect your handling of all the other questions.

4) If the examination is of the essay type and contains but a few questions, it is a moot point as to whether you should read all the questions before starting to answer any one. Of course, if you are given a choice – say five out of seven and the like – then it is essential to read all the questions so you can eliminate the two that are most difficult. If, however, you are asked to answer all the questions, there may be danger in trying to answer the easiest one first because you may find that you will spend too much time on it. The best technique is to answer the first question, then proceed to the second, etc.

5) Time your answers. Before the exam begins, write down the time it started, then add the time allowed for the examination and write down the time it must be completed, then divide the time available somewhat as follows:
    - If 3-1/2 hours are allowed, that would be 210 minutes. If you have 80 objective-type questions, that would be an average of 2-1/2 minutes per question. Allow yourself no more than 2 minutes per question, or a total of 160 minutes, which will permit about 50 minutes to review.
    - If for the time allotment of 210 minutes there are 7 essay questions to answer, that would average about 30 minutes a question. Give yourself only 25 minutes per question so that you have about 35 minutes to review.

6) The most important instruction is to *read each question* and make sure you know what is wanted. The second most important instruction is to *time yourself properly* so that you answer every question. The third most important instruction is to *answer every question*. Guess if you have to but include something for each question. Remember that you will receive no credit for a blank and will probably receive some credit if you write something in answer to an essay question. If you guess a letter – say "B" for a multiple-choice question – you may have guessed right. If you leave a blank as an answer to a multiple-choice question, the examiners may respect your feelings but it will not add a point to your score. Some exams may penalize you for wrong answers, so in such cases *only*, you may not want to guess unless you have some basis for your answer.

7) Suggestions
    a. Objective-type questions
        1. Examine the question booklet for proper sequence of pages and questions
        2. Read all instructions carefully
        3. Skip any question which seems too difficult; return to it after all other questions have been answered
        4. Apportion your time properly; do not spend too much time on any single question or group of questions

5. Note and underline key words – *all, most, fewest, least, best, worst, same, opposite,* etc.
6. Pay particular attention to negatives
7. Note unusual option, e.g., unduly long, short, complex, different or similar in content to the body of the question
8. Observe the use of "hedging" words – *probably, may, most likely,* etc.
9. Make sure that your answer is put next to the same number as the question
10. Do not second-guess unless you have good reason to believe the second answer is definitely more correct
11. Cross out original answer if you decide another answer is more accurate; do not erase until you are ready to hand your paper in
12. Answer all questions; guess unless instructed otherwise
13. Leave time for review

b. Essay questions
1. Read each question carefully
2. Determine exactly what is wanted. Underline key words or phrases.
3. Decide on outline or paragraph answer
4. Include many different points and elements unless asked to develop any one or two points or elements
5. Show impartiality by giving pros and cons unless directed to select one side only
6. Make and write down any assumptions you find necessary to answer the questions
7. Watch your English, grammar, punctuation and choice of words
8. Time your answers; don't crowd material

8) Answering the essay question

Most essay questions can be answered by framing the specific response around several key words or ideas. Here are a few such key words or ideas:

M's: manpower, materials, methods, money, management
P's: purpose, program, policy, plan, procedure, practice, problems, pitfalls, personnel, public relations

a. Six basic steps in handling problems:
1. Preliminary plan and background development
2. Collect information, data and facts
3. Analyze and interpret information, data and facts
4. Analyze and develop solutions as well as make recommendations
5. Prepare report and sell recommendations
6. Install recommendations and follow up effectiveness

b. Pitfalls to avoid
1. *Taking things for granted* – A statement of the situation does not necessarily imply that each of the elements is necessarily true; for example, a complaint may be invalid and biased so that all that can be taken for granted is that a complaint has been registered

2. *Considering only one side of a situation* – Wherever possible, indicate several alternatives and then point out the reasons you selected the best one
3. *Failing to indicate follow up* – Whenever your answer indicates action on your part, make certain that you will take proper follow-up action to see how successful your recommendations, procedures or actions turn out to be
4. *Taking too long in answering any single question* – Remember to time your answers properly

IX. AFTER THE TEST

Scoring procedures differ in detail among civil service jurisdictions although the general principles are the same. Whether the papers are hand-scored or graded by machine we have described, they are nearly always graded by number. That is, the person who marks the paper knows only the number – never the name – of the applicant. Not until all the papers have been graded will they be matched with names. If other tests, such as training and experience or oral interview ratings have been given, scores will be combined. Different parts of the examination usually have different weights. For example, the written test might count 60 percent of the final grade, and a rating of training and experience 40 percent. In many jurisdictions, veterans will have a certain number of points added to their grades.

After the final grade has been determined, the names are placed in grade order and an eligible list is established. There are various methods for resolving ties between those who get the same final grade – probably the most common is to place first the name of the person whose application was received first. Job offers are made from the eligible list in the order the names appear on it. You will be notified of your grade and your rank as soon as all these computations have been made. This will be done as rapidly as possible.

People who are found to meet the requirements in the announcement are called "eligibles." Their names are put on a list of eligible candidates. An eligible's chances of getting a job depend on how high he stands on this list and how fast agencies are filling jobs from the list.

When a job is to be filled from a list of eligibles, the agency asks for the names of people on the list of eligibles for that job. When the civil service commission receives this request, it sends to the agency the names of the three people highest on this list. Or, if the job to be filled has specialized requirements, the office sends the agency the names of the top three persons who meet these requirements from the general list.

The appointing officer makes a choice from among the three people whose names were sent to him. If the selected person accepts the appointment, the names of the others are put back on the list to be considered for future openings.

That is the rule in hiring from all kinds of eligible lists, whether they are for typist, carpenter, chemist, or something else. For every vacancy, the appointing officer has his choice of any one of the top three eligibles on the list. This explains why the person whose name is on top of the list sometimes does not get an appointment when some of the persons lower on the list do. If the appointing officer chooses the second or third eligible, the No. 1 eligible does not get a job at once, but stays on the list until he is appointed or the list is terminated.

X. HOW TO PASS THE INTERVIEW TEST

The examination for which you applied requires an oral interview test. You have already taken the written test and you are now being called for the interview test – the final part of the formal examination.

You may think that it is not possible to prepare for an interview test and that there are no procedures to follow during an interview. Our purpose is to point out some things you can do in advance that will help you and some good rules to follow and pitfalls to avoid while you are being interviewed.

What is an interview supposed to test?

The written examination is designed to test the technical knowledge and competence of the candidate; the oral is designed to evaluate intangible qualities, not readily measured otherwise, and to establish a list showing the relative fitness of each candidate – as measured against his competitors – for the position sought. Scoring is not on the basis of "right" and "wrong," but on a sliding scale of values ranging from "not passable" to "outstanding." As a matter of fact, it is possible to achieve a relatively low score without a single "incorrect" answer because of evident weakness in the qualities being measured.

Occasionally, an examination may consist entirely of an oral test – either an individual or a group oral. In such cases, information is sought concerning the technical knowledges and abilities of the candidate, since there has been no written examination for this purpose. More commonly, however, an oral test is used to supplement a written examination.

Who conducts interviews?

The composition of oral boards varies among different jurisdictions. In nearly all, a representative of the personnel department serves as chairman. One of the members of the board may be a representative of the department in which the candidate would work. In some cases, "outside experts" are used, and, frequently, a businessman or some other representative of the general public is asked to serve. Labor and management or other special groups may be represented. The aim is to secure the services of experts in the appropriate field.

However the board is composed, it is a good idea (and not at all improper or unethical) to ascertain in advance of the interview who the members are and what groups they represent. When you are introduced to them, you will have some idea of their backgrounds and interests, and at least you will not stutter and stammer over their names.

What should be done before the interview?

While knowledge about the board members is useful and takes some of the surprise element out of the interview, there is other preparation which is more substantive. It *is* possible to prepare for an oral interview – in several ways:

1) Keep a copy of your application and review it carefully before the interview

This may be the only document before the oral board, and the starting point of the interview. Know what education and experience you have listed there, and the sequence and dates of all of it. Sometimes the board will ask you to review the highlights of your experience for them; you should not have to hem and haw doing it.

2) Study the class specification and the examination announcement

Usually, the oral board has one or both of these to guide them. The qualities, characteristics or knowledges required by the position sought are stated in these documents. They offer valuable clues as to the nature of the oral interview. For example, if the job involves supervisory responsibilities, the announcement will usually indicate that knowledge of modern supervisory methods and the qualifications of the candidate as a supervisor will be tested. If so, you can expect such questions, frequently in the form of a hypothetical situation which you are expected to solve. NEVER go into an oral without knowledge of the duties and responsibilities of the job you seek.

3) Think through each qualification required

Try to visualize the kind of questions you would ask if you were a board member. How well could you answer them? Try especially to appraise your own knowledge and background in each area, *measured against the job sought*, and identify any areas in which you are weak. Be critical and realistic – do not flatter yourself.

4) Do some general reading in areas in which you feel you may be weak

For example, if the job involves supervision and your past experience has NOT, some general reading in supervisory methods and practices, particularly in the field of human relations, might be useful. Do NOT study agency procedures or detailed manuals. The oral board will be testing your understanding and capacity, not your memory.

5) Get a good night's sleep and watch your general health and mental attitude

You will want a clear head at the interview. Take care of a cold or any other minor ailment, and of course, no hangovers.

What should be done on the day of the interview?

Now comes the day of the interview itself. Give yourself plenty of time to get there. Plan to arrive somewhat ahead of the scheduled time, particularly if your appointment is in the fore part of the day. If a previous candidate fails to appear, the board might be ready for you a bit early. By early afternoon an oral board is almost invariably behind schedule if there are many candidates, and you may have to wait. Take along a book or magazine to read, or your application to review, but leave any extraneous material in the waiting room when you go in for your interview. In any event, relax and compose yourself.

The matter of dress is important. The board is forming impressions about you – from your experience, your manners, your attitude, and your appearance. Give your personal appearance careful attention. Dress your best, but not your flashiest. Choose conservative, appropriate clothing, and be sure it is immaculate. This is a business interview, and your appearance should indicate that you regard it as such. Besides, being well groomed and properly dressed will help boost your confidence.

Sooner or later, someone will call your name and escort you into the interview room. *This is it.* From here on you are on your own. It is too late for any more preparation. But remember, you asked for this opportunity to prove your fitness, and you are here because your request was granted.

What happens when you go in?

The usual sequence of events will be as follows: The clerk (who is often the board stenographer) will introduce you to the chairman of the oral board, who will introduce you to the other members of the board. Acknowledge the introductions before you sit down. Do not be surprised if you find a microphone facing you or a stenotypist sitting by. Oral interviews are usually recorded in the event of an appeal or other review.

Usually the chairman of the board will open the interview by reviewing the highlights of your education and work experience from your application – primarily for the benefit of the other members of the board, as well as to get the material into the record. Do not interrupt or comment unless there is an error or significant misinterpretation; if that is the case, do not hesitate. But do not quibble about insignificant matters. Also, he will usually ask you some question about your education, experience or your present job – partly to get you to start talking and to establish the interviewing "rapport." He may start the actual questioning, or turn it over to one of the other members. Frequently, each member undertakes the questioning on a particular area, one in which he is perhaps most competent, so you can expect each member to participate in the examination. Because time is limited, you may also expect some rather abrupt switches in the direction the questioning takes, so do not be upset by it. Normally, a board member will not pursue a single line of questioning unless he discovers a particular strength or weakness.

After each member has participated, the chairman will usually ask whether any member has any further questions, then will ask you if you have anything you wish to add. Unless you are expecting this question, it may floor you. Worse, it may start you off on an extended, extemporaneous speech. The board is not usually seeking more information. The question is principally to offer you a last opportunity to present further qualifications or to indicate that you have nothing to add. So, if you feel that a significant qualification or characteristic has been overlooked, it is proper to point it out in a sentence or so. Do not compliment the board on the thoroughness of their examination – they have been sketchy, and you know it. If you wish, merely say, "No thank you, I have nothing further to add." This is a point where you can "talk yourself out" of a good impression or fail to present an important bit of information. Remember, *you close the interview yourself*.

The chairman will then say, "That is all, Mr. _____, thank you." Do not be startled; the interview is over, and quicker than you think. Thank him, gather your belongings and take your leave. Save your sigh of relief for the other side of the door.

How to put your best foot forward

Throughout this entire process, you may feel that the board individually and collectively is trying to pierce your defenses, seek out your hidden weaknesses and embarrass and confuse you. Actually, this is not true. They are obliged to make an appraisal of your qualifications for the job you are seeking, and they want to see you in your best light. Remember, they must interview all candidates and a non-cooperative candidate may become a failure in spite of their best efforts to bring out his qualifications. Here are 15 suggestions that will help you:

1) Be natural – Keep your attitude confident, not cocky

If you are not confident that you can do the job, do not expect the board to be. Do not apologize for your weaknesses, try to bring out your strong points. The board is interested in a positive, not negative, presentation. Cockiness will antagonize any board member and make him wonder if you are covering up a weakness by a false show of strength.

2) Get comfortable, but don't lounge or sprawl

Sit erectly but not stiffly. A careless posture may lead the board to conclude that you are careless in other things, or at least that you are not impressed by the importance of the occasion. Either conclusion is natural, even if incorrect. Do not fuss with your clothing, a pencil or an ashtray. Your hands may occasionally be useful to emphasize a point; do not let them become a point of distraction.

3) Do not wisecrack or make small talk

This is a serious situation, and your attitude should show that you consider it as such. Further, the time of the board is limited – they do not want to waste it, and neither should you.

4) Do not exaggerate your experience or abilities

In the first place, from information in the application or other interviews and sources, the board may know more about you than you think. Secondly, you probably will not get away with it. An experienced board is rather adept at spotting such a situation, so do not take the chance.

5) If you know a board member, do not make a point of it, yet do not hide it

Certainly you are not fooling him, and probably not the other members of the board. Do not try to take advantage of your acquaintanceship – it will probably do you little good.

6) Do not dominate the interview

Let the board do that. They will give you the clues – do not assume that you have to do all the talking. Realize that the board has a number of questions to ask you, and do not try to take up all the interview time by showing off your extensive knowledge of the answer to the first one.

7) Be attentive

You only have 20 minutes or so, and you should keep your attention at its sharpest throughout. When a member is addressing a problem or question to you, give him your undivided attention. Address your reply principally to him, but do not exclude the other board members.

8) Do not interrupt

A board member may be stating a problem for you to analyze. He will ask you a question when the time comes. Let him state the problem, and wait for the question.

9) Make sure you understand the question

Do not try to answer until you are sure what the question is. If it is not clear, restate it in your own words or ask the board member to clarify it for you. However, do not haggle about minor elements.

10) Reply promptly but not hastily

A common entry on oral board rating sheets is "candidate responded readily," or "candidate hesitated in replies." Respond as promptly and quickly as you can, but do not jump to a hasty, ill-considered answer.

11) Do not be peremptory in your answers

A brief answer is proper – but do not fire your answer back. That is a losing game from your point of view. The board member can probably ask questions much faster than you can answer them.

12) Do not try to create the answer you think the board member wants

He is interested in what kind of mind you have and how it works – not in playing games. Furthermore, he can usually spot this practice and will actually grade you down on it.

13) Do not switch sides in your reply merely to agree with a board member

Frequently, a member will take a contrary position merely to draw you out and to see if you are willing and able to defend your point of view. Do not start a debate, yet do not surrender a good position. If a position is worth taking, it is worth defending.

14) Do not be afraid to admit an error in judgment if you are shown to be wrong

The board knows that you are forced to reply without any opportunity for careful consideration. Your answer may be demonstrably wrong. If so, admit it and get on with the interview.

15) Do not dwell at length on your present job

The opening question may relate to your present assignment. Answer the question but do not go into an extended discussion. You are being examined for a *new* job, not your present one. As a matter of fact, try to phrase ALL your answers in terms of the job for which you are being examined.

Basis of Rating

Probably you will forget most of these "do's" and "don'ts" when you walk into the oral interview room. Even remembering them all will not ensure you a passing grade. Perhaps you did not have the qualifications in the first place. But remembering them will help you to put your best foot forward, without treading on the toes of the board members.

Rumor and popular opinion to the contrary notwithstanding, an oral board wants you to make the best appearance possible. They know you are under pressure – but they also want to see how you respond to it as a guide to what your reaction would be under the pressures of the job you seek. They will be influenced by the degree of poise you display, the personal traits you show and the manner in which you respond.

ABOUT THIS BOOK

This book contains tests divided into Examination Sections. Go through each test, answering every question in the margin. We have also attached a sample answer sheet at the back of the book that can be removed and used. At the end of each test look at the answer key and check your answers. On the ones you got wrong, look at the right answer choice and learn. Do not fill in the answers first. Do not memorize the questions and answers, but understand the answer and principles involved. On your test, the questions will likely be different from the samples. Questions are changed and new ones added. If you understand these past questions you should have success with any changes that arise. Tests may consist of several types of questions. We have additional books on each subject should more study be advisable or necessary for you. Finally, the more you study, the better prepared you will be. This book is intended to be the last thing you study before you walk into the examination room. Prior study of relevant texts is also recommended. NLC publishes some of these in our Fundamental Series. Knowledge and good sense are important factors in passing your exam. Good luck also helps. So now study this Passbook, absorb the material contained within and take that knowledge into the examination. Then do your best to pass that exam.

EXAMINATION SECTION

EXAMINATION SECTION

TEST 1

DIRECTIONS: Each question or incomplete statement is followed by several suggested answers or completions. Select the one that BEST answers the question or completes the statement. *PRINT THE LETTER OF THE CORRECT ANSWER IN THE SPACE AT THE RIGHT.*

Questions 1-5.

DIRECTIONS: Each of Questions 1 through 5 consists of a passage which contains one word that is incorrectly used because it is not in keeping with the meaning that the quotation is evidently intended to convey. Determine which word is incorrectly used. Select from the choices lettered A, B, C, and D the word which, when substituted for the incorrectly used word, would BEST to convey the meaning of the quotation.

1. Whatever the method, the necessity to keep up with the dynamics of an organization is the point on which many classification plans go awry. The budgetary approach to "positions," for example, often leads to using for recruitment and pay purposes a position authorized many years earlier for quite a different purpose than currently contemplated—making perhaps the title, the class, and the qualifications required inappropriate to the current need. This happens because executives overlook the stability that takes place in job duties and fail to reread an initial description of the job before saying, as they scan a list of titles, "We should fill this position right away." Once a classification plan is adopted, it is pointless to do anything less than provide for continuous, painstaking maintenance on a current basis, else once different positions that have actually become similar to each other remain in different classes, and some former cognates that have become quite different continue in the same class. Such a program often seems expensive. But to stint too much on this out-of-pocket cost may create still higher hidden costs growing out of lowered morale, poor production, delayed operating programs, excessive pay for simple work, and low pay for responsible work (resulting in poorly qualified executives and professional men)—all normal concomitants of inadequate, hasty, or out-of-date classification. 1.____

    A. evolution   B. personnel   C. disapproved   D. forward

2. At first sight, it may seem that there is little or no difference between the usableness of a manual and the degree of its use. But there is a difference. A manual may have all the qualities which make up the usable manual and still not be used. Take this instance as an example: Suppose you have a satisfactory manual but issue instructions from day to day through the avenue of bulletins, memorandums, and other informational releases. Which will the employee use, the manual or the bulletin which passes over his desk? He will, 2.____

of course, use the latter, for some obsolete material will not be contained in this manual. Here we have a theoretically usable manual which is unused because of the other avenues by which procedural information may be issued.
    A. countermand   B. discard   C. intentional   D. worthwhile

3. By reconcentrating control over its operations in a central headquarters, a firm is able to extend the influence of automation to many, if not all, of its functions—from inventory and payroll to production, sales, and personnel. In so doing, businesses freeze all the elements of the corporate function in their relationship to one another and to the overall objectives of the firm. From this total systems concept, companies learn that computers can accomplish much more than clerical and accounting jobs. Their capabilities can be tapped to perform the traditional applications (payroll processing, inventory control, accounts payable, and accounts receivable) as well as newer applications such as spotting deviations from planned programs (exception reporting), adjusting planning schedules, forecasting business trends, simulating market conditions, and solving production problems. Since the officer manage is a manager of information and each of these applications revolve around the processing of data, he must take an active role in studying and improving the system under his care.
    A. maintaining   B. inclusion   C. limited   D. visualize

3.____

4. In addition to the formal and acceptance theories of the source of authority, although perhaps more closely related to the latter, is the belief that authority is generated by personal qualifies of technical competence. Under this heading is the individual who has made, in effect, subordinates of others through sheer force of personality, and the engineer or economist who exerts influence by furnishing answers or sound advice. These may have no actual organizational authority, yet their advice may be so eagerly sought and so unerringly followed that it appears to carry the weight of an order. But, above all, one cannot discount the importance of formal authority with its institutional foundations. Buttressed by the qualities of leadership implicit in the acceptance theory, formal authority is basic to the managerial job. Once abrogated, it may be delegated or withheld, used or misused, and be effective in capable hands or be ineffective in inept hands.
    A. selected   B. delegation   C. limited   D. possessed

4.____

5. Since managerial operations in organization, staffing, directing, and controlling are designed to support the accomplishment of enterprise objectives, planning logically precedes the execution of all other managerial functions. Although all the functions intermesh in practice, planning is unique in that it establishes the objectives necessary for all group effort. Besides, plans must be made to accomplish these objectives before the manager knows what kind of organization relationships and personal qualifications are needed, along which course subordinates are to be directed, and what kind of control is to be applied. And, of course, each of the other managerial functions must be planned if they are to be effective.

5.____

Planning and control are inseparable—the Siamese twins of management. Unplanned action cannot be controlled, for control involves keeping activities on course by correcting deviations from plans. Any attempt to control without plans would be meaningless, since there are no way anyone can tell whether he is going where he wants to go—the task of control—unless first he knows where he wants to go—the task of planning. Plans thus preclude the standards of control.

    A. coordinating   B. individual   C. furnish   D. follow

Questions 6-7.

DIRECTIONS: Questions 6 and 7 are to be answered SOLELY on the basis of information given in the following paragraph.

In-basket tests are often used to assess managerial potential. The exercise consists of a set of papers that would be likely to be found in the in-basket of an administrator or manager at any given time, and requires the individuals participating in the examination to indicate how they would dispose of each item found in the in-basket. In order to handle the in-basket effectively, they must successfully manage their time, refer and assign some work to subordinates, juggle potentially conflicting appointments and meetings, and arrange for follow-up of problems generated by the items in the in-basket. In other words, the in-basket test is attempting to evaluate the participants' abilities to organize their work, set priorities, delegate control, and make decisions.

6. According to the above paragraph, to succeed in an in-basket test, an administrator must
    A. be able to read very quickly
    B. have a great deal of technical knowledge
    C. know when to delegate work
    D. arrange a lot of appointments and meetings

6._____

7. According to the above paragraph, all of the following abilities are indications of managerial potential EXCEPT the ability to
    A. organize and control   B. manage time
    C. write effective reports   D. make appropriate decisions

7._____

Questions 8-9.

DIRECTIONS: Questions 8 and 9 are to be answered SOLELY on the basis of information given in the following paragraph.

One of the biggest mistakes of government executives with substantial supervisory responsibility is failing to make careful appraisals of performance during employee probationary periods. Many a later headache could have been avoided by prompt and full appraisal during the early months of an employee's assignment. There is not much more to say about this except to emphasize the common prevalence of this oversight, and to underscore that for its consequences, which are many and sad, the offending managers have no one to blame but themselves.

8. According to the above paragraph, probationary periods are	8._____
   A. a mistake, and should not be used by supervisors with large responsibilities
   B. not used properly by government executives
   C. used only for those with supervisory responsibility
   D. the consequences of management mistakes

9. The one of the following conclusions that can MOST appropriately be drawn from the above paragraph is that	9._____
   A. management's failure to appraise employees during their probationary period is a common occurrence
   B. there is not much to say about probationary periods, because they are unimportant
   C. managers should blame employees for failing to use their probationary periods properly
   D. probationary periods are a headache to most managers

Questions 10-12.

DIRECTIONS: Questions 11 and 12 are to be answered SOLELY on the basis of the information given in the following paragraph.

The common sense character of the merit system seems so natural to most Americans that many people wonder why it should ever have been inoperative. After all, the American economic system, the most phenomenal the world has ever known, is also founded on a rugged selective process which emphasizes the personal qualities of capacity, industriousness, and productivity. The criteria may not have always been appropriate and competition has not always been fair, but competition there was, and the responsibilities and the rewards—with exceptions, of course—have gone to those who could measure up in terms of intelligence, knowledge, or perseverance. This has been true not only in the economic area, in the money-making process, but also in achievement in the professions and other walks of life.

10. According to the above paragraph, economic awards in the United States have	10._____
    A. always been based on appropriate, fair criteria
    B. only recently been based on a competitive system
    C. not gone to people who compete too ruggedly
    D. usually gone to those people with intelligence, knowledge, and perseverance

11. According to the above paragraph, a merit system is	11._____
    A. an unfair criterion on which to base rewards
    B. unnatural to anyone who is not American
    C. based only on common sense
    D. based on the same principles as the American economic system

12. According to the above paragraph, it is MOST accurate to say that 12.____
    A. the United States has always had a civil service merit system
    B. civil service employees are very rugged
    C. the American economic system has always been based on a merit objective
    D. competition is unique to the American way of life

Questions 13-15.

DIRECTIONS: The management study of employee absence due to sickness is an effective tool in planning. Questions 13 through 15 are to be answered SOLELY on the data given below.

Number of Days Absent Per Worker (Sickness)	1	2	3	4	5	6	7	8 or Over
Number of Workers	76	23	6	3	1	0	1	0
Total Number of Workers	400							
Period Covered	January 1 – December 31							

13. The total number of man-days lost due to illness was 13.____
    A. 110   B. 137   C. 144   D. 164

14. What percent of the workers had 4 or more days absence due to sickness? 14.____
    A. .25%   B. 2.5%   C. 1.25%   D. 12.5%

15. Of the 400 workers studied, the number who lost no days due to sickness was 15.____
    A. 190   B. 236   C. 290   D. 346

Questions 16-18.

DIRECTIONS: In the graph below, the lines labeled "A" and "B" represent the cumulative progress in the work of two file clerks, each of whom was given 500 consecutively numbered applications to file in the proper cabinets over a five-day work week. Questions 16 through 18 are to be answered SOLELY upon the data provided in the graph.

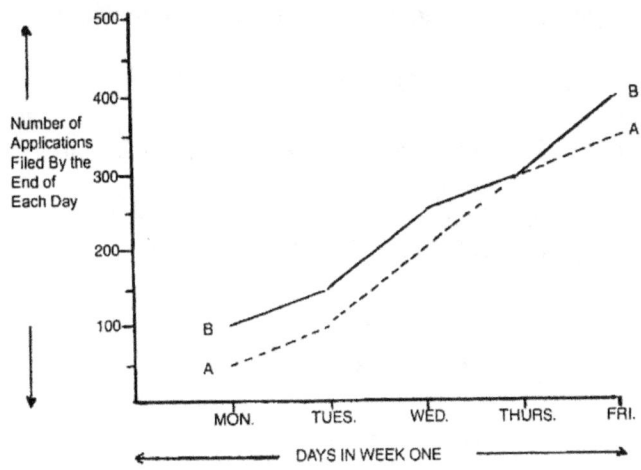

16. The day during which the LARGEST number of applications was filed by both clerks was
    A. Monday   B. Tuesday   C. Wednesday   D. Friday

16.____

17. At the end of the second day, the percentage of applications STILL to be filed was
    A. 25%   B. 50%   C. 66%   D. 75%

17.____

18. Assuming that the production pattern is the same the following week as the week shown in the chart, the day on which the file clerks will FINISH this assignment will be
    A. Monday   B. Tuesday   C. Wednesday   D. Friday

18.____

Questions 19-21.

DIRECTIONS: The following chart shows the differences between the rates of production of employees in Department D in 2009 and 2019. Questions 19 through 21 are to be answered SOLELY on the basis of the information given in the chart.

Number of Employees Producing Work-Units Within Range in 2009	Number of Work-Units Produced	Number of Employees Producing Work-Units Within Range in 2019
7	500 – 1000	4
14	1001 – 1500	11
26	1501 – 2000	28
22	2001 – 2500	36
17	2501 – 3000	39
10	3001 – 3500	23
4	3501 - 4000	9

19. Assuming that within each range of work-units produced the average production was at the mid-point at that range (e.g., category 500 – 1000 = 750), then the AVERAGE number of work-units produced per employee in 2009 fell into the range
    A. 1001 – 1500   B. 1501 – 2000   C. 2001 – 2500   D. 2501 – 3000

19.____

20. The ratio of the number of employees producing more than 2000 work-units in 2009 to the number of employees producing more than 2000 work-units in 2019 is MOST NEARLY
    A. 1:2   B. 2:3   C. 3:4   D. 4:5

20.____

21. In Department D, which of the following were GREATER in 2019 than in 2009?
    I. Total number of employees
    II. Total number of work-units produced
    III. Number of employees producing 2000 or fewer work-units
    The CORRECT answer is
    A. I, II, III   B. I, II   C. I, III   D. II, III

21.____

22. Unit S's production fluctuated substantially from one year to another. In 2018, Unit S's production was 100% greater than in 2017. In 2019, production decreased by 25% from 2018. In 2020, Unit S's production was 10% greater than in 2019.
On the basis of this information, it is CORRECT to conclude that Unit S's production in 2020 exceeded Unit S's production in 2017 by
  A. 65%   B. 85%   C. 95%   D. 135%

22._____

23. Agency "X" is moving into a new building. It has 1500 employees presently on its staff and does not contemplate much variance from this level. The new building contains 100 available offices, each with a maximum capacity of 30 employees. It has been decided that only 2/3 of the maximum capacity of each office will be utilized.
The TOTAL number of offices that will be occupied by Agency "X" is
  A. 30   B. 66   C. 75   D. 90

23._____

24. One typist completes a form letter every 5 minutes and another typist completes one every 6 minutes.
If the two typists start together, they will again start typing new letters simultaneously _____ minutes later and will have completed _____ letters by that time.
  A. 11; 30   B. 12; 24   C. 24; 12   D. 30; 11

24._____

25. During one week, a machine operator produces 10 fewer pages per hour of work than he usually does.
If it ordinarily takes him six hours to produce a 300-page report, it will take him _____ hours longer to produce that same 300-page report during the week when he produces more slowly.
  A. 1½   B. 1⅔   C. 2   D. 2¾

25._____

KEY (CORRECT ANSWERS)

		Incorrect Words
1.	A	stability
2.	D	obsolete
3.	D	freeze
4.	D	abrogated
5.	C	preclude

6.	C	16.	C
7.	C	17.	D
8.	B	18.	B
9.	A	19.	C
10.	D	20.	A
11.	D	21.	B
12	C	22.	A
13.	D	23.	C
14.	C	24.	D
15.	C	25.	A

EXAMINATION SECTION
TEST 1

DIRECTIONS: Each question or incomplete statement is followed by several suggested answers or completions. Select the one that BEST answers the question or completes the statement. *PRINT THE LETTER OF THE CORRECT ANSWER IN THE SPACE AT THE RIGHT.*

Questions 1-5.

DIRECTIONS: Questions 1 through 5 consist of sentences, each of which contains one underlined word whose meaning you are to identify by marking your answer either A, B, C, or D.

EXAMPLE

Public employees should avoid unethical conduct.
The word unethical, as used in the sentence, means MOST NEARLY
   A. fine   B. dishonest   C. polite   D. sleepy
The correct answer is *dishonest* (B). Therefore, you should mark your answer B.

1. Employees who can produce a considerable amount of good work are very valuable.
   The word *considerable*, as used in the sentence, means MOST NEARLY
      A. large   B. potential   C. necessary   D. frequent

2. No person should assume that he knows more than anyone else.
   The word *assume*, as used in the sentence, means MOST NEARLY
      A. verify   B. hope   C. suppose   D. argue

3. The parties decided to negotiate through the night.
   The word *negotiate*, as used in the sentence, means MOST NEARLY
      A. suffer   B. play   C. think   D. bargain

4. Employees who have severe emotional problems may create problems at work.
   The word *severe*, as used in the sentence, means MOST NEARLY
      A. serious   B. surprising   C. several   D. common

5. Supervisors should try to be as objective as possible when dealing with subordinates.
   The word *objective*, as used in the sentence, means MOST NEARLY
      A. pleasant   B. courteous   C. fair   D. strict

Questions 6-10.

DIRECTIONS: In each of Questions 6 through 10, one word is wrong because it is NOT in keeping with the intended meaning of the statement. First, decide which word is wrongly used; then select as your answer the right word which really belongs in its place.

EXAMPLE

The employee told ill and requested permission to leave early.
  A. felt   B. considered   C. cried   D. spoke

The word "*told*" is clearly wrong and not in keeping with the intended meaning of the quotation.
The word "*felt*" (A), however, would clearly convey the intended meaning of the sentence. Option A is correct. Your answer space, therefore, should be marked A.

6. Only unwise supervisors would deliberately overload their subordinates in order to create themselves look good.
  A. delegate   B. make   C. reduce   D. produce

7. In a democratic organization each employee is seen as a special individual kind of fair treatment.
  A. granted   B. denial   C. perhaps   D. deserving

8. In order to function the work flow in an office you should begin by identifying each important procedure being performed in that office.
  A. uniformity   B. study   C. standards   D. reward

9. A wise supervisor tries to save employees' time by simplifying forms or adding forms where possible.
  A. taxing   B. supervising   C. eliminating D. protecting

10. A public agency, whenever it changes its program, should give requirements to the need for retraining its employees.
  A. legislation   B. consideration
  C. permission   D. advice

Questions 11-15.

DIRECTIONS: Questions 11 through 15 are to be answered ONLY on the basis of the reading passage preceding each question.

11. Things may not always be what they seem to be. Thus, the wise supervisor should analyze his problems and determine whether there is something there that does not meet the eye. For example, what may seem on the surface to be a personality clash between two subordinates may really be a problem of faulty organization, bad communication, or bad scheduling.

Which one of the following statements BEST supports this passage?
- A. The wise supervisor should avoid personality clashes.
- B. The smart supervisor should figure out what really is going on.
- C. Bad scheduling is the result of faulty organization.
- D. The best supervisor is the one who communicates effectively.

12. Some supervisors, under the pressure of meeting deadlines, become harsh and dictatorial to their subordinates. However, the supervisor most likely to be effective in meeting deadlines is one who absorbs or cushions pressures from above.
    According to the passage, if a supervisor wishes to meet deadlines, it is MOST important that he
    - A. be informative to his superiors
    - B. encourage personal initiative among his subordinates
    - C. become harsh and dictatorial to his subordinates
    - D. protects his subordinates from pressures from above

13. When giving instructions, a supervisor must always make clear his meaning, leaving no room for misunderstanding. For example, a supervisor who tells a subordinate to do a task "as soon as possible" might legitimately be understood to mean either "it's top priority" or "do it when you can."
    Which of the following statements is BEST supported by the passage?
    - A. Subordinates will attempt to avoid work by deliberately distorting instructions.
    - B. Instructions should be short, since brief instructions are the clearest.
    - C. Less educated subordinates are more likely to honestly misunderstand instructions.
    - D. A supervisor should give precise instructions that cannot be misinterpreted.

14. Practical formulas are often suggested to simplify what a supervisor should know and how he should behave, such as the four F's (be firm, fair, friendly, and factual). But such simple formulas are really broad principles, not necessarily specific guides in a real situation.
    According to the passage, simple formulas for supervisory behavior
    - A. are superior to complicated theories and principles
    - B. not always of practical use in actual situations
    - C. useful only if they are fair and factual
    - D. would be better understood if written in clear language

15. Many management decisions are made far removed from the actual place of operations. Therefore, there is a great need for reliable reports and records and, the larger the organization, the greater is the need for such reports and records.
    According to the passage, management decisions made far from the place of operations are
    - A. dependent to a great extent on reliable reports and records
    - B. sometimes in error because of the great distances involved

C. generally unreliable because of poor communications
D. generally more accurate than on-the-scene decisions

16. Assume that you have just been advanced to a supervisory administrative position and have been assigned as supervisor to a new office with subordinates you do not know.
The BEST way for you to establish good relations with these new subordinates would be to
    A. announce that all actions of the previous supervisor are now cancelled
    B. hold a meeting and warn them that you will not tolerate loafing on the job
    C. reassign all your subordinates to new tasks on the theory that a thorough shake-up is good for morale
    D. act fairly and show helpful interest in their work

17. One of your subordinates asks you to let her arrive at work 15 minutes later than usual but leave for the day 15 minutes later than she usually does. This is temporarily necessary, your subordinate states, because of early morning medication she must give her sick child.
Which of the following would be the MOST appropriate action for you to take?
    A. Suggest to your subordinate that she choose another family doctor
    B. Warn your subordinate that untruthful excuses are not acceptable
    C. Tell your subordinate that you will consider the request and let her know very shortly
    D. Deny the request since late arrival at work interferes with work performance

18. A young newly-hired employee asked his supervisor several times for advice on private financial matters. The supervisor commented, in a friendly manner, that he considered it undesirable to give such advice.
The supervisor's response was
    A. *unwise*; the supervisor missed an opportunity to advise the employee on an important matter
    B. *wise*; if the financial advice was wrong, it could damage the supervisor's relationship with the subordinate
    C. *unwise*; the subordinate will take up the matter with his fellow workers and probably get poor advice
    D. *wise*; the supervisor should never advise subordinates on any matter

19. Which of the following is the MOST justified reason for a supervisor to pay any serious attention to a subordinate's off-the-job behavior? The
    A. subordinate's lifestyle is different from the supervisor's way of life
    B. subordinate has become well-known as a serious painter of fine art
    C. subordinate's work has become very poor as a result of his or her personal problems
    D. subordinate is a reserved person who, at work, seldom speaks of personal matters

20. One of your subordinates complains to you that you assign him to the least pleasant jobs more often than anyone else. You are disturbed by this complaint since you believe you have always rotated such assignments on a fair basis.
    Of the following, it would be BEST for you to tell the complaining subordinate that
    A. you will review your past assignment records and discuss the matter with him further
    B. complaints to supervisors are not the wise way to get ahead on the job
    C. disciplinary action will follow if the complaint is not justified
    D. he may be correct, but you do not have sufficient time to verify the complaint

21. Assume that you have called one of your subordinates into your office to talk about the increasing number of careless errors in her work. Until recently, this subordinate had been doing good work, but this is no longer so. Your subordinate does not seem to respond to your questions about the reason for her poor work.
    In these circumstances, your NEXT step should be to tell her
    A. that her continued silence will result in severe disciplinary action
    B. to request an immediate transfer from your unit
    C. to return when she is ready to respond
    D. to be more open with you so that her work problem can be identified

22. Assume that you are given a complicated assignment with a tight deadline set by your superior. Shortly after you begin work you realize that, if you are to do a top quality job, you cannot possibly meet the deadline.
    In these circumstances, what should be your FIRST course of action?
    A. Continue working as rapidly as possible, hoping that you will meet the deadline after all
    B. Request the assignment be given to an employee whom you believe works faster
    C. Advise your superior of the problem and see whether the deadline can be extended
    D. Advise your superior that the deadline cannot be met and, therefore, you will not start the job

23. Assume that a member of the public comes to you to complain about a long-standing practice of your agency. The complaint seems to be justified.
    Which one of the following is the BEST way for you to handle this situation?
    A. Inform the complainant that you will have the agency practice looked into and that he will be advised of any action taken
    B. Listen politely, express sympathy, and state that you see no fault in the practice
    C. Express agreement with the practice on the ground that it has been in effect for many years
    D. Advise the complainant that things will work out well in good time

24. One of your subordinates tells you that he sees no reason for having departmental safety rules.
Which one of the following replies would be BEST for you to make?
   A. Rules are meant to be obeyed without question
   B. All types of rules are equally important
   C. Safety rules are meant to protect people from injury
   D. If a person is careful enough, he doesn't have to observe safety rules

25. Assume that a supervisor, when he issues instructions to his subordinates, usually names his superior as the source of these instructions.
This practice is GENERALLY
   A. *wise*, since if things go wrong, the subordinates will know whom to blame
   B. *unwise*, since it may give the subordinates the impression that the supervisor doesn't really support the instructions
   C. *wise*, since it clearly invites the subordinates to go to higher authority if they don't like the instructions

KEY (CORRECT ANSWERS)

1.	A		11.	B
2.	C		12.	D
3.	D		13.	D
4.	A		14.	B
5.	C		15.	A
6.	B		16.	D
7.	D		17.	C
8.	B		18.	B
9.	C		19.	C
10.	B		20.	A

21.	D
22.	C
23.	A
24.	C
25.	B

TEST 2

DIRECTIONS: Each question or incomplete statement is followed by several suggested answers or completions. Select the one that BEST answers the question or completes the statement. *PRINT THE LETTER OF THE CORRECT ANSWER IN THE SPACE AT THE RIGHT.*

1. An office aide is assigned as a receptionist in a busy office. The office aide often has stretches of idle time between visitors.
   In this situation, the supervisor should
   A. give the receptionist non-urgent clerical jobs which can quickly be done at the reception desk
   B. offer all office aides an opportunity to volunteer for this assignment
   C. eliminate the receptionist assignment
   D. continue the arrangement unchanged, because receptionist duties are so important nothing should interfere with them

1.____

2. A supervisor can MOST correctly assume that an employee is not performing up to his usual standard when the employee does not handle a task as skillfully as
   A. do other employees who have received less training
   B. do similar employees having comparable work experience
   C. he has handled it in several recent instances
   D. the supervisor himself could handle it

2.____

3. Assume that you receive a suggestion that you direct all the typists in a typing pool to complete the identical quantity of work each day.
   For you to adopt this suggestion would be
   A. *advisable*; it will demonstrate the absence of supervisory favoritism
   B *advisable*; all employees in a given title should be treated identically
   C. *inadvisable*; a supervisor should decide on work standards without interference from others
   D. *inadvisable*; it ignores variations in specific assignments and individual skills

3.____

4. A certain supervisor encouraged her subordinates to tell her if they become aware of possible job problems.
   This practice is good MAINLY because
   A. early awareness of job problems allows more time for seeking solutions
   B. such expected job problems may not develop
   C. the supervisor will be able to solve the job problem without consulting other people
   D. the supervisor will be able to place responsibility for poor work

4.____

5. Some supervisors will discuss with a subordinate how he is doing on the job only when indicating his mistakes or faults.
   Which of the following is the MOST likely result of such a practice?
   A. The subordinate will become discouraged and frustrated.
   B. Management will set work standards too low.

5.____

C. The subordinate will be favorably impressed by the supervisor's frankness.
D. Supervisors will avoid creating any impression of favoritism.

6. A supervisor calls in a subordinate he supervises to discuss the subordinate's annual work performance, indicating his work deficiencies and also praising his job strengths. The subordinate nods his head as if in agreement with his supervisor's comments on both his strengths and weaknesses, but actually says nothing, even after the supervisor has completed his comments.
At this point, the supervisor should
   A. end the session and assume that the subordinate agrees completely with the evaluation
   B. end the session, since all the subordinate's good and bad points have been identified
   C. ask the supervisor whether the criticism is justified, and, if so, what he, the supervisor, can do to help
   D. thank the subordinate for being so fair-minded in accepting the criticism in a positive manner

6.____

7. The successful supervisor is often one who gives serious attention to his subordinates' needs for job satisfaction.
A supervisor who believes this statement is MOST likely to
   A. treat all subordinates in an identical manner, irrespective of individual differences
   B. permit each subordinate to perform his work as he wishes, within reasonable limits
   C. give all subordinates both criticism and praise in equal measure
   D. provide each subordinate with as much direct supervision as possible

7.____

8. Assume that you are supervising seven subordinates and have been asked by your superior to prepare an especially complex report due today. Its completion will take the rest of the day. You break down the assignment into simple parts and give a different part to each subordinate.
If you were to explain the work of each subordinate to more than one subordinate, your decision would be
   A. *wise*; this would prevent boredom
   B. *unwise*; valuable time would be lost
   C. *wise*; your subordinates would become well-rounded
   D. *unwise*; your subordinates would lose their competitive spirit

8.____

9. Suppose that an office associate whom you supervise has given you a well-researched report on a problem in an area in which he is expert. However, the report lacks solutions or recommendations. You know this office associate to be fearful of stating his opinions.
In these circumstances, you should tell him that
   A. you will seek recommendations on the problem from other, even if less expert, office associates
   B. his work is satisfactory, in hope of arousing him to greater assertiveness

9.____

3 (#2)

C. you need his advice and expertise, to help you reach a decision on the problem
D. his uncooperative behavior leaves you no choice but to speak to your superior

10. If a supervisor wishes to have the work of his unit completed on schedule, it is usually MOST important to
    A. avoid listening to employees' complaints, thereby discouraging dissatisfaction
    B. perform much of the work himself, since he is generally more capable
    C. observe employees continuously, so they do not slacken their efforts
    D. set up the work carefully, then stay informed as to how it is moving

10.____

11. Of the following agencies, the one MOST likely to work out a proposed budget close to its real needs is
    A. a newly-created agency staffed by inexperienced administrators
    B. funded with a considerable amount of money
    C. an existing agency which intends to install new, experimental systems for doing its work
    D. an existing agency which can base its estimate on its experience during the past few years

11.____

12. Assume that you are asked to prepare a report on the expected costs and benefits of a proposed new program to be installed in your office. However, you are aware that certain factors are not really measurable in dollars and cents.
    As a result, you should
    A. identify the non-measurable factors and state why they are important
    B. assign a fixed money value to all factors that are not really measurable
    C. recommend that programs containing non-measurable factors should be dropped
    D. assume that the non-measurable factors are really unimportant

12.____

13. Assume that you are asked for your opinion as to the necessity for hiring more employees to perform certain revenue-producing work in your office.
    The information that you will MOST likely need in giving an informed opinion is
    A. whether public opinion would favor hiring additional employees
    B. an estimate of the probable additional revenue compared with the additional personnel costs
    C. the total cost of all city operations in contrast to all city revenues
    D. the method by which present employees would be selected for promotion in an expanded operation

13.____

14. The MOST reasonable number of subordinate for a supervisor to have is BEST determined by the
    A. average number of subordinates other supervisors have
    B. particular responsibilities given to the supervisor
    C. supervisor's educational background
    D. personalities of the subordinates assigned to the supervisor

14.____

15. Most subordinates would need less supervision if they knew what they were supposed to do.
    An ESSENTIAL first step in fixing in subordinates' minds exactly what is required of them is to
    A. require that supervisors be firm in their supervision of subordinates
    B. encourage subordinates to determine their own work standards
    C. encourage subordinates to submit suggestions to improve procedures
    D. standardize and simplify procedures and logically schedule activities

16. Assume that you have been asked to recommend an appropriate office layout to correspond with a just completed office reorganization.
    Which of the following is it MOST advisable to recommend?
    A. Allocate most of the space for traffic flow
    B. Use the center area only for traffic flow
    C. Situate close to each other those units whose work is closely related
    D. Group in an out-of-the-way corner the supply and file cabinets

17. Although an organization chart will illustrate the formal structure of an agency, it will seldom show a true picture of its actual workings.
    Which of the following BEST explains this statement?
    Organization charts
    A. are often prepared by employees who may exaggerate their own importance
    B. usually show titles and sometimes names rather than the actual contacts and movements between employees
    C. are likely to discourage the use of official titles, and in so doing promote greater freedom in human relations
    D. usually show the informal arrangements and dealings between employees

18. Assume that a supervisor of a large unit has a variety of tasks to perform, and that he gives each of his subordinates just one set of tasks to do. He never rotates subordinates from one set of tasks to another.
    Which one of the following is the MOST likely advantage to be gained by this practice?
    A. Each subordinate will get to know all the tasks of the unit.
    B. The subordinate will be encouraged to learn all they can about all the unit's tasks.
    C. Each subordinate will become an expert in his particular set of tasks.
    D. The subordinates will improve their opportunities for promotion.

19. Listed below are four steps commonly used in trying to solve administrative problems. These four steps are not listed in the order in which they normally would be taken. If they were listed in the proper order, which step should be taken FIRST?
    I. Choosing the most practical solution to the problem
    II. Analyzing the essential facts about the problem
    III. Correctly identifying the problem
    IV. Following up to see if the solution chosen really works

5 (#2)

The CORRECT answer is:
A. III   B. I   C. II   D. IV

20. Assume that another agency informally tells you that most of your agency's reports are coming to them with careless errors made by many of your office aides.
Which one of the following is MOST likely to solve this problem?
   A. Require careful review of all outgoing reports by the supervisors of the office aides
   B. Request the other agency to make necessary corrections whenever such errors come to their attention
   C. Ask the other agency to submit a written report on this situation
   D. Establish a small unit to review all reports received from other agencies

20.____

21. Assume that you supervise an office which gets two kinds of work. One kind is high-priority and must be done within two days. The other kind of work must be done within two weeks.
Which one of the following instructions would be MOST reasonable for you to give to your subordinates in this office?
   A. If a backlog builds up during the day, clean the backlog up first, regardless of priority
   B. Spend half the day doing priority work and the other half doing non-priority work
   C. Generally do the priority work first as soon as it is received
   D. Usually do the work in the order in which it comes in, priority or non-priority

21.____

22. An experienced supervisor should do advance planning of his subordinates' work assignments and schedules.
Which one of the following is the BEST reason for such advance planning?
It
   A. enables the supervisor to do less supervision
   B. will assure the assignment of varied duties
   C. will make certain a high degree of discipline among subordinates
   D. helps make certain that essential operations are adequately covered

22.____

23. Agencies are required to evaluate the performance of their employees.
Which one of the following would generally be POOR evaluation practice by an agency rater?
The rater
   A. regularly observes the performance of the employee being rated
   B. in evaluating the employee, acquaints himself with the employee's job
   C. uses objective standards in evaluating the employee being rated
   D. uses different standards in evaluating men and women

23.____

19

24. A good supervisor should have a clear idea of the quantity and quality of his subordinates' work.
    Which one of the following sources would normally provide a supervisor with the LEAST reliable information about a subordinate's work performance?
    A. Discussion with a friend of the subordinate
    B. Comments by other supervisors who have worked recently with the subordinate
    C. Opinions of fellow workers who work closely with the subordinate on a daily basis
    D. Comparison with work records of others doing similar work during the same period of time

25. In order to handle the ordinary work of an office, a supervisor sets up standard work procedures.
    The MOST likely benefit of this is to reduce the need to
    A. motivate employees to do superior work
    B. rethink what has to be done every time a routine matter comes up
    C. keep record and write reports
    D. change work procedures as new situations come up

KEY (CORRECT ANSWERS)

1.	A	11.	D
2.	C	12.	A
3.	D	13.	B
4.	A	14.	B
5.	A	15.	D
6.	C	16.	C
7.	B	17.	B
8.	B	18.	C
9.	C	19.	A
10.	D	20.	A

21.	C
22.	D
23.	D
24.	A
25.	B

EXAMINATION SECTION
TEST 1

DIRECTIONS: Each question or incomplete statement is followed by several suggested answers or completions. Select the one that BEST answers the question or completes the statement. *PRINT THE LETTER OF THE CORRECT ANSWER IN THE SPACE AT THE RIGHT.*

1. In almost every organization there is a nucleus of highly important functions commonly designated as *management*.
   Which of the following statements BEST characterizes *management*?
   A. Getting things done through others
   B. The highest level of intelligence in any organization
   C. The process whereby democratic and participative activities are maximized
   D. The *first among equals*

   1.____

2. Strategies in problem-solving are important to anyone aspiring to advancement in the field of administration.
   Which of the following is BEST classified as the first step in the process of problem-solving?
   A. Collection and organization of data
   B. The formulation of a plan
   C. The definition of the problem
   D. The development of a method and methodology

   2.____

3. One of the objectives of preparing a budget is to
   A. create optimistic goals which each department can attempt to meet
   B. create an overall company goals by combining the budgets of the various departments
   C. be able to compare planned expenditures against actual expenditures
   D. be able to identify accounting errors

4. The rise in demand for *systems* personnel in industrial and governmental organizations over the past five years has been extraordinary.
   In which of the following areas would a *systems* specialist assigned to an agency be LEAST likely to be of assistance?
   A. Developing, recommending, and establishing an effective cost and inventory system
   B. Development and maintenance of training manuals
   C. Reviewing existing work procedures and recommending improvements
   D. Development of aptitude tests for new employees

   4.____

5. Management experts have come to the conclusion that the traditional forms of motivation used in industry and government, which emphasize authority over and economic rewards for the employee, are no longer appropriate.

   5.____

To which of the following factors do such experts attribute the GREATEST importance in producing this change?
- A. The desire of employees to satisfy material needs has become greater and more complex.
- B. The desire for social satisfaction has become the most important aspect of the job for the average worker.
- C. With greater standardization of work processes, there has been an increase in the willingness of workers to accept discipline.
- D. In general, employee organizations have made it more difficult for management to fire an employee.

6. In preparing a budget, it is usually considered advisable to start the initial phases of preparation at the operational level of management.
Of the following, the justification that management experts usually advance as MOST reasonable for this practice is that operating managers, as a consequence of their involvement, will
- A. develop a background in finance or accounting
- B. have an understanding of the organizational structure
- C. tend to feel responsible for carrying out budget activities
- D. have the ability to see the overall financial picture

7. An administrative officer has been asked by his superior to write a concise, factual report with objective conclusions and recommendations based on facts assembled by other researchers.
Of the following factors, the administrative officer should give LEAST consideration to
- A. the educational level of the person or persons for whom the report is being prepared
- B. the use to be made of the report
- C. the complexity of the problem
- D. his own feelings about the importance of the problem

8. In an agency, upon which of the following is a supervisor's effectiveness MOST likely to depend?
The
- A. degree to which a supervisor allows subordinates to participate in the decision-making process and the setting of objectives
- B. degree to which a supervisor's style meets management's objectives and subordinates' needs
- C. strength and forcefulness of the supervisor in pursuing his objectives
- D. expertise and knowledge of the supervisor has about the specific work to be done

9. For authority to be effective, which of the following is the MOST basic requirement?
Authority must be
- A. absolute   B. formalized   C. accepted   D. delegated

10. Management no longer abhors the idea of employees taking daily work breaks, but prefers to schedule such breaks rather than to allot to each employee a standard amount of free time to be taken off during the day as he wishes. Which of the following BEST expresses the reason management theorists give for the practice of scheduling such breaks?
    A. Many jobs fall into natural work units which are scheduled, and the natural time to take a break is at the end of the unit
    B. Taking a scheduled break permits socialization and a feeling of accomplishment
    C. Managers have concluded that scheduling rest periods seems to reduce the incidence of unscheduled ones
    D. Many office workers who really need such breaks are hesitant about taking them unless they are scheduled

11. The computer represents one of the major developments of modern technology. It is widely used in both scientific and managerial activities because of its many advantages.
    Which of the following is NOT an advantage gained by management in the use of the computer?
    A computer
    A. provides the manager with a greatly enlarged memory so that he can easily be provided with data for decision making
    B. relieves the manager of basic decision-making responsibility, thereby giving him more time for directing and controlling
    C. performs routine, repetitive calculations with greater precision and reliability than employees
    D. provides a capacity for rapid simulations of alternative solutions to problem solving

12. A supervisor of a unit in a division is usually responsible for all of the following EXCEPT
    A. the conduct of subordinates in the achievement of division objectives
    B. maintaining quality standards in the unit
    C. the protection and care of materials and equipment in the unit
    D. performing the most detailed tasks in the unit himself

13. You have been assigned to teach a new employee the functions and procedures of your office.
    In your introductory talk, which of the following approaches is PREFERABLE?
    A. Advise the new employee of the employee benefits and services available to him, over and above his salary
    B. Discuss honestly the negative aspects of departmental procedures and indicate methods available to overcome them
    C. Give the new employee an understanding of the general purpose of office procedures and functions and of their relevance to departmental objectives
    D. Give a basic and detailed explanation of the operations of your office, covering all functions and procedures

14. It is your responsibility to assign work to several clerks under your supervision. One of the clerks indignantly refuses to accept an assignment and asks to be given something else. He has not yet indicated why he does not want the assignment, but is sitting there glaring at you, awaiting your reaction.
Of the following, which is the FIRST action you should take?
    A. Ask the employee into your office in order to reprimand him and tell him emphatically that he must accept the assignment
    B. Talk to the employee privately in an effort to find the reason for his indignation and refusal, and then base your action upon your findings
    C. Let the matter drop for a day or two to allow the employee to cool off before you insist that he accept the assignment
    D. Inform the employee quietly and calmly that as his supervisor you have selected him for this assignment and that you fully expect him to accept it

15. Administrative officers are expected to be able to handle duties delegated to them by their supervisors and to be able, as they advance in status, to delegate tasks to assistants.
When considering whether to delegate tasks to a subordinate, which of the following questions should be LEAST important to an administrative officer?
In the delegated tasks,
    A. how significant are the decisions to be made, and how much consultation will be involved?
    B. to what extent is uniformity and close coordination of activity required?
    C. to what extent must speedy-on-the-spot decisions be made?
    D. to what extent will delegation relieve the administrative officer of his burden of responsibility?

16. A functional forms file is a collection of forms which are grouped by
    A. purpose   B. department   C. title   D. subject

17. All of the following are reasons to consult a records retention schedule except one.
Which one is that?
To determine
    A. whether something should be filed
    B. how long something should stay in file
    C. who should be assigned to filing
    D. when something on file should be destroyed

18. Listed below are four of the steps in the process of preparing correspondence for filing.
If they were to be put in logical sequence, the SECOND step would be
    A. preparing cross-reference sheets or cards
    B. coding the correspondence using a classification system
    C. sorting the correspondence in the order to be filed
    D. checking for follow-up action required and preparing a follow-up slip

5 (#1)

19. New material added to a file folder should USUALLY be inserted
    A. in the order of importance (the most important in front)
    B. in the order of importance (the most important in back)
    C. chronologically (most recent in front)
    D. chronologically (most recent in back)

20. An individual is looking for a name in the white pages of a telephone directory. Which of the following BEST describes the system of filing found there?
    A(n) _____ file
    A. alphabetic   B. sequential   C. locator   D. index

21. The MAIN purpose of a tickler file is to
    A. help prevent overlooking matters that require future attention
    B. check on adequacy of past performance
    C. pinpoint responsibility for recurring daily tasks
    D. reduce the volume of material kept in general files

22. Which of the following BEST describes the process of reconciling a bank statement?
    A. Analyzing the nature of the expenditures made by the office during the preceding month
    B. Comparing the statement of the bank with the banking records maintained in the office
    C. Determining the liquidity position by reading the bank statement carefully
    D. Checking the service charges noted on the bank statement

23. From the viewpoint of preserving agency or institutional funds, which of the following is the LEAST acceptable method for making a payment?
    A check made out to
    A. cash   B. a company
    C. an individual   D. a partnership

24. In general, the CHIEF economy of using multicopy forms is in
    A. the paper on which the form is printed
    B. printing the form
    C. employee time
    D. carbon paper

25. Suppose your supervisor has asked you to develop a form to record certain information needed.
    The FIRST thing you should do is to
    A. determine the type of data that will be recorded repeatedly so that it can be preprinted
    B. study the relationship of the form to the job to be accomplished so that the form can be planned
    C. determine the information that will be recorded in the same place on each copy of the form so that it can be used as a check
    D. find out who will be responsible for supplying the information so that space can be provided for their signatures

26. An administrative officer in charge of a small fund for buying office supplies has just written a check to Charles Laird, a supplier, and has sent the check by messenger to him. A half-hour later, the messenger telephones the administrative officer. He has lost the check.
Which of the following is the MOST important action for the administrative officer to take under these circumstances?
   A. Ask the messenger to return and write a report describing the loss of the check
   B. Make a note on the performance record of the messenger who lost the check
   C. Take the necessary steps to have payment stopped on the check
   D. Refrain from doing anything since the check may be found shortly

27. A petty cash fund is set up PRIMARILY to
   A. take care of small investments that must be made from time to time
   B. take care of small expenses that arise from time to time
   C. provide a fund to be used as the office wants to use it with little need to maintain records
   D. take care of expenses that develop during emergencies, such as machine breakdowns and fires

28. Of the following, which is usually the MOST important guideline in writing business letters?
A letter should be
   A. neat
   B. written in a formalized style
   C. written in clear language intelligible to the reader
   D. written in the past tense

29. Suppose you are asked to edit a policy statement. You note that personal pronouns like *you*, *we*, and *I* are used freely.
Which of the following statements BEST applies to this use of personal pronouns?
It
   A. is proper usage because written business language should not be different from carefully spoken business language
   B. requires correction because is it ungrammatical
   C. is proper because it is clearer and has a warmer tone
   D. requires correction because policies should be expressed in an impersonal manner

30. Good business letters are coherent.
To be coherent means to
   A. keep only one unifying idea in the message
   B. present the total message
   C. use simple, direct words for the message
   D. tie together the various ideas in the message

31. Proper division of a letter into paragraphs requires that the writer of business letters should, as much as possible, be sure that
    A. each paragraph is short
    B. each paragraph develops discussion of just one topic
    C. each paragraph repeats the theme of the total message
    D. there are at least two paragraphs for every message

32. An editor is given a letter with this initial paragraph:
    We have received your letter, which we read with interest, and we are happy to respond to your question. In fact, we talked with several people in our office to get ideas to send to you.
    Which of the following is MOST reasonable for the editor to conclude?
    The paragraph is
    A. concise
    B. communicating something of value
    C. unnecessary
    D. coherent

33. As soon as you pick up the phone, a very angry caller begins immediately to complain about city agencies and *red tape*. He says that he has been shifted to two or three different offices. It turns out that he is seeking information which is not immediately available to you. You believe you know, however, where it can be found.
    Which of the following actions is the BEST one for you to take?
    A. To eliminate all confusion, suggest that the caller write the mayor stating explicitly what he wants
    B. Apologize by telling the caller how busy city agencies now are, but also tell him directly that you do not have the information he needs
    C. Ask for the caller's telephone number and assure him you will call back after you have checked further
    D. Give the caller the name and telephone number of the person who might be able to help, but explain that you are not positive he will get results

34. Suppose that one of your duties is to dictate responses to routine requests from the public for information. A letter writer asks for information which, as expressed in a one-sentence, explicit agency rule, cannot be given out to the public.
    Of the following ways of answering the letter, which is the MOST efficient?
    A. Quote verbatim that section of the agency rules which prohibit giving this information to the public
    B. Without quoting the rule, explain why you cannot accede to the request and suggest alternative sources
    C. Describe how carefully the request was considered before classifying it as subject to the rule forbidding the issuance of such information
    D. Acknowledge receipt of the letter and advise that the requested information is not released to the public

35. Suppose you assist in supervising a staff which has rather high morale, and your own supervisor asks you to poll the staff to find out who will be able to work overtime this particular evening to help complete emergency work.
Which of the following approaches would be MOST likely to win their cooperation while maintaining their morale?
   A. Tell them that the better assignments will be given only to those who work overtime
   B. Tell them that occasional overtime is a job requirement
   C. Assure them they'll be doing you a personal favor
   D. Let them know clearly why the overtime is needed

36. Suppose that you have been asked to write and to prepare for reproduction new departmental vacation leave regulations.
After you have written the new regulations, all of which fit on one page, which one of the following would be the BESST method of reproducing 1,000 copies?
   A. An outside private printer, because you can best maintain confidentiality using this technique
   B. Xeroxing, because the copies will have the best possible appearance
   C. Typing copies, because you will be certain that there are the fewest possible errors
   D. Including it in the next company newsletter

37. Administration is the center, but not necessarily the source, of all ideas for procedural improvement.
The MOST significant implication that this principle bears for the administrative officer is that
   A. before procedural improvements are introduced, they should be approved by a majority of the staff
   B. it is the unique function of the administrative officer to derive and introduce procedural improvements
   C. the administrative officer should derive ideas and suggestions for procedural improvement from all possible sources, introducing any that promise to be effective
   D. the administrative officer should view employee grievances as the chief source of procedural improvements

38. Your bureau is assigned an important task.
Of the following, the function that you, as an administrative officer, can LEAST reasonably be expected to perform under these circumstances is
   A. division of the large job into individual tasks
   B. establishment of *production lines* within the bureau
   C. performance personally of a substantial share of all the work
   D. check up to see that the work has been done well

39. Suppose that you have broken a complex job into its smaller components before making assignments to the employees under your jurisdiction.
Of the following, the LEAST advisable procedure to follow from that point is to
   A. give each employee a picture of the importance of his work for the success of the total job
   B. establish a definite line of work flow and responsibility
   C. post a written memorandum of the best method for performing each job
   D. teach a number of alternative methods for doing each job

40. As an administrative officer, you are requested to draw up an organization chart of the whole department.
Of the following, the MOST important characteristic of such a chart is that it will
   A. include all peculiarities and details of the organization which distinguish it from any other
   B. be a schematic representation of purely administrative functions within the department
   C. present a modification of the actual departmental organization in the light of principles of scientific management
   D. present an accurate picture of the lines of authority and responsibility

KEY (CORRECT ANSWERS)

1.	A	11.	B	21.	A	31.	B
2.	C	12.	D	22.	B	32.	C
3.	C	13.	C	23.	A	33.	C
4.	D	14.	B	24.	C	34.	A
5.	D	15.	D	25.	B	35.	D
6.	C	16.	A	26.	C	36.	B
7.	D	17.	C	27.	B	37.	C
8.	B	18.	A	28.	C	38.	C
9.	C	19.	C	29.	D	39.	D
10.	C	20.	A	30.	D	40.	D

TEST 2

DIRECTIONS: Each question or incomplete statement is followed by several suggested answers or completions. Select the one that BEST answers the question or completes the statement. *PRINT THE LETTER OF THE CORRECT ANSWER IN THE SPACE AT THE RIGHT.*

Questions 1-10.

DIRECTIONS: In each of Questions 1 through 10, a pair of related words written in capital letters is followed by four other pairs of words. For each question, select the pair of words which MOST closely expresses a relationship similar to that of the pair in capital letters.

    SAMPLE QUESTION:
      BOAT – DOCK

    A. air plane – hangar   B. rain – snow
    C. cloth – cotton   D. hunger - food

Choice A is the answer to this sample question since, of the choices given, the relationship between airplane and hangar is most similar to the relationship between boat and dock.

1. AUTOMOBILE – FACTORY
   A. tea – lemon
   B. wheel – engine
   C. pot – flower
   D. paper – mill

2. GIRDER – BRIDGE
   A. petal – flower
   B. street – sidewalk
   C. meat – vegetable
   D. sun – storm

3. RADIUS – CIRCLE
   A. brick – building
   B. tie – tracks
   C. spoke – wheel
   D. axle – tire

4. DISEASE – RESEARCH
   A. death – poverty
   B. speech – audience
   C. problem – conference
   D. invalid – justice

5. CONCLUSION – INTRODUCTION
   A. commencement – beginning
   B. housing – motor
   C. caboose – engine
   D. train – cabin

6. SOCIETY – LAW
   A. baseball – rules
   B. jury – law
   C. cell – prisoner
   D. sentence – jury

7. PLAN – ACCOMPLISHMENT
   A. deed – fact
   B. method – success
   C. graph – chart
   D. rules – manual

8. ORDER – GOVERNMENT
   A. chaos – administration
   B. confusion – pandemonium
   C. rule – stability
   D. despair – hope

9. TYRANNY – FREEDOM
   A. despot – mob
   B. wealth – poverty
   C. nobility – commoners
   D. dictatorship – democracy

10. FAX – LETTER
    A. hare – tortoise
    B. lie – truth
    C. number – word
    D. report – research

Questions 11-16.

DIRECTIONS: Questions 11 through 16 are to be answered SOLELY on the basis of the information given in the passage below.

Inherent in all organized endeavors is the need to resolve the individual differences involved in conflict. Conflict may be either a positive or negative factor, since it may lead to creativity, innovation, and progress, on the one hand, or it may result, on the other hand, in a deterioration or even destruction of the organization. Thus, some forms of conflict are desirable, whereas others are undesirable and ethically wrong.

There are three management strategies which deal with interpersonal conflict. In the "divide-and-rule strategy," management attempts to maintain control by limiting the conflict to those directly involved and preventing their disagreement from spreading to the larger group. The "suppression –of-differences strategy" entails ignoring conflicts or pretending they are irrelevant. In the "working-through-differences strategy," management actively attempts to solve or resolve intergroup or interpersonal conflicts. Of the three strategies, only the last directly attacks and has the potential for eliminating the causes of conflict. An essential part of this strategy, however, is its employment by a committed and relatively mature management team.

11. According to the above passage, the *divide-and-rule strategy* for dealing with conflict is the attempt to
    A. involve other people in the conflict
    B. restrict the conflict to those participating in it
    C. divide the conflict into positive and negative factors
    D. divide the conflict into a number of smaller ones

12. The word *conflict* is used in relation to both positive and negative factors in this passage.
    Which one of the following words is MOST likely to describe the activity which the word *conflict*, in the sense of the passage, implies?
    A. Competition   B. Cooperation   C. Confusion   D. Aggression

13. According to the above passage, which one of the following characteristics is shared by both the *suppression-of-difference strategy* and the *divide-and-rule strategy*?   13.____
    A. Pretending that conflicts are irrelevant
    B. Preventing conflicts from spreading to the group situation
    C. Failure to directly attack the causes of conflict
    D. Actively attempting to resolve interpersonal conflict

14. According to the above passage, the successful resolution of interpersonal conflict requires   14.____
    A. allowing the group to mediate conflicts between two individuals
    B. division of the conflict into positive and negative factors
    C. involvement of a committed, mature management team
    D. ignoring minor conflicts until they threaten the organization

15. Which can be MOST reasonably inferred from the above passage? A conflict between two individuals is LEAST likely to continue when management uses   15.____
    A. the *working-through-differences strategy*
    B. the *suppression-of-differences strategy*
    C. the *divide-and-rule strategy*
    D. a combination of all three strategies

16. According to the above passage, a DESIRABLE result of conflict in an organization is when conflict   16.____
    A. exposes production problems in the organization
    B. can be easily ignored by management
    C. results in advancement of more efficient managers
    D. leads to development of new methods

Questions 17-23.

DIRECTIONS: Questions 17 through 23 are to be answered SOLELY on the basis of the information given in the passage below.

Modern management places great emphasis on the concept of communication. The communication process consists of the steps through which an idea or concept passes from its inception by one person, the sender, until it is acted upon by another person, the receiver. Through an understanding of these steps and some of the possible barriers that may occur, more effective communication may be achieved. The first step in the communication process is ideation by the sender. This is the formation of the intended content of the message he wants to transmit. In the next step, encoding, the sender organizes his ideas into a series of symbols designed to communicate his message to his intended receiver. He selects suitable words or phrases that can be understood by the receiver, and he also selects the appropriate media to be used—for example, memorandum, conference, etc. The third step is transmission of the encoded message through selected channels in the organizational structure. In the fourth step, the receiver enters the process by tuning in to receive the message. If the receiver does not function, however, the message is lost. For example, if the message is oral, the receiver must be a good listener. The fifth step is decoding of the message by the receiver, as for example, by changing words into ideas. At this step, the decoded message may not be the same idea that the sender originally encoded because the sender and receiver have different perceptions regarding the meaning of certain words.

Finally, the receiver acts or responds. He may file the information, ask for more information, or take other action. There can be no assurance, however, that communication has taken place unless there is some type of feedback to the sender in the form of an acknowledgement that the message was received.

17. According to the above passage, *ideation* is the process by which the 17.____
    A. sender develops the intended content of the message
    B. sender organizes his ideas into a series of symbols
    C. receiver tunes in to receive the message
    D. receiver decodes the message

18. In the last sentence of the passage, the word *feedback* refers to the process by which the sender is assured that the 18.____
    A. receiver filed the information
    B. receiver's perception is the same as his own
    C. message was received
    D. message was poorly interpreted

19. Which one of the following BEST shows the order of the steps in the communication process as described in the passage? 19.____
    A. 1 – ideation   2 – encoding
       3 – decoding   4 – transmission
       5 – receiving   6 – action
       7 – feedback to the sender
    B. 1 – ideation   2 – encoding
       3 – transmission   4 – decoding
       5 – receiving   6 – action
       7 – feedback to the sender
    C. 1 – ideation   2 – decoding
       3 – transmission   4 – receiving
       5 – encoding   6 – action
       7 – feedback to the sender
    D. 1 – ideation   2 – encoding
       3 – transmission   4 – receiving
       5 – decoding   6 – action
       7 – feedback to the sender

20. Which one of the following BEST expresses the main theme of the passage? 20.____
    A. Different individuals have the same perceptions regarding the meaning of words.
    B. An understanding of the steps in the communication process may achieve better communication.
    C. Receivers play a passive role in the communication process.
    D. Senders should not communicate with receivers who transmit feedback.

21. The above passage implies that a receiver does NOT function properly when he 21._____
    A. transmits feedback
    B. files the information
    C. is a poor listener
    D. asks for more information

22. Which of the following, according to the above passage, is included in the SECOND step of the communication process? 22._____
    A. Selecting the appropriate media to be used in transmission
    B. Formulation of the intended content of the message
    C. Using appropriate media to respond to the receiver's feedback
    D. Transmitting the message through selected channels in the organization

23. The above passage implies that the *decoding* process is MOST NEARLY the reverse of the _____ process. 23._____
    A. transmission   B. receiving   C. feedback   D. encoding

Questions 24-27.

DIRECTIONS: Questions 24 through 27 are to be answered SOLELY on the basis of the information given in the passage below.

A personnel researcher has at his disposal various approaches for obtaining information, analyzing it, and arriving at conclusions that have value in predicting and affecting the behavior of people at work. The type of method to be used depends on such factors as the nature of the research problem, the available data, and the attitude of those people being studied to the various kinds of approaches. While the experimental approach, with its use of control groups, is the most refined type of study, there are others that are often found useful in personnel research. Surveys, in which the researcher obtains facts on a problem from a variety of sources, are employed in research on wages, fringe benefits, and labor relations. Historical studies are used to trace the development of problems in order to understand them better and to isolate possible causative factors. Case studies are generally developed to explore all the details of a particular problem that is representative of other similar problems. A researcher chooses the most appropriate form of study for the problem he is investigating. He should recognize, however, that the experimental method, commonly referred to as the scientific method, if used validly and reliably, gives the most conclusive results.

24. The above statement discusses several approaches used to obtain information on particular problems. 24._____
    Which of the following may be MOST reasonably concluded from the passage? A(n)
    A. historical study cannot determine causative factors
    B. survey is often used in research on fringe benefits
    C. case study is usually used to explore a problem that is unique and unrelated to other problems
    D. experimental study is used when the scientific approach to a problem fails

6 (#2)

25. According to the above passage, all of the following are factors that may determine the type of approach a researcher uses EXCEPT
    A. the attitudes of people toward being used in control groups
    B. the number of available sources
    C. his desire to isolate possible causative factors
    D. the degree of accuracy he requires

    25._____

26. The words *scientific method*, used in the last sentence of the paragraph, refer to a type of study which, according to the paragraph,
    A. uses a variety of sources
    B. traces the development of problems
    C. uses control group
    D. analyzes the details of a representative problem

    26._____

27. Which of the following can be MOST reasonably concluded from the above passage?
    In obtaining and analyzing information on a particular problem, a researcher employs the method which is the
    A. most accurate
    B. most suitable
    C. least expensive
    D. least time-consuming

    27._____

Questions 28-31.

DIRECTIONS: Questions 28 through 31 are to be answered according to the information given in the following graph, which indicates at 5-year intervals the number of citations issued for various offenses from the year 2000 to the year 2020.

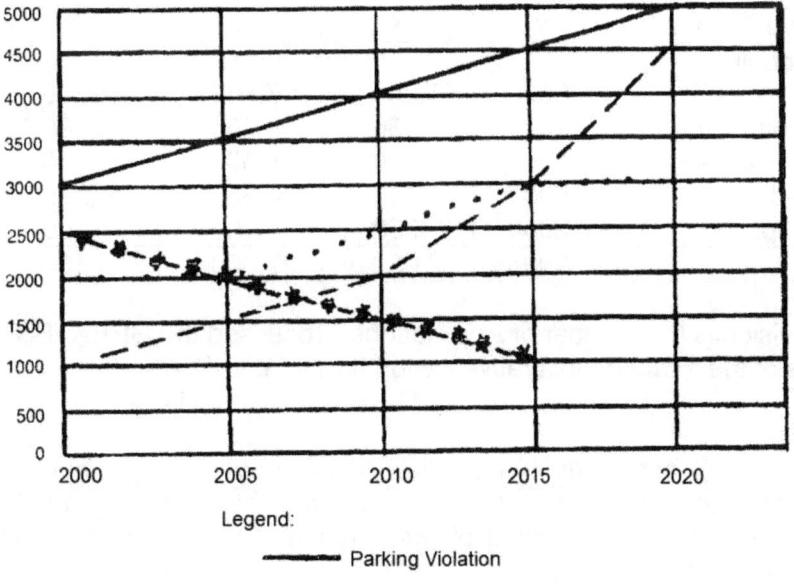

Legend:
——— Parking Violation
— — — Drug Use
· · · · Dangerous Weapons
✱–✱–✱–✱ Improper Dress

35

28. Over the 20-year period, which offense shows an AVERAGE rate of increase of more than 150 citations per year?
    A. Parking Violations
    B. Dangerous Weapons
    C. Drug Use
    D. None of the above

28._____

29. Over the 20-year period, which offense shows a CONSTANT rate of increase or decrease?
    A. Parking Violations
    B. Drug Use
    C. Dangerous Weapons
    D. Improper Dress

29._____

30. Which offense shows a TOTAL INCREASE OR DECREASE of 50% for the full 20-year period?
    A. Parking Violations
    B. Drug Use
    C. Dangerous Weapons
    D. Improper Dress

30._____

31. The percentage increase in total citations issued from 2005 to 2010 is MOST NEARLY
    A. 7%   B. 11%   C. 21%   D. 41%

31._____

Questions 32-35.

DIRECTIONS: Questions 32 through 35 are to be answered SOLELY on the basis of the information given in the following chart, which shows the annual number of administrative actions completed for the four divisions of a bureau. Assume that the figures remain stable from year to year.

	DIVISIONS				
Administrative Actions	W	X	Y	Z	TOTALS
Telephone Inquiries Answered	8,000	6,800	7,500	4,800	27,100
Interviews Conducted	500	630	550	500	2,180
Applications Processed	15,000	18,000	14,500	9,500	57,000
Letters Typed	2,500	4,400	4,350	3,250	14,500
Reports Completed	200	250	100	50	600
Totals	26,200	30,080	27,000	18,100	101,380

32. In which division is the number of Applications Processed the GREATEST percentage of the total Administrative Action for that division?
    A. W   B. X   C. Y   D. Z

32._____

33. The bureau chief is considering a plant that would consolidate the typing of letters in a separate unit. This unit would be responsible for the typing of letters for all divisions in which the number of letters typed exceeds 15% of the total number of Administrative Actions.
    Under this plan, which of the following divisions would CONTINUE to type its own letters?
    A. W and X   B. W, X, and Y   C. X and Y   D. X and Z

33._____

8 (#2)

34. The setting up of a central information service that would be capable of answering 25% of the whole bureau's telephone inquiries is under consideration. Under such a plan, the divisions would gain for other activities that time previously spent on telephone inquiries.
Approximately how much total time would such a service gain for all four divisions if it requires 5 minutes to answer the average telephone inquiry?
_____ hours.
A. 500   B. 515   C. 565   D. 585

34._____

35. Assume that the rate of production shown in the table can be projected as accurate for the coming year and that monthly output is constant for each type of administrative action within a division. Division Y is scheduled to work exclusively on a 4-month long special project during that year. During the period of the project, Division Y's regular workload will be divided evenly among the remaining divisions.
Using the figures in the table, what would be MOST NEARLY the percentage increase in the total Administrative Actions completed by Division Z for the year?
A. 8%   B. 16%   C. 25%   D. 50%

35._____

36. You have conducted a traffic survey a 10 two-lane bridges and find the traffic between 4:30 and 5:30 P.M. average 665 cars per bridge that hour. You can't find the tabulation sheet for Bridge #7, but you know that 6066 cars were counted at the other 9 bridges.
Determine from this how many must have been counted at Bridge #7.
A. 584   B. 674   C. 665   D. 607

36._____

37. You pay temporary help $11.20 per hour and regular employees $12.00 per hour. Your workload is temporarily heavy, so you need 20 hours of extra regular employees' time to catch up. If you do this on overtime, you must pay time-and-a-half. If you use temporary help, it takes 25% more time to do the job.
What is the difference in cost between the two alternatives?
A. $20 more for temporary   B. $40 more for temporary
C. $80 more for regular   D. $136 more for regular

37._____

38. An experienced clerk can process the mailing of annual forms in 9 day. A new clerk takes 14 days to process them.
If they work together, how many days MOST NEARLY will it take to do the processing?
A. 4½   B. 5½   C. 6½   D. 7

38._____

39. A certain administrative aide is usually able to successfully handle 27% of all telephone inquiries without assistance. In a particular month, he receives 1,200 inquiries and handles 340 of them successfully on his own.
How many more inquiries has he handled successfully in that month than would have been expected of him based on his usual rate?
A. 10   B. 16   C. 24   D. 44

39._____

9 (#2)

40. Suppose that on a scaled drawing of an office building floor, ½ inch represents three feet of actual floor dimensions.
A floor which is, in fact, 75 feet wide and 132 feet long has which of the following dimensions on this scaled drawing? _____ inches wide and _____ inches long.
  A. 9.5; 20.5   B. 12.5; 22   C. 17;32   D. 25; 44

40._____

41. In a division of clerks and stenographers, 15 people are currently employed, 20% of whom are stenographers.
If management plans are to maintain the current number of stenographers, but to increase the clerical staff to the point where 12% of the total staff are stenographers, what is the MAXIMUM number of additional clerks that should be hired to meet these plans?
  A. 3   B. 8   C. 10   D. 12

41._____

42. Suppose that a certain agency had a 2018 budget of $1,200,500. The 2019 budget was 7% higher than that of 2018, and the 2020 budget was 8% higher than that of 2019.
Of the following, which one is MOST NEARLY that agency's budget for 2020?
  A. $1,177,624   B. $1,261,737   C. $1,265,575   D. $1,271,738

42._____

Questions 43-50.

DIRECTIONS: Your office keeps a file card record of the work assignments for all the employees in a certain bureau. On each card is the employee's name, a work assignment code number, and the date of this assignment. In this filing system, the employee's name is filed alphabetically, the work assignment code is filed numerically, and the date of assignment is filed chronologically (earliest date first).

Each of Questions 43 through 50 represents five cards to be filed, numbered (1) through (5) shown in Column I. Each card is made up of the employee's name, a work assignment code number shown in parentheses, and the date of this assignment. The cards are to be filed according to the following rules:

First: File in alphabetical order.
Second: When two or more cards have the same employee's name, file according to the work assignment number, beginning with the lowest number.
Third: When two or more cards have the same employee's name and same assignment number, file according to the assignment date beginning with earliest date.

Column II shows the cards arranged in four different orders. Pick the answer (A, B, C, or D) in Column II which shows the cards arranged correctly according to the above filing rules.

10 (#2)

SAMPLE QUESTION:
		Column I		Column II
(1)	Cluney	(486503)	6/17/07	A. 2, 3, 4, 1, 5
(2)	Roster	(246611)	5/10/06	B. 2, 5, 1, 3, 4
(3)	Altool	(711433)	10/15/07	C. 3, 2, 1, 4, 5
(4)	Cluney	(527610)	12/18/06	D. 3, 5, 1, 4, 2
(5)	Cluney	(486500)	4/8/07	

The CORRECT way to file the cards is:
(3)	Altool	(711433)	10/15/07
(5)	Cluney	(486500)	4/8/07
(1)	Cluney	(486503)	6/17/07
(4)	Cluney	(527610)	12/18/06
(2)	Roster	(246611)	5/10/06

The correct filing order is shown by the numbers in front of each name (3, 5, 1, 4, 2). The answer to the sample question is the letter in Column II in front of the numbers 3, 5, 1, 4, 2. This answer is D.

		Column I		Column II	
43.	(1) Prichard	(013469)	4/6/06	A. 5, 4, 3, 2, 1	43.____
	(2) Parks	(678941)	2/7/06	B. 1, 2, 5, 3, 4	
	(3) Williams	(551467)	3/6/05	C. 2, 1, 5, 3, 4	
	(4) Wilson	(551466)	8/9/02	D. 1, 5, 4, 3, 2	
	(5) Stanhope	(300014)	8/9/02		
44.	(1) Ridgeway	(623809)	8/11/06	A. 5, 1, 3, 4, 2	44.____
	(2) Travers	(305439)	4/5/02	B. 5, 1, 3, 2, 4	
	(3) Tayler	(818134)	7/5/03	C. 1, 5, 3, 2, 4	
	(4) Travers	(305349)	5/6/05	D. 1, 5, 4, 2, 3	
	(5) Ridgeway	(62309)	10/9/06		
45.	(1) Jaffe	(384737)	2/19/06	A. 3, 5, 2, 4, 1	45.____
	(2) Inez	(859176)	8/8/07	B. 3, 5, 2, 1, 4	
	(3) Ingrahm	(946460)	8/6/04	C. 2, 3, 5, 1, 4	
	(4) Karp	(256146)	5/5/05	D. 2, 3, 5, 4, 1	
	(5) Ingrahm	(946460)	6/4/05		
46.	(1) Marrano	(369421)	7/24/04	A. 1, 5, 3, 4, 2	46.____
	(2) Marks	(652910)	2/23/06	B. 3, 5, 4, 2, 1	
	(3) Netto	(556772)	3/10/07	C. 2, 4, 1, 5, 3	
	(4) Marks	(652901)	2/17/07	D. 4, 2, 1, 5, 3	
	(5) Netto	(556772)	6/17/05		
47.	(1) Abernathy	(712467)	6/23/05	A. 5, 3, 1, 2, 4	47.____
	(2) Acevedo	(680262)	6/23/03	B. 5, 4, 2, 3, 1	
	(3) Aaron	(967647)	1/17/04	C. 1, 3, 5, 2, 4	
	(4) Acevedo	(680622)	5/14/02	D. 2, 4, 1, 5, 3	
	(5) Aaron	(967647)	4/1/00		

48.	(1) Simon	(645219)	8/19/05	A. 4, 1, 2, 5, 3	48.____
	(2) Simon	(645219)	9/2/03	B. 4, 5, 2, 1, 3	
	(3) Simons	(645218)	7/7/05	C. 3, 5, 2, 1, 4	
	(4) Simms	(646439)	10/12/06	D. 5, 1, 2, 3, 4	
	(5) Simon	(645219)	10/16/02		
49.	(1) Rappaport	(312230)	6/11/06	A. 4, 3, 1, 2, 5	49.____
	(2) Rascio	(777510)	2/9/05	B. 4, 3, 1, 5, 2	
	(3) Rappaport	(312230)	7/3/02	C. 3, 4, 1, 5, 2	
	(4) Rapaport	(312330)	9/6/05	D. 5, 2, 4, 3, 1	
	(5) Rascio	(777501)	7/7/05		
50.	(1) Johnson	(843250)	6/8/02	A. 1, 3, 2, 4, 5	50.____
	(2) Johnson	(843205)	4/3/05	B. 1, 3, 2, 5, 4	
	(3) Johnson	(843205)	8/6/02	C. 3, 2, 1, 4, 5	
	(4) Johnson	(843602)	3/8/06	D. 3, 2, 1, 5, 4	
	(5) Johnson	(843602)	8/3/05		

KEY (CORRECT ANSWERS)

1.	D	11.	B	21.	C	31.	B	41.	C
2.	A	12.	A	22.	A	32.	B	42.	D
3.	C	13.	C	23.	D	33.	A	43.	C
4.	C	14.	C	24.	B	34.	C	44.	A
5.	C	15.	A	25.	D	35.	B	45.	C
6.	A	16.	D	26.	C	36.	A	46.	D
7.	B	17.	A	27.	B	37.	C	47.	A
8.	C	18.	C	28.	C	38.	B	48.	B
9.	D	19.	D	29.	A	39.	B	49.	B
10.	A	20.	B	30.	C	40.	B	50.	D

EXAMINATION SECTION

TEST 1

DIRECTIONS: Each question or incomplete statement is followed by several suggested answers or completions. Select the one that BEST answers the question or completes the statement. *PRINT THE LETTER OF THE CORRECT ANSWER IN THE SPACE AT THE RIGHT.*

1. Assume that you are a supervisor of a unit which is about to start work on an urgent job. One of your subordinates starts to talk to you about the urgent job but seems not to be saying what is really on his mind.
   What is the BEST thing for you to say under these circumstances?
   A. I'm not sure I understand. Can you explain that?
   B. Please come to the point. We haven't got all day.
   C. What is it? Can't you see I'm busy?
   D. Haven't you got work to do? What do you want?

   1.____

2. Assume that you have recently been assigned a new subordinate. You have explained to this subordinate how to fill out certain forms which will constitute the major portion of her job. After the first day, you find that she has filled out the forms correctly but has not completed as many as most other workers normally complete in a day.
   Of the following, the MOST appropriate action for you to take is to
   A. tell the subordinate how many forms she is expected to complete
   B. instruct the subordinate in the correct method filling out the forms
   C. monitor the subordinate's production to see if she improves
   D. reassign the job of filling out the forms to a more experienced worker in the unit

   2.____

3. One of the problems commonly met by the supervisor is the *touchy* employee who imagines slights when none are intended.
   Of the following, the BEST way to deal with such an employee is to
   A. ignore him, until he sees the error of his behavior
   B. frequently reassure him of his value as a person
   C. advise him that oversensitive people get promoted
   D. issue written instructions to him to avoid misinterpretation

   3.____

4. The understanding supervisor should recognize that a certain amount of anxiety is common to all newly-hired employees.
   If you are a supervisor of a unit and a newly-hired employee has been assigned to you, you can usually assume that the LEAST likely worry that the new employee has is worry about
   A. the job and the standards required in the job
   B. his acceptance by the other people in your unit
   C. the difficulty of advancing to top positions in the agency
   D. your fairness in evaluating his work

   4.____

5. In assigning work to subordinates, it is often desirable for you to tell them the overall or ultimate objective of the assignment.
Of the following, the BEST reason for telling him the objective is that it will
   A. assure them that you know what you are doing
   B. eliminate most of the possible complaints about the assignment
   C. give them confidence in their ability to do the assignment
   D. help them to make decisions consistent with the objective

6. Generally a supervisor wishes to increase the likelihood that instructions given to subordinates will be carried out properly.
Of the following, the MOST important action for the supervisor to take to accomplish this objective when giving instructions to subordinates is to
   A. tailor the instructions to fit the interests of the subordinate
   B. use proper timing in giving the instruction
   C. make sure that the subordinate understand the instructions
   D. include only those instructions that are essential to the task at hand

7. Suppose that a supervisor, because of his heavy workload, has decided to delegate to his subordinates some of the duties that he has been performing.
Of the following attitudes of the supervisor, the one that is LEAST conducive toward effective delegation is his belief that
   A. his subordinates will make some mistakes in performing these duties
   B. controls will be necessary to make sure the work is done
   C. performance of these duties may be slowed down temporarily
   D. much of his time will be spent supervising performance of these duties

8. In attempting to determine why one of his subordinates has frequently been coming to work late, a supervisor begins an interview with the subordinate by asking her whether everything is all right on the job and at home.
The BEST of the following reasons for beginning the interview in this manner is that a question specifically about the reason for the lateness
   A. might indicate insecurity on the part of the supervisor
   B. might limit the responses of the subordinate
   C. will offend the subordinate
   D. might reveal the purpose of the interview

9. Of the following, the BEST use to which a supervisor should put his knowledge of human relations is to
   A. enhance his image among his subordinates
   B. improve interpersonal relationships with the organization
   C. prompt the organization to awareness of mental health
   D. resolve technical difference of opinion among employees

10. Which of the following types of information would come tribute LEAST to a measure of the quality of working conditions for employees in various jobs?
   A. Data reflecting a view of working conditions as seen through the eyes of workers
   B. Objective data relating to problems in working conditions, such as occupational safety statistics

C. The considered opinion of recognized specialists in relevant fields
D. The impressionistic accounts of journalists in feature articles

Questions 11-15.

DIRECTIONS: Questions 11 through 15 each consist of a sentence which may or may not be an example of good English usage. Consider grammar, punctuation, spelling, capitalization, verbosity, awkwardness, etc. Examine each sentence, and then choose the correct statement about it from the four choices below it. If the English usage in the sentence is better as given than with any of the changes suggested in options B, C, or D, choose option A. Do NOT choose an option that will change the meaning of the sentence.

11. The clerk could have completed the assignment on time if he knows where these materials were located.
    A. This is an example of acceptable writing.
    B. The word *knows* should be replaced by *had known*.
    C. The word *were* should be replaced by *had been*.
    D. The words *where these materials were located* should be replaced by *the location of these materials*.

11.____

12. All employees should be given safety training. Not just those who have accidents.
    A. This is an example of acceptable writing.
    B. The period after the word *training* should be changed to a colon.
    C. The period after the word *training* should be changed to a semicolon, and the first letter of the word *Not* should be changed to a small *n*.
    D. The period after the word *training* should be changed to a comma, and the first letter of the word *Not* should be changed to a small *n*.

12.____

13. This proposal is designed to promote employee awareness of the suggestion program, to encourage employee participation in the program, and to increase the number of suggestions submitted.
    A. This is an example of acceptable writing.
    B. The word *proposal* should be spelled *proposal*.
    C. The words *to increase the number of suggestions submitted* should be changed to *an increase in the number of suggestions is expected*.
    D. The word *promote* should be changed to *enhance* and the word *increase* should be changed to *add to*.

13.____

14. The introduction of inovative managerial techniques should be preceded by careful analysis of the specific circumstances and conditions in each department.
    A. This is an example of acceptable writing.
    B. The word *techniques* should be spelled *techneques*.
    C. The word *inovative* should be spelled *innovative*.
    D. A comma should be placed after the word *circumstance* and after the word *conditions*.

14.____

15. This occurrence indicates that such criticism embarrasses him. 15.____
    A. This is an example of acceptable writing.
    B. The word *occurrence* should be spelled *occurence*.
    C. The word *criticism* should be spelled *criticizm*.
    D. The word *embarrasses* should be spelled *embarasses*.

Questions 16-18.

DIRECTIONS: Questions 16 through 18 each consist of four sentences. Choose the one sentence in each set of four that would be BEST for a *formal* letter or report. Consider grammar and appropriate usage.

16. A. Most all the work he completed before he become ill. 16.____
    B. He completed most of the work before becoming ill.
    C. Prior to him becoming ill his work was mostly completed.
    D. Before he became ill most of the work he had completed.

17. A. Being that the report lacked a clearly worded recommendation, it did not matter that it contained enough information. 17.____
    B. There was enough information in the report, although it, including the recommendation, were not clearly worded.
    C. Although the report contained enough information, it did not have a clearly worded recommendation.
    D. Though the report did not have a recommendation that was clearly worded, and the information therein contained was enough.

18. A. Having already overlooked the important mistake, the one which she found were not as important toward the end of the letter. 18.____
    B. Toward the end of the letter she had already overlooked the important mistake, so that which she had found were not as important.
    C. The mistakes which she had already overlooked were not as important as those which near the end of letter she had found.
    D. The mistakes which she found near the end of the letter were not as important as those which she had already overlooked.

19. Examine the following sentence, and then choose from below the words which should be inserted in the blank spaces to produce the BEST sentence. The unit has exceeded _____ goals and the employees are satisfied with _____ accomplishments. 19.____
    A. their; it's   B. it's; it's   C. its; there   D. its; their

20. Examine the following sentence, and then choose from below the words which should be inserted in the blank spaces to produce the BEST sentence. Research indicates that employees who _____ no opportunity for clos social relationships often find their work unsatisfying, and this _____ of satisfaction often reflects itself in low production. 20.____
    A. have; lack   B. have; excess   C. has; lack   D. has; excess

KEY (CORRECT ANSWERS)

1.	A	11.	B
2.	C	12.	D
3.	B	13.	A
4.	C	14.	C
5.	D	15.	A
6.	C	16.	B
7.	D	17.	C
8.	B	18.	D
9.	B	19.	D
10.	D	20.	A

TEST 2

DIRECTIONS: Each question or incomplete statement is followed by several suggested answers or completions. Select the one that BEST answers the question or completes the statement. *PRINT THE LETTER OF THE CORRECT ANSWER IN THE SPACE AT THE RIGHT.*

1. Of the following, the GREATEST *pitfall* in interviewing is that the result may be effected by the
    A. bias of the interviewee
    B. bias of the interviewer
    C. educational level of the interviewee
    D. educational level of the interviewer

    1.____

2. Assume that you have been asked to interview each of several students who have been hired to work part-time.
    Which of the following could *ordinarily* be accomplished LEAST effectively in such an interview?
    A. Providing information about the organization or institution in which the students will be working
    B. Directing the students to report for work each afternoon at specified times
    C. Determining experience and background of the students so that appropriate assignments can be made
    D. changing the attitudes of the students toward the importance of parental controls

    2.____

3. Assume that someone you are interviewing is reluctant to give you certain information.
    He would probably be MORE responsive if you show him that
    A. all the other persons you interviewed provided you with the information
    B. it would serve his own best interests to give you the information
    C. the information is very important to you
    D. you are businesslike and take a no-nonsense approach

    3.____

4. Taking notes while you are interviewing someone is MOST likely to
    A. arouse doubts as to your trustworthiness
    B. give the interviewee confidence in your ability
    C. insure that you record the facts you think are important
    D. make the responses of the interviewee unreliable

    4.____

5. Assume that you have been asked to get all the pertinent information from an employee who claims that she witnessed a robbery.
    Which of the following questions is LEAST likely to influence the witness's response?
    A. Can you describe the robber's hair?
    B. Did the robber have a lot of hair?
    C. Was the robber's hair black or brown?
    D. Was the robber's hair very dark?

    5.____

6. If you are to interview several applicants for jobs and rate them on five different factors on a scale of 1 to 5, you should be MOST careful to insure that your
   A. rating on one factor does not influence your rating on another factor
   B. ratings on all factors are interrelated with a minimum of variation
   C. overall evaluation for employment exactly reflects the arithmetic average of your ratings
   D. overall evaluation for employment is unrelated to your individual ratings

7. In answering questions asked by students, faculty, and the public, it is MOST important that
   A. you indicate your source of information
   B. you are not held responsible for the answers
   C. the facts you give be accurate
   D. the answer cover every possible aspect of each question

8. One of the applicants for a menial job is a tall, stooped, husky individual with a low forehead, narrow eyes, a protruding chin, and a tendency to keep his mouth open.
   In interviewing him, you SHOULD
   A. check him more carefully than the other applicants regarding criminal background
   B. disregard any skills he might have for other jobs which are vacant
   C. make your vocabulary somewhat simpler than with the other applicants
   D. make no assumption regarding his ability on the basis of his appearance

9. Of the following, the BEST approach for you to us at the beginning of an interview with a job applicant is to
   A. caution him to use his time economically and to get to the point
   B. ask him how long he intends to remain on the job if hired
   C. make some pleasant remarks to put him at ease
   D. emphasize the importance of the interview in obtaining the job

10. Of the following, the BEST reason for conducting an *exit interview* with an employee is to
    A. make certain that he returns all identification cards and office keys
    B. find out why he is leaving
    C. provide a useful training device for the exit interviewer
    D. discover if his initial hiring was in error

11. Suppose that a visitor to an office asks a receptionist for a specific person by name. The person is available, but the visitor refuses to state the purpose of the visit, saying that it is personal.
    Which of the following is the MOST appropriate response for the receptionist to make?
    A. Does M_____ know you?
    B. I'm sorry, M_____ is busy.
    C. M_____ won't be able to help you unless you're more specific.
    D. M_____ is not able to see you.

12. When writing a reply to a letter you received, it is proper to mention the subject of the letter.
    However, you should ordinarily NOT summarize the contents or repeat statements made in the letter you received PRIMARILY because
    A. a letter writer answers people, not letters
    B. direct answers will help you avoid sounding pompous
    C. the response will thus be more confidential
    D. the sender usually knows what he or she wrote

    12.____

13. Assume that you are a supervisor in an office which gets approximately equal quantities of urgent work and work that is not urgent. The volume of work is high during some periods and low during others.
    In order to level out the fluctuations in workload, it would be BEST for you to schedule work so that
    A. urgent work which comes up in a period of high work volume can be handled expeditiously by the use of voluntary overtime
    B. urgent work is postponed for completion in periods of low volume
    C. work is completed as it comes into the office, except that when urgent work arises, other work is laid aside temporarily
    D. work is completed chronologically, that is, on the basis of *first in, first out*

    13.____

14. Suppose that a supervisor sets up a pick-up and delivery messenger system to cover several nearby buildings. Each building has at least one station for both pick-up and delivery. Three messenger trips are scheduled for each day, and the messenger is instructed to make pick-up and deliveries at the same time.
    In this situation, telling the messenger to visit each pick-up and delivery station even though there is nothing to deliver to it is
    A. *advisable;* messengers are generally not capable of making decisions for themselves
    B. *advisable*; there may be material for the messenger to pick up
    C. *inadvisable*; the system must be made flexible to meet variable workload conditions
    D. *inadvisable*; postponing the visit until there is something to deliver is more efficient

    14.____

15. You, as a unit head, have been asked to submit budget estimates of staff, equipment and supplies in terms of programs for your unit for the coming fiscal year.
    In addition to their use in planning, such unit budget estimates can be BEST used to
    A. reveal excessive costs in operations
    B. justify increases in the debt limit
    C. analyze employee salary adjustments
    D. predict the success of future programs

    15.____

4 (#2)

Questions 16-21.

DIRECTIONS: Questions 6 through 21 involve calculations of annual grade averages for college students who have just completed their junior year. These averages are to be based on the following table showing the number of credit hours for each student during the year at each of the grade levels: A, B, C, D, and F. How these letter grades may be translated into numerical grades is indicated in the first column of the table.

Grade Value	Credit Hours – Junior Year					
	King	Lewis	Martin	Nonkin	Ottly	Perry
A = 95	12	12	9	15	6	3
B = 85	9	12	9	12	918	6
C = 75	6	6	9	3	33	21
D = 65	3	3	3	3	6-	--
F = 0	-	--	3	-	--	--

Calculating a grade average for an individual student is a 4-step process:
I. Multiply each grade value by the number of credit hours for which the student received that grade.
II. Add these multiplication products for each student.
III. Add the student's total credit hours.
IV. Divide the multiplication product total by the total number of credit hours.
V. Round the result, if there is a decimal place, to the nearest whole number. A number ending in .5 would be rounded to the next higher number.

EXAMPLE

Using student King's grades as an example, his grade average can be calculated by going through the following four steps.

I. 95 x 12 = 1140
   85 x 9 = 765
   75 x 6 = 450
   65 x 3 = 195
   65 x 3 =   0

II. Total   2550

III. 12
     9
     6
     2
     0
    30 Total Credit Hours

IV. Divide 2550 by 30: $\frac{2550}{30} = 85$

King's grade average is 85.

Questions 16 through 21 are to be answered on the basis of the information given above.

16. The grade average of Lewis is
    A. 83   B. 84   C. 85   D. 86

16.____

17. The grade average of Martin is
    A. 72   B. 73   C. 74   D. 75

18. The grade average of Nonkin is
    A. 85   B. 86   C. 87   D. 88

19. Student Ottly must attain a grade average of 90 in each of his years in college to be accepted into the graduate school of his choice.
    If, in summer school during his junior year, he takes two 3-credit courses and receives a grade of 95 in each one, his grade average for his junior year will then be MOST NEARLY
    A. 79   B. 80   C. 81   D. 82

20. If Perry takes an additional 3-credit course during the year and receives a grade of 95. his grade average will be increased to approximately
    A. 79   B. 80   C. 81   D. 82

21. What has been the effect of automation in data processing on the planning of managerial objectives?
    A. Paperwork can be virtually eliminated from the planning process.
    B. The information on which such planning is based can be more precise and up-to-date.
    C. Planning must be done much more frequently because of the constantly changing nature of the objectives.
    D. Planning can be done much less frequently because of the increased stability of objectives.

22. Which of the following is the BEST reason for budgeting a new calculating machine for an office?
    A. The clerks in the office often make mistakes adding.
    B. The machine would save time and money.
    C. It was budgeted last year but never received.
    D. All the other offices have calculating machines.

23. Which of the following is MOST likely to reduce the volume of paperwork in a unit responsible for preparing a large number of reports?
    A. Changing the office layout so that there will be a minimum of backtracking and delay
    B. Acquiring additional adding and calculating machines
    C. Consolidating some of the reports
    D. Inaugurating a *records retention policy* to reduce the length of time office papers are retained

24. With regard to typed correspondence received by most offices, which of the following is the GREATEST problem?
    A. Verbosity   B. Illegibility
    C. Improper folding   D. Excessive copies

25. Of the following, the GREATEST advantage of electronic typewriters over electric typewriters is that they usually 25._____
    A. are less expensive to repair
    B. are smaller and lighter
    C. produce better looking copy
    D. require less training for the typist

KEY (CORRECT ANSWERS)

1.	B		11.	A
2.	D		12.	D
3.	B		13.	C
4.	C		14.	B
5.	A		15.	A
6.	A		16.	C
7.	C		17.	D
8.	D		18.	C
9.	C		19.	B
10.	B		20.	B

21.	B
22.	B
23.	C
24.	A
25.	C

EXAMINATION SECTION
TEST 1

DIRECTIONS: Each question or incomplete statement is followed by several suggested answers or completions. Select the one that BEST answers the question or completes the statement. *PRINT THE LETTER OF THE CORRECT ANSWER IN THE SPACE AT THE RIGHT.*

1. A certain system for handling office supplies requires that supplies be issued to the various agency offices only on a bi-weekly basis and that all supply requisitions be authorized by the unit supervisor.
   The BEST reason for establishing this supplies system is to
   A. standardize ordering descriptions and stock identification codes
   B. prevent the disordering of stock shelves and cabinets by unauthorized persons searching for supplies
   C. ensure that unit supervisors properly exercise their right to make determinations on supply orders
   D. encourage proper utilization of supplies to control the workload

   1.____

2. It is important that every office have a retention and disposal program for filing material. Suppose that you have been appointed administrative assistant in an office with a poorly organized records-retention program.
   In establishing a revised program for the transfer or disposal of records, the step which would logically be taken THIRD in the process is
   A. preparing a safe and inexpensive storage area and setting up an indexing system for records already in storage
   B. determining what papers to retain and for how long a period
   C. taking an inventory of what is filed, where it is filed, how much is filed, and how often it is used
   D. moving records from active to inactive files and destroying useless records

   2.____

3. In the effective design of office forms, the FIRST step to take is to
   A. decide what information should be included
   B. decide the purpose for which the form will be used
   C. identify the form by name and number
   D. identify the employees who will be using the form

   3.____

4. Some designers of office forms prefer to locate the instructions on how to fill out the form at the bottom of it.
   The MOST logical objection to placing such instructions at the bottom of the form is that
   A. instructions at the bottom require an excess of space
   B. all form instructions should be outlined with a separate paragraph
   C. the form may be partly filled out before the instructions are seen
   D. the bottom of the form should be reserved only for authorization and signature

   4.____

53

5. A formal business report may consist of many parts, including the following:
   I. Table of Contents
   II. List of References
   III. Preface
   IV. Index
   V. List of Tables
   VI. Conclusions or Recommendations

   Of the following, in setting up a formal report, the PROPER order of the six parts listed is
   A. I, III, VI, V, II, IV
   B. IV, III, II, V, VI, I
   C. III, I, V, VI, II, IV
   D. II, V, III, I, IV, VI

6. Three of the basic functions of office management are considered to be planning, controlling, and organizing.
   Of the following, the one which might BEST be considered ORGANIZING activity is
   A. assigning personnel and materials to work units to achieve agreed-upon objectives
   B. determining future objectives and indicating conditions affecting the accomplishment of the goals
   C. evaluating accomplishments and applying necessary corrective measures to insure results
   D. motivating employees to perform their work in accordance with objectives

7. The following four statements relate to office layout.
   I. Position supervisors' desks at the front of their work group so that they can easily be recognized as persons in authority.
   II. Arrange file cabinets and frequently used equipment near the employees who utilize them most often.
   III. Locate the receptionist's desk near the entrance of the office so that visitor traffic will not distract other workers.
   IV. Divide a large office area into many smaller offices by using stationary partitions so that all employees may have privacy and prestige.

   According to authorities in office management and administration, which of these statements are generally recommended guides to effective office layout?
   A. I, II, III   B. II, III, IV   C. II, III   D. All of the above

8. For which of the following purposes would a flow chart have the GREATEST applicability?
   A. Training new employees in performance of routine duties
   B. Determining adequacy of performance of employees
   C. Determining the accuracy of the organization chart
   D. Locating causes of delays in carrying out an operation

9. Office work management concerns tangible accomplishment or production. It has to do with results; it does not deal with the amount of energy expended by the individual who produces the results.
   According to this statement, the production in which of the following kinds of jobs would be MOST difficult to measure accurately?

A(n)
- A. file clerk
- B. secretary
- C. computer operator
- D. office administrator

10. The FIRST step in the statistical analysis of a great mass of data secured from a survey is to
    - A. scan the data to determine which is atypical of the survey
    - B. determine the number of deviations from the average
    - C. arrange the data into groups on the basis of likenesses and differences
    - D. plot the drama on a graph to determine trends

11. Suppose that, as an administrative assistant in charge of an office, you are required to change the layout of your office to accommodate expanding functions.
    The LEAST important factor to be considered in planning the revised layout is the
    - A. relative productivity of individuals in the office
    - B. communication and work flow needs
    - C. need for screening confidential activities from unauthorized persons
    - D. areas of noise concentration

12. Suppose you have instructed a new employee to follow a standardized series of steps to accomplish a job. He is to use a rubber stamp, then a red pencil on the first paper, and a numbering machine on the second. Then, he is to staple the two sheets of paper together and put them to one side. You observe, however, that he sometimes uses the red pencil first, sometimes the numbering machine first. At other times, he does the stapling before using the numbering machine.
    For you as supervisor to suggest that the clerk use the standardized method when doing this job would be
    - A. *bad*, because the clerk should be given a chance to use his independent judgment on the best way to do his job
    - B. *good*, because the clerk's sequence of actions results in a loss of efficiency
    - C. *bad*, because it is not wise to interrupt the work habit the clerk has already developed
    - D. *good*, because the clerk should not be permitted to make unauthorized changes in standard office routines

13. Suppose study of the current records management system for students' transcripts reveals needless recopying of transcript data throughout various offices within the university. On this basis, a recommendation is made that this unnecessary recopying of information be eliminated.
    This decision to eliminate waste in material, time, and space is an application of the office management principle of
    - A. work simplification
    - B. routing and scheduling
    - C. job analysis
    - D. cost and budgetary control

14. It is generally LEAST practical for an office manager to prepare for known peak work periods by
    A. putting job procedures into writing so that they can be handled by more than one person
    B. arranging to make assignments of work on a short-interval scheduling basis
    C. cleaning up as much work as possible ahead of known peak periods
    D. rotating jobs and assignments among different employees to assure staff flexibility

15. The four statements below are about office manuals used for various purposes. If you had the job of designing and controlling several kinds of office manuals to be used in your agency, which one of these statements would BEST apply as a general rule for you to follow?
    A. Office manual content should be classified into main topics with proper subdivisions arranged in strict alphabetical order.
    B. Manual additions and revisions should be distributed promptly to all holders of manuals for their approval, correction, and criticism.
    C. The language used in office manuals should be simple, and charts and diagrams should be interspersed within the narrative material for further clarity.
    D. Office manual content should be classified into main topics arranged in strict alphabetical order with subtopics in sequence according to importance.

16. Suppose that, as an administrative assistant, you have been assigned to plan the reorganization of an office which has not been operating efficiently because of the uncoordinated manner in which new functions have been assigned to it over the past year.
    The FIRST thing you should so is
    A. call a meeting of the office staff and explain the purposes of the planned reorganization
    B. make a cost-value analysis of the present operations to determine what should be changed or eliminated
    C. prepare a diagram of the flow of work as you think it should be
    D. define carefully the current objectives to be achieved by this reorganization

17. Effective organization requires that specific actions be taken in proper sequence. The following are four actions essential to effective organization:
    I. Group activities on the basis of human and material resources
    II. Coordinate functions and provide for good communications
    III. Formulate objectives, policies, and plans
    IV. Determine activities necessary to accomplish goals

    The PROPER sequence of these four actions is:
    A. III, II, IV, I   B. IV, III, I, II   C. III, IV, I, II   D. IV, I, III, II

18. For an administrative assistant to give each of his subordinates exactly the same type of supervision is
    A. *advisable*, because he will gain a reputation for being fair and impartial
    B. *inadvisable*, because subordinates work more diligently when they think they are receiving preferential treatment
    C. *advisable*, because most human problems can be classified into categories which make them easier to handle
    D. *inadvisable*, because people differ and there is no one supervisory procedure that applies in every case to dealing with individuals

19. Suppose that, as an administrative assistant, you find that some of your subordinates are coming to you with complaints you think are trivial.
    For you to hear them through is
    A. *poor practice*; subordinates should be trained to come to you only with major grievances
    B. *good practice*; major grievances sometimes are the underlying cause of minor complaints
    C. *poor practice*; you should delegate this kind of matter and spend your time on more important problems
    D. *good practice*; this will make you more popular with your subordinates

20. Suppose that a new departmental policy has just been established which you feel may be resented by your subordinates, but which they must understand and follow.
    Which would it be MOST advisable for you as their supervisory to do FIRST?
    A. Make clear to your subordinates that you are not responsible for making this policy.
    B. Tell your subordinates that you agree with the policy whether you do or not.
    C. Explain specifically to your subordinates the reasons for the policy and how it is going to affect them.
    D. Distribute a memo outlining the new policy and require your subordinates to read it.

21. An office assistant under your supervision tells you that she is reluctant to speak to one of her subordinates about poor work habits because this subordinate is strong-willed, and she does not want to antagonize her.
    For you to refuse the office assistant's request that you speak to her subordinate about this matter is
    A. *inadvisable*, since you are in a position of greater authority
    B. *advisable*, since supervision of his subordinate is a basic responsibility of that office assistant
    C. *inadvisable*, since the office assistant must work more closely with her subordinate than you do
    D. *advisable*, since you should not risk antagonizing her subordinate yourself

22. The GREATEST advantage to a supervisor of using oral communication as compared to written is the
    A. opportunity provided for immediate feedback
    B. speed with which orders can be given and carried out
    C. reduction in amount of paper work
    D. establishment of an informal atmosphere

23. Of the following, the MOST important reason for an administrative assistant to have private, face-to-face discussions with subordinates about their performance is
    A. encourage a more competitive spirit among employees
    B. give special praise to employees who perform well
    C. discipline employees who perform poorly
    D. help employees improve their work

24. For a supervisor to keep records of reprimands to subordinates about violations of rules is
    A. *poor practice*; such records are evidence of the supervisor's inability to maintain discipline
    B. *good practice*; these records are valuable to support disciplinary actions recommended or taken
    C. *poor practice*; the best way to prevent recurrences is to apply penalties without delay
    D. *good practice*; such records are evidence that the supervisor is doing a good job

25. As an administrative assistant supervising a small office, you decide to hold a staff meeting to try to find an acceptable solution to s problem that is causing serious conflicts within the group.
    At this meeting, your role should be to prevent the problem and
    A. see that the group keeps the problem in focus and does not discuss irrelevant matters
    B. act as chairman of the meeting, but take no other part in the discussion
    C. see to it that each member of the group offers a suggestion for its solution
    D. state you views on the matter before any discussion gets under way

KEY (CORRECT ANSWERS)

1. D
2. A
3. B
4. C
5. C

6. A
7. C
8. D
9. D
10. C

11. A
12. B
13. A
14. B
15. C

16. D
17. C
18. D
19. B
20. C

21. B
22. A
23. D
24. B
25. A

TEST 2

DIRECTIONS: Each question or incomplete statement is followed by several suggested answers or completions. Select the one that BEST answers the question or completes the statement. *PRINT THE LETTER OF THE CORRECT ANSWER IN THE SPACE AT THE RIGHT.*

1. Suppose that one of your subordinates who supervises two young office assistants has been late for work a number of times and you have decided to talk to him about it.
   In your discussion, it would be MOST constructive for you to emphasize that
   A. personal problems cannot be used as an excuse for these latenesses
   B. the department suffers financially when he is late
   C. you will be forced to give him a less desirable assignment if his latenesses continue
   D. his latnesses set a bad example to those he supervises

   1.____

2. Suppose that, as a newly-appointed administrative assistant, you are in charge of a small but very busy office. Your four subordinates are often required to make quick decisions on a wide range of matters while answering telephone or in-person inquiries.
   You can MOST efficiently help your subordinates meet such situations by
   A. delegating authority to make such decisions to only one or two trusted subordinates
   B. training each subordinate in the proper response for each kind of inquiry that might be made
   C. making certain that subordinates understand clearly the basic policies that affect these decisions
   D. making each subordinate an expert in one area

   2.____

3. Of the following, the MOST recent development in methods of training supervisors that involves the human relations approach is
   A. conference training   B. the lecture method
   C. the case method   D. sensitivity training

   3.____

4. Which of the following is MOST likely to result in failure as a supervisor?
   A. Showing permissiveness in relations with subordinates
   B. Avoiding delegation of tasks to subordinates
   C. Setting high performance standards for subordinates
   D. Using discipline only when necessary

   4.____

5. The MOST important long-range benefit to an organization of proper delegation of work by supervisors is generally that
   A. subordinates will be developed to assume greater responsibilities
   B. subordinates will perform the work as their supervisors would
   C. errors in delegated work will be eliminated
   D. more efficient communication among organizational components will result

   5.____

6. Which of the following duties would it be LEAST appropriate for an administrative assistant in charge of an office to delegate to an immediate subordinate?
   A. Checking of figures to be used in a report to the head of the department
   B. On-the-job training of newly appointed college office assistants
   C. Reorganization of assignments for higher level office staff
   D. Contacting other school offices for needed information

7. Decisions should be delegated to the lowest point in the organization at which they can be made effectively.
   The one of the following which is MOST likely to be a result of the application of this accepted management principle is that
   A. upward communications will be facilitated
   B. potential for more rapid decisions and implementation is increased
   C. coordination of decisions that are made will be simplified
   D. no important factors will be overlooked in making decisions

8. The lecture-demonstration method would be LEAST desirable in a training program set up for
   A. changing the attitudes of long-term employees
   B. informing subordinates about new procedures
   C. explaining how a new office machine works
   D. orientation of new employees

9. Which one of the following conditions would be LEAST likely to indicate a need for employee training?
   A. Large number of employee suggestions
   B. Large amount of overtime
   C. High number of chronic latenesses
   D. Low employee morale

10. An administrative assistant is planning to make a recommendation to change a procedure which would substantially affect the work of his subordinates. For this supervisor to consult with his subordinates about the recommendation before sending it through would be
    A. *undesirable*; subordinates may lose respect for a supervisor who evidences such indecisiveness
    B. *desirable*; since the change in procedure would affect their work, subordinates should decide whether the change should be made
    C. *undesirable*; since subordinates would not receive credit if the procedure were changed, their morale would be lowered
    D. *desirable*; the subordinates may have some worthwhile suggestions concerning the recommendation

11. The BEST way to measure improvement in a selected group of office assistants who have undergone a training course in the use of specific techniques is to
    A. have the trainees fill out questionnaires at the completion of the course as to what they have learned and giving their opinions as to the value of the course

B. compare the performance of the trainees who completed the course with the performance of office assistants who did not take the course
C. compare the performance of the trainees in these techniques before and after the training course
D. compare the degree of success on the next promotion examination of trainees and non-trainees

12. When an administrative assistant finds it necessary to call in a subordinate for a disciplinary interview, his MAIN objective should be to
    A. use techniques which can penetrate any deception and get at the truth
    B. stress correction of, rather than punishment for, past errors
    C. maintain a reputation for being an understanding superior
    D. decide on disciplinary action that is consistent with penalties applied for similar infractions

12._____

13. Suppose that a newly promoted office assistant does satisfactory work during the first five months of her probationary period. However, her supervisor notices shortly after this time that her performance is falling below acceptable standards. The supervisor decides to keep records of this employee's performance, and if there is no significant improvement by the end of 11 months, to recommend that this employee not be given tenure in the higher title.
    This, as the sole course of action, is
    A. *justified*; employees who do not perform satisfactorily should not be promoted
    B. *unjustified*; the supervisor should attempt to determine the cause of the poor performance as soon as possible
    C. *justified*; the supervisor will have given the subordinate the full probationary period to improve herself
    D. *unjustified*; the subordinate should be demoted to her previous title as soon as her work becomes unsatisfactory

13._____

14. Suppose that you are conducting a conference-style training course for a group of 12 office assistants. Miss Jones is the only conferee who has not become involved in the discussion.
    The BEST method of getting Miss Jones to participate is to
    A. ask her to comment on remarks made by the best-informed participant
    B. ask her to give a brief talk at the next session on a topic that interests her
    C. set up a role-play situation and assign her to take a part
    D. ask her a direct questions which you know she can answer

14._____

15. Which of the following is NOT part of the *control* function of office management?
    A. Deciding on alternative courses of action
    B. Reporting periodically on productivity
    C. Evaluating performance against the standards
    D. Correcting deviations when required

15._____

16. Which of the following is NOT a principal aspect of the process of delegation?
    A. Developing improvements in methods used to carry out assignments
    B. Granting of permission to do what is necessary to carry out assignments
    C. Assignment of duties by a supervisor to an immediate subordinate
    D. Obligation on the part of a subordinate to carry out his assignment

17. Reluctance of a supervisor to delegate work effectively may be due to any or all of the following EXCEPT the supervisor's
    A. unwillingness to take calculated risks
    B. lack of confidence in subordinates
    C. inability to give proper directions as to what he wants done
    D. retention of ultimate responsibility for delegated work

18. A man cannot serve two masters.
    This statement emphasizes the importance in an organization of following the principle of
    A. specialization of work   B. unity of command
    C. uniformity of assignment   D. span of control

19. In general, the number of subordinates an administrative assistant can supervise effectively tends to vary
    A. *directly* with both similarity and complexity of their duties
    B. *directly* with similarity of their duties and *inversely* with complexity of their duties
    C. *inversely* with both similarity and complex of their duties
    D. *inversely* with similarity of their duties and *directly* with complexity of their duties

20. When an administrative assistant practices *general* rather than *close* supervision, which one of the following is MOST likely to happen?
    A. His subordinates will not be as well-trained as employees who are supervised more closely.
    B. Standards are likely to be lowered because subordinates will be under pressures and will not be motivated to work toward set goals.
    C. He will give fewer specific orders and spend more time on planning and coordinating than those supervisors who practice close supervision.
    D. This supervisor will spend more time checking and correcting mistakes made by subordinates than would one who supervises closely.

Questions 21-25.

DIRECTIONS: Questions 21 through 25 are to be answered SOLELY on the basis of the information contained in the following paragraph.

Since an organization chart is pictorial in nature, there is a tendency for it to be drawn in an artistically balanced and appealing fashion, regardless of the realities of actual organizational structure. In addition to being subject to this distortion, there is the difficulty of communicating in any organization chart the relative importance or the relative size of various component parts of an organizational structure. Furthermore, because of the need for simplicity of design, an organization chart can never indicate the full extent of the interrelationships among the component parts of an organization. These interrelationships are often just as vital as the specifications which an organization chart endeavors to indicate. Yet, if an organization chart were to be drawn with all the wide variety of criss-crossing communication and cooperation networks existent within a typical organization, the chart would probably be much more confusing than informative. It is also obvious that no organization chart as such can "prove" or "disprove" that the organizational structure it represents is effective in realizing the objectives of the organization. At best, an organization chart can only illustrate some of the various factors to be taken into consideration in understanding, devising, or altering organizational arrangements.

21. According to the above paragraph, an organization chart can be expected to portray the
    A. structure of the organization along somewhat ideal lines
    B. relative size of the organizational units quite accurately
    C. channels of information distribution within the organization graphically
    D. extent of the obligation of each unit to meet the organizational objectives

21._____

22. According to the above paragraph, those aspects of internal functioning which are NOT shown on an organization chart
    A. can be considered to have little practical application in the operations of the organization
    B. might well be considered to be as important as the structural relationships which a chart does present
    C. could be the cause of considerable confusion in the operation of an organization which is quite large
    D. would be most likely to provide the information needed to determine the overall effectiveness of an organization

22._____

23. In the above paragraph, the one of the following conditions which is NOT implied as being a defect of an organization chart is that an organization chart may
    A. present a picture of the organizational structure which is different from the structure that actually exists
    B. fail to indicate the comparative size of various organizational units
    C. be limited in its ability to convey some of the meaningful aspects of organizational relationships
    D. become less useful over a period of time during which the organizational facts which it illustrated have changed

23._____

24. The one of the following which is the MOST suitable title for the above paragraph is
    A. The Design and Construction of an Organization Chart
    B. The Informal Aspects of an Organization Chart
    C. The Inherent Deficiencies of an Organization Chart
    D. The Utilization of a Typical Organization Chart

24._____

25. It can be INFERRED from the above paragraph that the function of an organization chart is to
    A. contribute to the comprehension of the organization form and arrangements
    B. establish the capabilities of the organization to operate effectively
    C. provide a balanced picture of the operations of the organization
    D. eliminate the need for complexity in the organization's structure

KEY (CORRECT ANSWERS)

1.	D	11.	C
2.	C	12.	B
3.	D	13.	B
4.	B	14.	D
5.	A	15.	A
6.	C	16.	A
7.	B	17.	D
8.	A	18.	B
9.	A	19.	B
10.	D	20.	C

21.	A
22.	B
23.	D
24.	C
25.	A

TEST 3

DIRECTIONS: Each question or incomplete statement is followed by several suggested answers or completions. Select the one that BEST answers the question or completes the statement. *PRINT THE LETTER OF THE CORRECT ANSWER IN THE SPACE AT THE RIGHT.*

1. Of the following problems that might affect the conduct and outcome of an interview, the MOST troublesome and usually the MOST difficult for the interviewer to control is the
    A. tendency of the interviewee to anticipate the needs and preferences of the interviewer
    B. impulse to cut the interviewee off when he seems to have reached the end of an idea
    C. tendency of interviewee attitudes to bias the results
    D. tendency of the interviewer to do most of the talking

1.____

2. The administrative assistant MOST likely to be a good interviewer is one who
    A. is adept at manipulating people and circumstances toward his objectives
    B. is able to put himself in the position of the interviewee
    C. gets the more difficult questions out of the way at the beginning of the interview
    D. develops one style and technique that can be used in any type of interview

2.____

3. A good interviewer guards against the tendency to form an overall opinion about an interviewee on the basis of a single aspect of the interviewee's make-up
    A. assumption error
    B. expectancy error
    C. extension effect
    D. halo effect

3.____

4. In conducting an exit interview with an employee who is leaving voluntarily, the interviewer's MAIN objective should be to
    A. see that the employee leaves with a good opinion of the organization
    B. learn the true reasons for the employee's resignation
    C. find out if the employee would consider a transfer
    D. try to get the employee to remain on the job

4.____

5. During an interview, an interviewee discloses a relevant but embarrassing personal fact.
   It would be BEST for the interviewer to
    A. listen calmly, avoiding any gesture or facial expression that would suggest approval or disapproval of what is related
    B. change the subject, since further discussion in this area may reveal other embarrassing, but irrelevant, personal facts
    C. apologize to the interviewee for having led him to reveal such a fact and promise not to do so again
    D. bring the interview to a close as quickly as possible in order to avoid a discussion which may be distressful to the interviewee

5.____

6. Suppose that while you are interviewing an applicant for a position in your office, you notice a contradiction in facts in two of his responses.
   For you to call the contradictions to his attention would be
   A. *inadvisable*, because it reduces the interviewee's level of participation
   B. *advisable*, because getting the facts is essential to a successful interview
   C. *inadvisable*, because the interviewer should use more subtle techniques to resolve any discrepancies
   D. *advisable*, because the interviewee should be impressed with the necessity for giving consistent answers

7. An interviewer should be aware that an undesirable result of including *leading questions* in an interview is to
   A. cause the interviewee to give *yes* or *no* answers with qualification or explanation
   B. encourage the interviewee to discuss irrelevant topics
   C. encourage the interviewee to give more meaningful information
   D. reduce the validity of the information obtained from the interviewee

8. The kind of interview which is PARTICULARLY helpful in getting an employee to tell about his complaints and grievances is one in which
   A. a pattern has been worked out involving a sequence of exact questions to be asked
   B. the interviewee is expected to support his statements with specific evidence
   C. the interviewee is not made to answer specific questions but is encouraged to talk freely
   D. the interviewer has specific items on which he wishes to get or give information

9. Suppose you are scheduled to interview a student aide under your supervision concerning a health problem. You know that some of the questions you will be asked him will seem embarrassing to him, and that he may resist answering these questions.
   In general, to hold these questions for the last part of the interview would be
   A. *desirable*; the intervening time period gives the interviewer an opportunity to plan how to ask these sensitive questions
   B. *undesirable*; the student aide will probably feel that he has been tricked when he suddenly must answer embarrassing questions
   C. *desirable*; the student aide will probably have increased confidence in the interviewer and be more willing to answer these questions
   D. *undesirable*; questions that are important should not be deferred until the end of the interview

10. The House passed an amendment to delete from the omnibus higher education bill a section that would have prohibited coeducational colleges and universities from considering sex as a factor in their admissions policy.
    According to the above passage, consideration of sex as a factor in the admissions policy of coeducational colleges and universities would

A. be permitted by the omnibus higher education bill if passed without further amendment
B. be prohibited by the amendment to the omnibus higher education bill
C. have been prohibited by the deletion of a section from the omnibus higher education bill
D. have been permitted if the house had failed to pass the amendment

Questions 11-14.

DIRECTIONS: Questions 11 through 14 are to be answered SOLELY according to the information given in the following passage.

The proposition that administrative activity is essentially the same in all organizations appears to underlie some of the practices in the administration of private higher education. Although the practice is unusual in public education, there are numerous instances of industrial, governmental, or military administrators being assigned to private institutions of higher education and, to a lesser extent, of college and university presidents assuming administrative positions in other types of organizations. To test this theory that administrators are interchangeable, there is a need for systematic observation and classification. The myth that an educational administrator must first have experience in the teaching profession is firmly rooted in a long tradition that has historical prestige. The myth is bound up in the expectations of the public and personnel surrounding the administrator. Since administrative success depends significantly on how well an administrator meets the expectations others have of him, the myth may be more powerful than the special experience in helping the administrator attain organizational and educational objectives. Educational administrators who have risen through the teaching profession have often expressed nostalgia for the life of a teacher or scholar, but there is no evidence that this nostalgia contributes to administrative success.

11. Which of the following statements as completed is MOST consistent with the above passage?
The greatest number of administrators has moved from
    A. industry and the military to government and universities
    B. government and universities to industry and the military
    C. government, the armed forces, and industry to colleges and universities
    D. colleges and universities to government, the armed forces, and industry

11.____

12. Of the following, the MOST reasonable inference from the above passage is that a specific area requiring research is the
    A. place of myth in the tradition and history of the educational profession
    B. relative effectiveness of educational administrators from inside and outside the teaching profession
    C. performance of administrators in the administration of public colleges
    D. degree of reality behind the nostalgia for scholarly pursuits often expressed by educational administrators

12.____

13. According to the above passage, the value to an educational administrator of experience in the teaching profession
    A. lies in the first-hand knowledge he has acquired of immediate educational problems
    B. may lie in the belief of his colleagues, subordinates, and the public that such experience is necessary
    C. has been supported by evidence that the experience contributes to administrative success in educational fields
    D. would be greater if the administrator were able to free himself from nostalgia for his former duties

14. Of the following, the MOST appropriate title for the above passage is
    A. Educational Administration, Its problems
    B. The Experience Needed for Educational Administration
    C. Administration in Higher Education
    D. Evaluating Administrative Experience

Questions 15-20.

DIRECTIONS: Questions 15 through 20 are to be answered SOLELY according to the information contained in the following paragraph.

Methods of administration of office activities, much of which consists of providing information and "know-how" needed to coordinate both activities within that particular office and other offices, have been among the last to come under the spotlight of management analysis. Progress has been rapid during the past decade, however, and is now accelerating at such a pace that an "information revolution" in office management appears to be in the making. Although triggered by technological breakthroughs in electronic computers and other giant steps in mechanization, this information revolution must be attributed to underlying forces, such as the increased complexity of both governmental and private enterprise, and ever-keener competition. Size, diversification, specialization of function, and decentralization are among the forces which make coordination of activities both more imperative and more difficult. Increased competition, both domestic and international, leaves little margin for error in managerial decisions. Several developments during recent years indicate an evolving pattern. In 1960, the American Management Association expanded the scope of its activities and changed the name of its Office Management Division to Administrative Service Division. Also in 1960, the magazine Office Management merged with the magazine American Business, and this new publication was named Administrative Management.

15. A REASONABLE inference that can be made from the information in the above paragraph is that an important role of the office manager today is to
    A. work toward specialization of functions performed by his subordinates
    B. inform and train subordinates regarding any new developments in computer technology and mechanization
    C. assist the professional management analysts with the management analysis work in the organization
    D. supply information that can be used to help coordinate and manager the other activities of the organization

16. An IMPORTANT reason for the "information revolution" that has been taking place in office management is the
    A. advance made in management analysis in the past decade
    B. technological breakthrough in electronic computers and mechanization
    C. more competitive and complicated nature of private business and government
    D. increased efficiency of office management techniques in the past ten years

16.____

17. According to the above paragraph, specialization of function in an organization is MOST likely to result in
    A. the elimination of errors in managerial decisions
    B. greater need to coordinate activities
    C. more competition with other organizations, both domestic and international
    D. a need for office managers with greater flexibility

17.____

18. The word *evolving*, as used in the third from last sentence in the above paragraph, means MOST NEARLY
    A. developing by gradual changes
    B. passing on to others
    C. occurring periodically
    D. breaking up into separate, constituent parts

18.____

19. Of the following, the MOST reasonable implication of the changes in names mentioned in the last part of the above paragraph is that these groups are attempting to
    A. professionalize the field of office management and the title of Office Manager
    B. combine two publications into one because of the increased costs of labor and materials
    C. adjust to the fact that the field of office management is broadening
    D. appeal to the top managerial people rather than the office management people in business and government

19.____

20. According to the above paragraph, intense competition among domestic and international enterprises makes it MOST important for an organization's managerial staff to
    A. coordinate and administer office activities with other activities in the organization
    B. make as few errors in decision-making as possible
    C. concentrate on decentralization and reduction of size of the individual divisions of the organization
    D. restrict decision-making only to top management officials

20.____

KEY (CORRECT ANSWERS)

1.	A	11.	C
2.	B	12.	B
3.	D	13.	B
4.	B	14.	B
5.	A	15.	D
6.	B	16.	C
7.	D	17.	B
8.	C	18.	A
9.	C	19.	C
10.	A	20.	B

EXAMINATION SECTION
TEST 1

DIRECTIONS: Each question or incomplete statement is followed by several suggested answers or completions. Select the one that BEST answers the question or completes the statement. *PRINT THE LETTER OF THE CORRECT ANSWER IN THE SPACE AT THE RIGHT.*

Questions 1-6.

DIRECTIONS: Questions 1 through 6 each consist of four sentences. Choose the one sentence in each set of four that would be BEST for a formal letter or report. Consider grammar and appropriate usage.

1. A. These statements can be depended upon, for their truth has been guaranteed by reliable city employees.
   B. Reliable city employees guarantee the facts with regards to the truth of these statements.
   C. Most all these statements have been supported by city employees who are reliable and can be depended upon.
   D. The city employees which have guaranteed these statements are reliable.

   1._____

2. A. I believe the letter was addressed to either my associate or I.
   B. If properly addressed, the letter will reach my associate and I.
   C. My associate's name, as well as mine, was on the letter.
   D. The letter had been addressed to myself and my associate.

   2._____

3. A. The secretary would have corrected the errors if she knew that the supervisor would see the report.
   B. The supervisor reprimanded the secretary, whom she believed had made careless errors.
   C. Many errors were found in the report which she typed and could not disregard them.
   D. The errors in the typed report were so numerous that they could hardly be overlooked.

   3._____

4. A. His consultant was as pleased as he with the success of the project.
   B. The success of the project pleased both his consultant and he.
   C. he and also his consultant was pleased with the success of the project.
   D. Both his consultant and he was pleased with the success of the project.

   4._____

5. A. Since the letter did not contain the needed information, it was not real useful to him.
   B. Being that the letter lacked the needed information, he could not use it.
   C. Since the letter lacked the needed information, it was of no use to him.
   D. This letter was useless to him because there was no needed information in it.

   5._____

6. A. Scarcely had the real estate tax increase been declared than the notices were sent out.
   B. They had no sooner declared the real estate tax increases when they sent the notices to the owners.
   C. The city had hardly declared the real estate tax increase till the notices were prepared for mailing.
   D. No sooner had the real estate tax been declared than the notices were sent out.

6._____

Questions 7-14.

DIRECTIONS: Questions 7 through 14 are to be answered on the basis of the following passage.

Important figures in education and in public affairs have recommended development of a private organization sponsored in part by various private foundations which would offer installment payment plans to full-time matriculated students in accredited colleges and universities in the United States and Canada. Contracts would be drawn to cover either tuition and fees, or tuition, fees, room and board in college facilities, from one year up to and including six years. A special charge, which would vary with the length of the contract, would be added to the gross repayable amount. This would be in addition to interest at a rate which would vary with the income of the parents. There would be a 3% annual interest charge for families with total income, before income taxes of $10,000 or less. The rate would increase by 1/10 of 1% for every $200 of additional net income in excess of $10,000 up to a maximum of 10% interest. Contracts would carry an insurance provision on the life of the parent or guardian who signs the contract; all contracts must have the signature of a parent or guardian. Payment would be scheduled in equal monthly installments.

7. Which of the following students would be eligible for the payment plan described in the above passage? A
   A. matriculated student taking 6 semester hours toward a graduate degree at CCNY
   B. matriculated student taking 17 semester hours toward an undergraduate degree at Brooklyn College
   C. CCNY graduate matriculated at the University of Mexico, taking 18 semester hours toward a graduate degree
   D. student taking 18 semester hours in a special pre-matriculation program at Hunter College

7._____

8. According to the above passage, the organization described would be sponsored in part by
   A. private foundations   B. colleges and universities
   C. persons in the field of education   D. persons in public life

8._____

9. Which of the following expenses could NOT be covered by a contract with the organization described in the above passage?
   A. Tuition amounting to $4,000 per year
   B. Registration and laboratory fees
   C. Meals at restaurants near the college
   D. Rent for an apartment in a college dormitory

9.____

10. The total amount to be paid would include ONLY the
    A. principal
    B. principal and interest
    C. principal, interest, and special charge
    D. principal, interest, special charge, and fee

10.____

11. The contract would carry insurance on the
    A. life of the student
    B. life of the student's parents
    C. income of the parents of the student
    D. life of the parent who signed the contract

11.____

12. The interest rate for an annual loan of $5,000 from the organization described in the passage for a student whose family's net income was $11,000 should be
    A. 3%   B. 3.5%   C. 4%   D. 4.5%

12.____

13. The interest rate for an annual loan of $7,000 from the organization described in the passage for a student whose family's net income was $20,000 should be
    A. 5%   B. 8%   C. 9%   D. 10%

13.____

14. John Lee has submitted an application for the installment payment plan described in the passage. John's mother and father have a store which grossed $100,000 last year, but the income which the family received from the store was $18,000 before taxes. They also had $1,000 income from stock dividends. They paid $2,000 in income taxes.
    The amount of income upon which the interest should be based is
    A. $17,000   B. $18,000   C. $19,000   D. $21,000

14.____

15. One of the MOST important techniques for conducting good interviews is
    A. asking the applicant questions in rapid succession, thereby keeping the conversation properly focused
    B. listening carefully to all that the applicant has to say, making mental notes of possible areas for follow-up
    C. indicating to the applicant the criteria and standards on which you will base your judgment
    D. making sure that you are interrupted above five minutes before you wish to end so that you can keep on schedue

15.____

16. You are planning to conduct preliminary interviews of applicants for an important position in your department.
    Which of the following planning considerations is LEAST likely to contribute to successful interviews?
    A. Make provisions to conduct interviews in privacy
    B. Schedule your appointments so that interviews will be short
    C. Prepare a list of your objectives
    D. Learn as much as you can about the applicant before the interview

17. In interviewing job applicants, which of the following usually does NOT have to be done before the end of the interview?
    A. Making a decision to hire an applicant
    B. Securing information from applicants
    C. Giving information to applicants
    D. Establishing a friendly relationship with applicants

18. In the process of interviewing applicants for a position on your staff, the one of the following which would be BEST is to
    A. make sure all applicants are introduced to the other members of your staff prior to the formal interview
    B. make sure the applicant does not ask questions about the job or the department
    C. avoid having the applicant talk with the staff under any circumstances
    D. introduce applicants to some of the staff at the conclusion of a successful interview

19. While interviewing a job applicant, you ask why the applicant left his last job. The applicant does not answer immediately.
    Of the following, the BEST action to take at that point is to
    A. wait until he answers
    B. ask another question
    C. repeat the question in a loud voice
    D. ask him why he does not answer

20. Which of the following actions would be LEAST desirable for you to take when you have to conduct an interview?
    A. Set a relaxed and friendly atmosphere
    B. Plan your interview ahead of time
    C. Allow the person interviewed to structure the interview as he wishes
    D. Include some stock or standard question which you ask everyone

21. You know that a student applying for a job in your office has done well in college except for two courses in science. However, when you ask him about his grades, his reply is vague and general.
    It would be BEST for you to
    A. lead the applicant to admitting doing poorly in science to be sure that the facts are correct
    B. judge the applicant's tact and skill in handling what may be for him a personally sensitive question

C. immediately confront the applicant with the facts and ask for an explanation
D. ignore the applicant's response since you have the transcript

22. A college student has applied for a position with your department. Prior to conducting an interview of the job applicant, it would be LEAST helpful for you to have
    A. a personal resume
    B. a job description
    C. references
    D. hiring requirements

23. Job applicants tend to be nervous during interviews.
    Which of the following techniques is MOST likely to put such an applicant at ease?
    A. Try to establish rapport by asking general questions which are easily answered by the applicant
    B. Ask the applicant to describe his career objectives immediately, thus minimizing the anxiety caused by waiting
    C. Start the interview with another member of the staff present so that the applicant does not feel alone
    D. Proceed as rapidly as possible, since the emotional state of the applicant is none of your concern

24. Of the following abilities, the one which is LEAST important in conducting an interview is the ability to
    A. ask the interviewee pertinent questions
    B. evaluate the interviewee on the basis of appearance
    C. evaluate the responses of the interviewee
    D. gain the cooperation of the interviewee

25. One of the techniques of management often used by supervisors is performance appraisal.
    Which of the following is NOT one of the objectives of performance appraisal?
    A. Improve staff performance
    B. Determine individual training needs
    C. Improve organizational structure
    D. Set standards and performance criteria for employees

KEY (CORRECT ANSWERS)

1.	A		11.	D
2.	C		12.	B
3.	D		13.	B
4.	A		14.	C
5.	C		15.	B
6.	D		16.	B
7.	B		17.	A
8.	A		18.	D
9.	C		19.	A
10.	C		20.	C

21. B
22. C
23. A
24. B
25. C

TEST 2

DIRECTIONS: Each question or incomplete statement is followed by several suggested answers or completions. Select the one that BEST answers the question or completes the statement. *PRINT THE LETTER OF THE CORRECT ANSWER IN THE SPACE AT THE RIGHT.*

1. Examine the following sentence, and then choose the BEST statement about it from the choices below.
   Clerks are expected to receive visitors, to answer telephones, and miscellaneous clerical work must be done.
   A. This sentence is an example of effective writing.
   B. This is a run-on sentence.
   C. The three ideas in this sentence are not parallel, and therefore they should be divided into separate sentences.
   D. The three ideas in this sentence are parallel, but they are not expressed in parallel form.

   1._____

2. Examine the following sentence, and then choose from below the word which should be inserted in the blank space.
   Mr. Luce is a top-notch interviewer, _____ he is very reliable.
   A. but   B. and   C. however   D. for

   2._____

3. Examine the following sentence, and then choose from below the words which should be inserted in the blank spaces.
   The committee _____ sent in _____ report.
   A. has; it's   B. has; their   C. have; its   D. has; its

   3._____

4. Examine the following sentence, and then choose from below the words which should be inserted in the blank spaces.
   An organization usually contains more than just a few people; usually the membership is _____ enough so that close personal relationships among _____ impossible.
   A. large; are   B. large; found
   C. small; becomes   D. small; is

   4._____

5. Of the following, the BEST reference book to use to find a synonym for a common word is a(n)
   A. thesaurus   B. dictionary
   C. encyclopedia   catalog

   5._____

Questions 6-10.

DIRECTIONS: Questions 6 through 10 concern college students who have just completed their junior year for whom you must calculate grade averages for the year. These averages are to be based on the following table showing the number of credit hours for each student during the year at each of the grade levels: A, B, C, D, and F. How these letter grades may be translated into numerical grades is indicated in the first column of the table.

Grade Value	Credit Hours – Junior Year					
	King	Lewis	Martin	Nonkin	Ottly	Perry
A = 95	12	6	15	3	9	-
B = 85	9	15	6	12	9	3
C = 75	6	9	9	12	3	27
D = 65	3	-	3	3	6	-
F = 0	-	-	-	3	-	-

Calculating a grade average for an individual student is a 4-step process:
I. Multiply each grade value by the number of credit hours for which the student received that grade.
II. Add these multiplication products for each student.
III. Add the student's total credit hours.
IV. Divide the multiplication product total by the total number of credit hours.
V. Round the result, if there is a decimal place, to the nearest whole number. A number ending in .5 would be rounded to the next higher number.

EXAMPLE

Using student King's grades as an example, his grade average can be calculated by going through the following four steps.

I. 95 x 12 = 1140
    85 x 9 = 765
    75 x 6 = 450
    65 x 3 = 195
    65 x 3 =   0

II. Total   2550

III. 12
     9
     6
     2
     0
30 Total Credit Hours

IV. Divide 2550 by 30: $\frac{2550}{30} = 85$

King's grade average is 85.

Questions 6 through 10 are to be answered on the basis of the information given above.

6. The grade average of Lewis is
    A. 83   B. 84   C. 85   D. 86

6.____

7. The grade average of Martin is
    A. 83   B. 84   C. 85   D. 86

7.____

8. The grade average of Nonkin is
    A. 72   B. 73   C. 79   D. 80

8.____

3 (#2)

9. Student Ottly must attain a grade average of 85 in each of his years in college to be accepted into graduate school.
If, in summer school during his junior year, he takes two 3-credit courses and receives a grade of 85 in one and 95 in the other, his grade average for his junior year will then be MOST NEARLY
   A. 82
   B. 83
   C. 84
   D. 85

9._____

10. If Perry takes an additional 3-credit course during the year and receives a grade of 95. his grade average will be increased to approximately
    A. 74
    B. 76
    C. 78
    D. 80

10._____

11. You are in charge of verifying employees' qualifications. This involves telephoning previous employers and schools. One of the applications which you are reviewing contains information which you are almost certain is correct on the basis of what the employee has told you.
The BEST thing to do is to
    A. check the information again with the employee
    B. perform the required verification procedures
    C. accept the information as valid
    D. ask a superior to verify the information

11._____

12. The practice of immediately identifying oneself and one's place of employment when contacting persons on the telephone is
    A. *good*, because the receiver of the call can quickly identify the caller and establish a frame of reference
    B. *good*, because it helps to set the caller at ease with the other party
    C. *poor*, because it is not necessary to divulge that information when making general calls
    D. *poor*, because it takes longer to arrive at the topic to be discussed

12._____

13. A supervisor, Miss Smith, meets with a group of subordinates and tells them how they should perform certain tasks. The meeting is highly successful. She then attends a meeting to discuss common problems with a group of fellow supervisors with duties similar to her own. When she tells them how their subordinates should perform the same tasks, some of the other supervisors become angry.
Of the following, the MOST likely reason for this anger is that
    A. tension is to be expected in situations in which supervisors deal with each other
    B. the other supervisors are jealous of Miss Smith's knowledge
    C. Miss Smith should not tell other supervisors what methods she uses
    D. Miss Smith does not correctly perceive her role in relation to other supervisors

13._____

14. There is considerable rivalry among employees in a certain department over location of desks. It is the practice of the supervisor to assign desks without any predetermined plan. The supervisor is reconsidering his procedure.

14._____

81

In assigning desks, PRIMARY consideration should ordinarily be given to
A. past practices
B. flow of work
C. employee seniority
D. social relations among employees

15. Assume that, when you tell some of the typists under your supervision that the letters they prepare have too many errors, they contend that the letters are readable and that they obtain more satisfaction from their jobs if they do not have to be as concerned about errors.
These typists are
A. *correct*, because the ultimate objective should be job satisfaction
B. *incorrect*, because every job should be performed perfectly
C. *correct*, because they do not compose the letters themselves
D. *incorrect*, because their satisfaction is not the only consideration

16. Which of the following possible conditions is LEAST likely to represent a hindrance to effective communication?
A. The importance of a situation may not be apparent.
B. Words may mean different things to different people.
C. The recipient of a communication may respond to it, sometimes unfavorably
D. Communications may affect the self-interest of those communicating.

17. You are revising the way in which your unit handle records.
One of the BEST ways to make sure that the change will be implemented with a minimum of difficulty is to
A. allow everyone on the staff who is affected by the change to have an opportunity to contribute their ideas to the new procedures
B. advise only the key member of your staff in advance so that they can help you enforce the new method when it is implemented
C. give the assignment of implementation to the newest member of the unit
D. issue a memorandum announcing the change and stating that complaints will not be tolerated

18. One of your assistants is quite obviously having personal problems that are affecting his work performance.
As a supervisor, it would be MOST appropriate for you to
A. avoid any inquiry into the nature of the situation since this is not one of your responsibilities
B. avoid any discussion of personal problems on the basis that there is nothing you could do about them anyhow
C. help the employee obtain appropriate help with these problems
D. advise the employee that personal problems cannot be considered when evaluating work performance

19. The key to improving communication with your staff and other departments is the development of an awareness of the importance of communication.
Which of the following is NOT a good suggestion for developing this awareness?
   A. Be willing to look at your own attitude toward how you communicate
   B. Be sensitive and receptive to reactions to what you tell people
   C. Make sure all communication is in writing
   D. When giving your subordinates directions, try to put yourself in their place and see if your instructions still make sense

20. One of the assistants on your staff has neglected to complete an important assignment on schedule. You feel that a reprimand is necessary.
When speaking to the employee, it would usually be LEAST desirable to
   A. display your anger to show the employee how strongly you feel about the problem
   B. ask several questions about the reasons for failure to complete the assignment
   C. take the employee aside so that nobody else is present when you discuss the matter
   D. give the employee as much time as he needs to explain exactly what happened

KEY (CORRECT ANSWERS)

1.	D	11.	B
2.	B	12	A
3.	D	13.	D
4.	A	14.	B
5.	A	15.	D
6.	B	16.	C
7.	C	17.	A
8.	B	18.	C
9.	C	19.	C
10.	C	20.	A

EXAMINATION SECTION
TEST 1

DIRECTIONS: Each question or incomplete statement is followed by several suggested answers or completions. Select the one that BEST answers the question or completes the statement. *PRINT THE LETTER OF THE CORRECT ANSWER IN THE SPACE AT THE RIGHT.*

1. One of the things that can ruin morale in a work group is the failure to exercise judgment in the assignment of overtime work to your subordinates.
   Of the following, the MOST desirable supervisory practice in assigning overtime work is to
   A. rotate overtime on a uniform basis among all your subordinates
   B. assign overtime to those who are *moonlighting* after regular work hours
   C. rotate overtime as much as possible among employees willing to work additional hours
   D. assign overtime to those employees who take frequent long weekend vacations

2. The consistent delegation of authority by you to experienced and reliable subordinates in your work group is generally considered
   A. *undesirable*, because your authority in the group may be threatened by an unscrupulous subordinate
   B. *undesirable*, because it demonstrates that you cannot handle your own workload
   C. *desirable*, because it shows that you believe that you have been accepted by your subordinates
   D. *desirable*, because the development of subordinates creates opportunities for assuming broader responsibilities yourself

3. The MOST effective way for you to deal with a false rumor circulating among your subordinates is to
   A. have a trusted subordinate state a counter-rumor
   B. recommend disciplinary action against the rumor mongers
   C. point out to your subordinates that rumors degrade both listener and initiator
   D. furnish your subordinates with sufficient authentic information

4. Two of your subordinates tell you about a mistake they made in a report that has already been sent the top management.
   Which of the following questions is most likely to elicit the MOST valuable information from your subordinates?
   A. Who is responsible?
   B. How can we explain this to top management?
   C. How did it happen?
   D. Why weren't you more careful?

5. Assume that you are responsible for implementing major changes in work flow patterns and personnel assignments in the unit of which you are in charge. The one of the following actions which is MOST likely to secure the willing cooperation of those persons who will have to change their assignments?
   A. having the top administrators of the agency urge their cooperation at a group meeting
   B. issuing very detailed and carefully planned instructions to the affected employees regarding the changes
   C. integrating employee participation into the planning of the changes
   D. reminding the affected employees that career advancement depends upon compliance with organizational objectives

6. Of the following, the BEST reason for using face-to-face communication instead of written communication is that face-to-face communication
   A. allows for immediate feedback
   B. is more credible
   C. enables greater use of detail and illustration
   D. is more polite

7. Of the following, the MOST likely disadvantage of giving detailed instructions when assigning a task to a subordinate is that such instructions may
   A. conflict with the subordinate's ideas of how the task should be done
   B. reduce standardization of work performance
   C. cause confusion in the mind of the subordinate
   D. inhibit the development of new procedures by the subordinate

8. Assume that you are a supervisor of a unit consisting of a number of subordinates and that one subordinate, whose work is otherwise acceptable, keeps on making errors in one particular task assigned to him in rotation. This task consists of routine duties which all your subordinates should be able to perform.
   Of the following, the BEST way for you to handle this situation is to
   A. do the task yourself when the erring employee is scheduled to perform it and assign this employee other duties
   B. reorganize work assignments so that the task in question is no longer performed in rotation but assigned full-time to your most capable subordinate
   C. find out why this subordinate keeps on making the errors in question and see that he learns how to do the task properly
   D. maintain a well-documented record of such errors and, when the evidence is overwhelming, recommend appropriate disciplinary action

9. In the past, Mr. T, one of your subordinates, had been generally withdrawn and suspicious of others, but he had produced acceptable work. However, Mr. T has lately started to get into arguments with his fellow workers during which he displays intense rage. Friction between this subordinate and the others in your unit is mounting and the unit's work is suffering.

Of the following, which would be the BEST way for you to handle this situation?
- A. Rearrange work schedules and assignments so as to give Mr. T no cause for complaint
- B. Instruct the other workers to avoid Mr. T and not to respond to any abuse
- C. Hold a unit meeting and appeal for harmony and submergence of individual differences in the interest of work
- D. Maintain a record of incidents and explore with Mr. T the possibility of seeking professional help

10. You are responsible for seeing to it that your unit is functioning properly in the accomplishment of its budgeted goals.
    Which of the following will provide the LEAST information on how well you are accomplishing such goals?
    - A. Measurement of employee performance
    - B. Identification of alternative goals
    - C. Detection of employee errors
    - D. Preparation of unit reports

11. Some employees see an agency training program as a threat.
    Of the following, the MOST likely reason for such an employee attitude toward training is that the employee involved feel that
    - A. some trainers are incompetent
    - B. training rarely solves real work-a-day problems
    - C. training may attempt to change comfortable behavior patterns
    - D. training sessions are boring

12. Of the following, the CHIEF characteristic which distinguishes a good supervisor from a poor supervisor is the good supervisor's
    - A. ability to favorably impress others
    - B. unwillingness to accept monotony or routine
    - C. ability to deal constructively with problem situations
    - D. strong drive to overcome opposition

13. Of the following, the MAIN disadvantage of on-the-job training is that, generally,
    - A. special equipment may be needed
    - B. production may be slowed down
    - C. the instructor must maintain an individual relationship with the trainee
    - D. the on-the-job instructor must be better qualified than the classroom instructor

14. All of the following are correct methods for a supervisor to use in connection with employee discipline EXCEPT
    - A. trying not to be too lenient or too harsh
    - B. informing employees of the rules and the penalties for violations of the rules
    - C. imposing discipline immediately after the violation is discovered
    - D. making sure, when you apply discipline, that the employee understands that you do not want to do it

15. Of the following, the MAIN reason for a supervisor to establish standard procedures for his unit is to
    A. increase the motivation for his subordinates
    B. make it easier for the subordinates to submit to authority
    C. reduce the number of times that his subordinates have to consult him
    D. reduce the number of mistakes that his subordinates will make

16. Of the following, the BEST reason for using form letters in correspondence is that they are
    A. concise and businesslike
    B. impersonal in tone
    C. uniform in appearance
    D. economical for large mailings

17. The use of loose-leaf office manuals for the guidance of employees on office policy, organization, and office procedures has won wide acceptance.
    The MAIN advantage of the loose-leaf format is that it
    A. allows speedy reference
    B. facilitates revisions and changes
    C. includes a complete index
    D. presents a professional appearance

18. Office forms sometimes consist of several copies, each of a different color.
    The MAIN reason for using different colors is to
    A. make a favorable impression on the users of the form
    B. distinguish each copy from the others
    C. facilitate the appearance of legible carbon copies
    D. reduce cost, since using colored stock permits recycling of paper

19. Which of the following is the BEST justification for obtaining a photocopying machine for the office?
    A. A photocopying machine can produce an unlimited number of copies at a low fixed cost per copy.
    B. Employees need little training in operating a photocopying machine.
    C. Office costs will be reduced and efficiency increased.
    D. The legibility of a photocopy generally is superior to copy produced by any other office duplicating device.

20. Which one of the following should be the MOST important overall consideration when preparing a recommendation to automate a large-scale office activity?
    The
    A. number of models of automated equipment available
    B. benefits and costs of automation
    C. fears and resistance of affected employees
    D. experience of offices which have automated similar activities

21. A tickler file is MOST appropriate for filing materials
    A. chronologically according to date they were received
    B. alphabetically by name
    C. alphabetically by subject
    D. chronologically according to date they should be followed up

22. Which of the following is the BEST reason for decentralizing rather than centralizing the use of duplicating machines?
    A. Developing and retaining efficient duplicating machine operators
    B. Facilitating supervision of duplicating services
    C. Motivating employees to produce legible duplicated copies
    D. Placing the duplicating machines where they are most convenient and most frequently used

22.____

23. Window envelopes are sometimes considered preferable to individually addressed envelopes PRIMARILY because
    A. window envelopes are available in standard sizes for all purposes
    B. window envelopes are more attractive and official-looking
    C. the use of window envelopes eliminates the risk of inserting a letter in the wrong envelope
    D. the use of window envelopes requires neater typing

23.____

24. In planning the layout of a new office, the utilization of space and the arrangement of staff, furnishings and equipment should usually be MOST influenced by the
    A. gross square footage
    B. status differences in the chain of command
    C. framework of informal relationships among employees
    D. activities to be performed

24.____

25. When delegating responsibility for an assignment to a subordinate, it is MOST important that you
    A. retain all authority necessary to complete the assignment
    B. make yourself generally available for consultation with the subordinate
    C. inform your superiors that you are no longer responsible for the assignment
    D. decrease the number of subordinates whom you have to supervise

25.____

KEY (CORRECT ANSWERS)

1.	C		11.	C
2.	D		12.	C
3.	D		13.	B
4.	D		14.	D
5.	C		15.	C
6.	A		16.	D
7.	D		17.	B
8.	C		18.	B
9.	D		19.	C
10.	B		20.	B

21. D
22. D
23. C
24. D
25. B

TEST 2

DIRECTIONS: Each question or incomplete statement is followed by several suggested answers or completions. Select the one that BEST answers the question or completes the statement. *PRINT THE LETTER OF THE CORRECT ANSWER IN THE SPACE AT THE RIGHT.*

Questions 1-5.

DIRECTIONS: Questions 1 through 5 are to be answered on the basis of the following passage.

The most effective control mechanism to prevent gross incompetence on the part of public employees is a good personnel program. The personnel officer in the line departments and the central personnel agency should exert positive leadership to raise levels of performance. Although the key factor is the quality of the personnel recruited, staff members other than personnel officers can make important contributions to efficiency. Administrative analysts, now employed in many agencies, make detailed studies of organization and procedures, with the purpose of eliminating delays, waste, and other inefficiencies. Efficiency is, however, more than a question of good organization and procedures; it is also the product of the attitudes and values of the public employees. Personal motivation can provide the will to be efficient. The best management studies will not result in substantial improvement of the performance of those employees who feel no great urge to work up to their abilities.

1. The passage indicates that the key factor in preventing gross incompetence of public employees is the
    A. hiring of administrative analysts to assist personnel people
    B. utilization of effective management studies
    C. overlapping of responsibility
    D. quality of the employees hired

2. According to the above passage, the central personnel agency staff should
    A. work more closely with administrative analysts in the line departments than with personnel officers
    B. make a serious effort to avoid jurisdictional conflicts with personnel officers in line departments
    C. contribute to improving the quality of work of public employees
    D. engage in a comprehensive program to change the public's negative image of public employees

3. The passage indicates that efficiency in an organization can BEST be brought about by
    A. eliminating ineffective control mechanisms
    B. instituting sound organizational procedures
    C. promoting competent personnel
    D. recruiting people with desire to do good work

4. According to the passage, the purpose of administrative analysis in a public agency is to
   A. prevent injustice to the public employee
   B. promote the efficiency of the agency
   C. protect the interests of the public
   D. ensure the observance of procedural due process

5. The passage implies that a considerable rise in the quality of work of public employees can be brought about by
   A. encouraging positive employee attitudes toward work
   B. controlling personnel officers who exceed their powers
   C. creating warm personal associations among public employees in an agency
   D. closing loopholes in personnel organization and procedures

6. Typist X can type 20 forms per hour and Typist I can type 30 forms per hour. If there are 30 forms to be typed and both typists are put to work on the job, how soon should they be expected to finish the work? _____ minutes.
   A. 32   B. 34   C. 36   D. 38

7. Assume that there were 18 working days in February and that the six clerks in your unit had the following number of absences:
   Clerk F – 3 absences
   Clerk G – 2 absences
   Clerk H – 8 absences
   Clerk I – 1 absence
   Clerk J – 0 absences
   Clerk K – 5 absences
   The average percentage attendance for the six clerks in your unit in February was MOST NEARLY
   A. 80%   B. 82%   C. 84%   D. 86%

8. A certain employee is paid at the rate of $15.00 per hour, with time-and-a-half for overtime. Hours in excess of 40 hours a week count as overtime. During the past week, the employee put in 48 working hours.
   The employee's gross wages for the week are MOST NEARLY
   A. $600   B. $700   C. $720   D. $840

9. You are making a report on the number of inside and outside calls handled by a particular switchboard. Over a 15-day period, the total number of all inside and outside calls handled by the switchboard was 5,760. The average number of inside calls per day was 234. You cannot find one day's tally of outside calls, but the total number of outside calls for the other fourteen days was 2,065. From this information, how many outside calls must have been reported on the missing tally?
   A. 175   B. 185   C. 195   D. 205

10. A floor plan has been prepared for a new building, drawn to a scale of ¾ inch = 1 foot. A certain area is drawn 1 and ½ feet long and 6 inches wide on the floor plan.
What are the ACTUAL dimensions of this area in the new building?
_____ feet long and _____ feet wide.
A. 21; 8   B. 24; 8   C. 27; 9   D. 30; 9

10.____

Questions 11-15.

DIRECTIONS: In answering Questions 11 through 15, assume that you are in charge of public information for an office which issues reports and answers questions from other offices and from the public on changes in land use. The following charts represent comparative land use in four neighborhoods. The area of each neighborhood is expressed in city blocks. Assume that all city blocks are the same size.

NEIGHBORHOOD A – 16 CITY BLOCKS   NEIGHBORHOOD B – 24 CITY BLOCKS

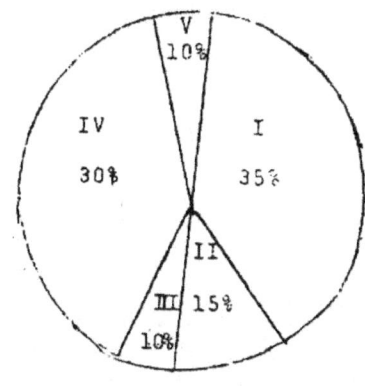
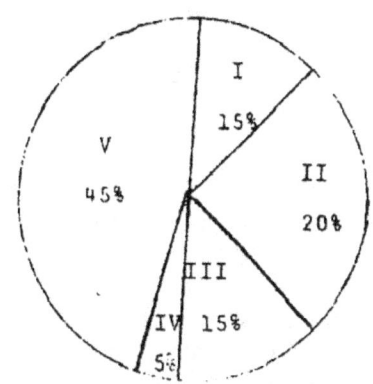

NEIGHBORHOOD C – 20 CITY BLOCKS   NEIGHBORHOOD D – 12 CITY BLOCKS

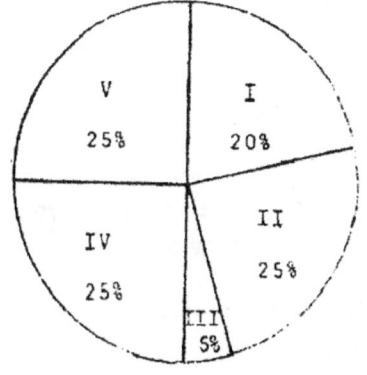
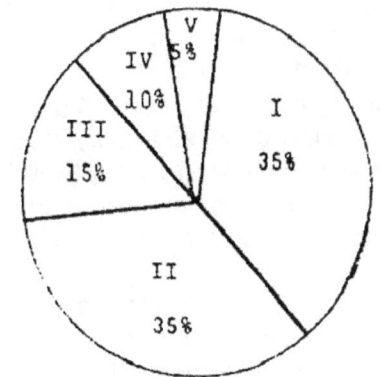

KEY: I: One- and two-family houses
II: Apartment buildings
III: Office buildings
IV: Rental Stores
V: Factories and warehouses

11. In how many of these neighborhoods does residential use (Categories I and II together) account for at least 50% of the land use?
    A. One   B. Two   C. Three   D. Four

11.____

12. Which neighborhood has the largest land area occupied by apartment buildings? Neighborhood
    A. A   B. B   C. C   D. D

12.____

13. In which neighborhood is the largest percentage of the land devoted to both office buildings and retail stores? Neighborhood _____.
    A. A   B. B   C. C   D. D

13.____

14. What is the difference, to the nearest city block, between the amount of land devoted to retail stores in Neighborhood B and the amount devoted to similar use in Neighborhood C? _____ block(s).

14.____

15. Which one of the following types of buildings occupies the same amount of land area in Neighborhood B as the amount of land area occupied by retail stores in Neighborhood A?
    A. 1   B. 2   C. 4   D. 6

15.____

Questions 16-20.

DIRECTIONS: Questions 16 through 20 are to be answered on the basis of the following passage.

For a period of nearly fifteen years, beginning in the mid-1960's, higher education sustained a phenomenal rate of growth. The factors principally responsible were continuing improvement in the rate of college entrance by high school graduates, a 50-percent increase in the size of the college-age (eighteen to twenty-one) group, and—until about 1977—a rapid expansion of university research activity supported by the federal government.

Today, as one looks ahead to the year 2030, it is apparent that each of these favorable stimuli will either be abated or turn into a negative factor. The rate of growth of the college-age group has already diminished, and from 2020 to 2025 the size of the college-age group will shrink annually almost as fast as it grew from 1975 to 1980. From 2025 to 2030, this annual decrease will slow down so that by 2030 the age-group will be about the same size as it was in 2029. This substantial net decrease in the size of the college-age group over the next fifteen years will dramatically affect college enrollments since, currently, 83 percent of undergraduates are twenty-one and under, and another 11 percent are twenty-one to twenty-four.

16. Which one of the following factors is NOT mentioned in the above passage as contributing to the high rate of growth of higher education?
    A. A larger increase in the size of the eighteen to twenty-one age group
    B. The equalization of educational opportunities among socio-economic groups
    C. The federal budget impact on research and development spending in the higher education sector
    D. The increasing rate at which high school graduates enter college

16.____

5 (#2)

17. Based on the information in the above passage, the size of the college-age group in 2030 will be
    A. larger than it was in 2029
    B. larger than it was in 2015
    C. smaller than it was in 2025
    D. about the same as it was in 2020

    17._____

18. According to the above passage, the tremendous rate of growth of higher education started around
    A. 1960   B. 1965   C. 1970   D. 1975

    18._____

19. The percentage of undergraduates who are over age 24 is MOST NEARLY
    A. 6%   B. 8%   C. 11%   D. 17%

    19._____

20. Which one of the following conclusions can be substantiated by the information given in the above passage?
    A. The college-age group will be about the same size in 2020 as it was in 1975.
    B. The annual decrease in the size of the college-age group from 2020 to 2025 will be about the same as the annual increase from 1975 to 1980.
    C. The overall decrease in the size of the college-age group from 2020 to 2025 will be followed by an overall increase in its size from 2025 to 2030.
    D. The size of the college-age group will decrease at a fairly constant rate from 2005 to 2020.

    20._____

21. Because higher status is important to many employees, they will often make an effort to achieve it as an end in itself.
    Of the following, the BEST course of action for the supervisor to take on the basis of the preceding statement is to
    A. attach higher status to that behavior of subordinates which is directed toward reaching the goals of the organization
    B. avoid showing sympathy toward subordinates' wishes for increased wages, improved working conditions, or other benefits
    C. foster interpersonal competitiveness among subordinates so that personal friendliness is replaced by the desire to protect individual status
    D. reprimand subordinates whenever their work is in some way unsatisfactory in order to adjust their status accordingly

    21._____

22. Assume that a large office in a certain organization operates long hours and is thus on two shifts with a slight overlap. Those employees, including supervisors, who are most productive are given their choice of shifts. The earlier shift is considered preferable by most employees.
    As a result of this method of assignment, which of the following is MOST likely to result?
    A. Most non-supervisory employees will be assigned to the late shift; most supervisors will be assigned to the early shift.
    B. Most supervisors will be assigned to the late shift; most non-supervisory employees will be assigned to the early shift.
    C. The early shift will be more productive than the late shift.
    D. The late shift will be more productive than the early shift.

    22._____

23. Assume that a supervisor of a unit in which the employees are of average friendliness tells a newly-hired employee on her first day that her co-workers are very friendly. The other employees hear his remarks to the new employee. Which of the following is the MOST likely result of this action of the supervisor? The
    A. newly-hired employee will tend to feel less friendly than if the supervisor had said nothing
    B. newly-hired employee will tend to believe that her co-workers are very friendly
    C. other employees will tend to feel less friendly toward one another
    D. other employees will tend to see the newly-hired employee as insincerely friendly

24. A recent study of employee absenteeism showed that, although unscheduled absence for part of a week is relatively high for young employees, unscheduled absence for a full week is low. However, although full-week unscheduled absence is least frequent for the youngest employees, the frequency of such absence increases as the age of employees increases.
    Which of the following statements is the MOST logical explanation for the greater full-week absenteeism among older employees?
    A. Older employees are more likely to be males.
    B. Older employees are more likely to have more relatively serious illnesses.
    C. Younger employees are more likely to take longer vacations.
    D. Younger employees are more likely to be newly-hired.

25. An employee can be motivated to fulfill his needs as he sees them. He is not motivated by what others think he ought to have, but what he himself wants. Which of the following statements follows MOST logically from the foregoing viewpoint?
    A. A person's different traits may be separately classified, but they are all part of one system comprising a whole person.
    B. Every job, however simple, entitles the person who does it to proper respect and recognition of his unique aspirations and abilities.
    C. No matter what equipment and facilities an organization has, they cannot be put to use except by people who have been motivated.
    D. To an observer, a person's need may be unrealistic but they ae still controlling.

KEY (CORRECT ANSWERS)

1.	D	11.	B
2.	C	12.	C
3.	D	13.	A
4.	B	14.	C
5.	A	15.	D
6.	C	16.	B
7.	B	17.	C
8.	D	18.	B
9.	B	19.	A
10.	B	20.	B

21. A
22. C
23. B
24. B
25. D

EXAMINATION SECTION
TEST 1

DIRECTIONS: Each question or incomplete statement is followed by several suggested answers or completions. Select the one that BEST answers the question or completes the statement. *PRINT THE LETTER OF THE CORRECT ANSWER IN THE SPACE AT THE RIGHT.*

Questions 1-5.

DIRECTIONS: Questions 1 to 5 refer to the table below.

TABLE 1: NEW HOUSING UNITS STARTED 2000-2005
(Hypothetical)

YEAR	TOTAL IN THOUSANDS	PERCENT CHANGE[1]	PRIVATELY OWNED (in thousands)		PUBLICLY OWNED IN THOUSANDS
			TOTAL	1-UNIT STRUCTURE	
2000	1,398	-20.4	1,250	990	I
2001	II	4.9	1,370	1,120	96
2002	1,524	4.0	III	1,236	104
2003	1,420	-6.8	1,325	1,164	95
2004	1,380	-2.8	1,260	IV	120
2005	1,690	V	1,520	1,415	170

[1] Change from previous year
Minus sign (-) denotes decrease

1. What is the value of I?

    A. 148
    B. 150
    C. 146
    D. 248
    E. None of the above, or cannot be calculated from the data provided

1.____

2. What is the value of II?

    A. 1,216
    B. 2,495
    C. 1,466
    D. 1,464
    E. None of the above, or cannot be calculated from the data provided

2.____

3. What is the value of III?

    A. 288
    B. 1,420
    C. 1,132
    D. 1,430
    E. None of the above, or cannot be calculated from the data provided

3.____

4. What is the value of IV?

   A. 1,140
   B. 1,380
   C. 1,102
   D. 1,094
   E. None of the above, or cannot be calculated from the data provided

5. What is the value of V?

   A. 18.3
   B. 81.7
   C. 21.5
   D. 22.5
   E. None of the above, or cannot be calculated from the data provided

Questions 6-10.

DIRECTIONS: Questions 6 to 10 test the applicant's ability to determine whether or not conclusions are true based on a given set of premises. The examinee should first read the premises that are given; then, look at the conclusion. Assume that the premises are true and decide whether the conclusion is:

   A. Necessarily true
   B. Probably, but not necessarily true
   C. Indeterminable, cannot be determined
   D. Probably, but not necessarily false
   E. Necessarily false

6. *Premises:* If the Commission approves the new proposal, the agency will move to a new location immediately. If the agency moves, five new supervisors will be appointed immediately. The Commission approved the new proposal.

   Conclusion: No new supervisors were appointed.

7. *Premises:* If the director retires, John Jackson, the associate director, will not be transferred to another agency. Jackson will be promoted to director if he is not transferred. The director retired.

   Conclusion: Jackson will be promoted to director.

8. *Premises:* If the maximum allowable income for food stamp recipients is increased, the number of food stamp recipients will increase. If the number of food stamp recipients increases, more funds must be allocated to the food stamp program, which will require a tax increase. Taxes cannot be raised without the approval of Congress. Congress probably will not approve a tax increase.

   Conclusion: The maximum allowable income for food stamp recipients will increase.

9. *Premises:* If prices are raised and sales remain constant, profits will increase. Prices were raised and sales levels will probably be maintained.

   Conclusion: Profits will increase.

   9.____

10. *Premises:* Some employees in the personnel department are technicians. Most of the technicians working in the personnel department are test development specialists. Lisa Jones works in the personnel department.

    Conclusion: Lisa Jones is a technician.

    10.____

Questions 11-15.

DIRECTIONS: Many jobs require skill in analyzing, understanding, and interpreting written material of varying levels of difficulty. These questions are primarily designed to test the applicant's comprehension and interpretation abilities. Therefore, Questions 11 to 15 require examinees to understand a given paragraph and to choose an answer based on their comprehension of the general concept used in the written passage. The right answer is usually a repetition in different terminology of the main concept(s) found in the passage. It may also be a conclusion drawn from the content of the paragraph that is equivalent to a restatement. The applicant should read each passage and select the one of the five statements that is BEST supported by the contents of the passage.

11. *A viable affirmative action program must contain specific procedures designed to achieve equal employment opportunities for specified groups. Appropriate procedures, without necessary determination to carry them out, are useless. Determination, without well-defined procedures, will achieve only partial success.*
    The paragraph BEST supports the statement that:

    11.____

    A. Well-defined procedures will assure the success of an affirmative action program
    B. A high degree of determination is necessary and sufficient for a highly successful affirmative action program
    C. It is impossible for an agency to develop a viable affirmative action program
    D. An agency may guarantee success of its affirmative action program by developing and implementing well-defined procedures
    E. Two important ingredients of a successful affirmative action program are well-defined procedures and a sincere resolve to implement those procedures

12. *Claimants who have become unemployed by voluntarily leaving the job, by refusing to accept suitable work, or due to misconduct should be temporarily disqualified from receiving benefits. However, the disqualification period should never be longer than the average period required for a worker to find employment. Unemployment insurance is designed to alleviate hardship due to unemployment. Benefits should definitely be paid if unemployment continues beyond a certain point and the claimant can show that he has made an honest effort to find employment.*
    The paragraph BEST supports the statement that:

    12.____

    A. If a claimant cannot find work after a certain period of time, he/she should no longer receive benefits
    B. In cases of willful misconduct, disqualification should continue indefinitely
    C. The reasons for unemployment change as the period of unemployment gets longer

D. If a claimant cannot find employment after a certain period of time, he/she should be allowed to receive unemployment insurance benefits
E. If a claimant chooses voluntary unemployment, he/she should receive unemployment insurance benefits immediately

13. *Education in the United States is a state responsibility, a local function, and a federal concern. Unlike other social service programs, this arrangement also places state governments between the federal government and local governing bodies.*
The paragraph BEST supports the statement that:

   A. Enforcement of federal education policies is left to state discretion
   B. The federal government plays an advisory role only in matters concerning education
   C. Federal educational policies are generally implemented by local governments under the direction of the state
   D. No federal funds are used to support local educational programs
   E. Federal aid is often used to induce local school systems to implement federal policies

13._____

14. *Technological and psychological conditions are changing so rapidly that most agencies and organizations must continually adapt to new situations in order to remain viable.*
The paragraph BEST supports the statement that:

   A. Changes in general conditions determine the effectiveness of an organization
   B. The effectiveness of an organization depends more on technological advances than on psychological changes
   C. Organizations must be able to adapt to technological and psychological changes in order to maintain effectiveness
   D. The effectiveness of an organization is equally dependent upon technological advances and psychological changes
   E. The effectiveness of an organization is dependent upon its technological and psychological advances

14._____

15. *A disability may be defined as the inability to perform one or more activities essential to normal everyday living. Some examples are basic care of self, earning a living, and social competence. Some basic causes are physical impairment due to illness or injury, mental impairment, and physical or mental deprivation*
The paragraph BEST supports the statement that a disability is

   A. a term utilized to denote any lessening of an individual's ability to perform normal daily activities
   B. any acute or chronic condition that may be permanent or long-range in nature
   C. any physical or mental impairment which inhibits higher order intellectual pursuits
   D. an acute or chronic condition that can be described by the pathology underlying the condition
   E. defined as the inability to perform any activity essential to normal everyday living

15._____

Questions 16-20.

DIRECTIONS: Many occupations require skill in solving quantitative problems of varying degrees of difficulty. Questions 16 to 20 are designed to test these abilities. Read each statement carefully before attempting to solve the problem.

16. Angela Winston processed 300 applications for food stamps during the month of June. During the month of July, she processed 10% fewer applications. Determine the number she processed in July. 16.____

    A. 220 B. 240 C. 270
    D. 280 E. None of the above

17. A personnel officer drove from Lake Charles to a conference in Baton Rouge. The total distance for the round trip was 240 miles. The time required to travel one way to Baton Rouge was two hours. Due to heavy traffic during the return trip to Lake Charles, an extra hour was required.
    How much *slower* was the personnel officer traveling on the return trip? 17.____

    A. 10 mph B. 15 mph C. 20 mph
    D. 25 mph E. None of the above

18. Ten employment security interviewers interviewed a total of 800 applicants in five days. Sixty percent of those interviewed were placed on jobs.
    If each interviewer worked 8 hours each day, what was the AVERAGE number of applicants placed on jobs each hour by each interviewer? 18.____

    A. 1.2 B. 0.8 C. 0.5
    D. 1.5 E. None of the above

19. A state park *is* budgeted at an amount 9 times the amount budgeted for a nearby city park.
    If the combined yearly budget of both parks is $1,000,000, what is the average monthly budget of the city park? 19.____

    A. $8,111.00 B. $8,222.22 C. $8,333.33
    D. $8,444.44 E.

20. The estimated completion time for a 100-item test is 3 1/3 hours. Ten applicants actually took the test and completed it in 3 hours.
    What is the difference, in seconds, between the actual and estimated rate of completion per item? 20.____

    A. 10 B. 12 C. 14
    D. 16 E. None of the above

KEY (CORRECT ANSWERS)

1.	A	11.	E
2.	C	12.	D
3.	B	13.	C
4.	E	14.	C
5.	D	15.	E
6.	E	16.	C
7.	A	17.	C
8.	D	18.	A
9.	B	19.	C
10.	C	20.	B

SOLUTIONS TO PROBLEMS

1. The answer is 148 or A. The figure represents the number of publicly-owned units which is obtained by subtracting the number of privately-owned units from the total: 1,398 - 1,250 = 148.

2. The answer is 1,466 or C. The figure represents the total number of housing units which is obtained by adding the total number of privately-owned units to the number of publicly-owned units: 1,370 + 96 = 1,466. Alternative A represents the sum of the total number of publicly-owned units and the number of 1-unit, privately-owned structures. Alternatives B and D are irrelevant values.

3. The answer is 1,420 or B. It is obtained by subtracting the number of publicly-owned units from the total number of housing units: 1,524 - 104 = 1,420. Alternative A is obtained by subtracting the number of 1-unit, privately-owned structures from the total number of units. Alternatives C and D are irrelevant values.

4. The answer is E. The number of privately-owned 1-unit structures cannot be calculated since the number of privately-owned multi-unit structures is not given in the table. Alternative A represents the difference between the number of privately-owned units and the number of publicly-owned units. Alternative B represents the sum of publicly-owned units and privately-owned units. Alternatives C and D are irrelevant values.

5. The answer is 22.5 or D. The percent change is calculated by computing the increase or decrease and dividing the result by the number that existed before the change: 1,690 - 1,380 = 310 and 310/1380 = 22.46 or 22.5. Alternative A erroneously divides 310 by 1,690, and Alternative B was found by erroneously dividing 1,380 by 1,690. Alternative C is an irrelevant value.

6. The correct answer is E. The new proposal was approved. According to the premises, approval means that the agency will move, and moving to a new location means that five new supervisors will be appointed.

7. The correct answer is A. According to the premises, the director retired, which means that Jackson will not be transferred and, therefore, will be promoted to director.

8. The correct answer is D (probably, but not necessarily false). Since Congress probably will not approve a tax increase, the maximum allowable income for food stamp recipients probably will not increase.

9. The correct answer is B (probably, but not necessarily true). According to the premises, profits will increase if prices are raised and sales remain constant. It is known that prices were raised. Although sales levels will probably be maintained, this is not certain.

10. The correct answer is C (indeterminable, cannot be determined). The premises give no indication of the proportion of employees who are technicians. Therefore, no conclusion can be drawn with respect to the probability that any one employee is a technician.

11. The correct alternative, E, restates the idea presented in the paragraph. Statements A and B each contain only one of the ingredients. Alternative D overstates the implications of the paragraph.

12. The correct alternative, D, summarizes the meaning of the passage as a whole. Alternative A concerns the length of time the claimant should receive benefits. Alternatives B and E contradict parts of the passage and the idea expressed in Alternative C is not addressed in the paragraph.

13. Correct alternative, C, is supported by the paragraph. The ideas expressed in Alternatives A, B, and D are not addressed in the paragraph. Although Alternative E is probably true, it is not mentioned in the paragraph.

14. Correct alternative, C, effectively restates the essence of the paragraph. In contrast to Alternatives A and B, the paragraph states that organizations must adapt to changes. Alternatives D and E imply that effectiveness of an organization depends on change; however, the paragraph states that effectiveness depends on an organization's ability to adapt to change.

15. Correct alternative E is supported by the first sentence of the paragraph. Alternatives B, C, and D are not supported by the paragraph. Although Alternative A is supported by the paragraph to some extent, its lack of specificity makes it less acceptable than Alternative

16. The answer is C. First, compute 10% of 300: 300 x .10 = 30. Second, subtract the result from 300: 300 - 30 = 270.

17. The answer is C. First, compute the distance one way: 1/2 x 240 = 120 miles. Second, calculate the rate going: 120 miles ÷ 2 hours = 60 mph. Third, calculate the rate returning: 120 miles ÷ 3 hours = 40 mph. Fourth, compute the difference: 60 mph - 40 mph = 20 mph.

18. The answer is A. The total number of applicants placed on jobs equals 60% of 800: .60 x 800 = 480. The total placed per day equals 480 divided by the number of days: 480 ÷ 5 = 96. The total placed per hour equals 96 divided by hours per day: 96 ÷ 8 = 12. The total placed per hour per interviewer equals the total placed per hour divided by the number of interviewers: 12 ÷ 10 = 1.2.

19. The correct answer is C. Let x = the annual city park budget and 9x = the annual state park budget. Therefore, 10x = $1,000,000, and x = $100,000. $100,000 divided by 12 = $8,333.33, the average monthly city park budget.

20. The answer is B. The estimated time per item equals the estimated time divided by the number of items:

$$\frac{3\,1/3 \times 60}{100} = \frac{10/3 \times 60}{100} = \frac{10 \times 20}{100} = \frac{200}{100} = 2 \text{ minutes}$$

The actual time equals 3 hours or 180 minutes. The actual time per item equals 180 minutes divided by the number of items: 180 ÷ 100 = 1.8 minutes. The difference in estimated time and actual time equals 2 minutes minus 1.8 minutes: 2.0 - 1.8 = .2 minutes or .2 x 60 seconds = 12 seconds.

LOGICAL REASONING
EVALUATING CONCLUSIONS IN LIGHT OF KNOWN FACTS
EXAMINATION SECTION
TEST 1

COMMENTARY

This section is designed to provide practice questions in evaluating conclusions when you are given specific data to work with.

We suggest you do the questions three at a time, consulting the answer key and then the solution section for any questions you may have missed. It's a good idea to try the questions again a week before the exam.

In the validity of conclusion type of question, you are first given a reading passage which describes a particular situation. The passage may be on any topic, as it is not your knowledge of the topic that is being tested, but your reasoning abilities. The passage is likely to detail several proposed courses of action and factors affecting these proposals. The reading passage is followed by a conclusion based on the facts in the passage, or a description of a decision taken regarding the situation. The conclusion is followed by a number of statements which have a possible connection to the conclusion. For each statement, you are to determine whether:

- A. The statement proves the conclusion.
- B. The statement supports the conclusion but does not prove it.
- C. The statement disproves the conclusion.
- D. The statement weakens the conclusion but does not disprove it.
- E. The statement has no relevance to the conclusion.

Remember that the conclusion after the passage is to be accepted as the outcome of what actually happened, and that you are being asked to evaluate the impact each statement would have had on the conclusion.

Questions 1-8.

DIRECTIONS: Questions 1 through 8 are based on the following paragraph.

In May of 2018, Mr. Bryan inherited a clothing store on Main Street in a small New England town. The store has specialized in selling quality men's and women's clothing since 1920. Business has been stable throughout the years, neither increasing nor decreasing. He has an opportunity to buy two adjacent stores which would enable him to add a wider range and style of clothing. In order to do this, he would have to borrow a substantial amount of money. He also risks losing the goodwill of his present clientele.

CONCLUSION: On November 7, 2018, Mr. Bryan tells the owner of the two adjacent stores that he has decided not to purchase them. He feels that it would be best to simply maintain his present marketing position, as there would not be enough new business to support an expansion.

A. The statement proves the conclusion.
B. The statement supports the conclusion but does not prove it.
C. The statement disproves the conclusion.
D. The statement weakens the conclusion.
E. The statement is irrelevant to the conclusion.

1. A large new branch of the county's community college holds its first classes in September. 1.____

2. The town's largest factory shuts down with no indication that it will reopen. 2.____

3. The United States Census showed that the number of children per household dropped from 2.4 to 2.1 since the last census. 3.____

4. Mr. Bryan's brother tells him of a new clothing boutique specializing in casual women's clothing which is opening soon. 4.____

5. Mr. Bryan's sister buys her baby several items for Christmas at Mr. Bryan's store. 5.____

6. Mrs. McIntyre, the President of the Town Council, brings Mr. Bryan a home-baked pumpkin pie in honor of his store's 100th anniversary. They discuss the changes that have taken place in the town, and she comments on how his store has maintained the same look and feel over the years. 6.____

7. In October, Mr. Bryan's aunt lends him $50,000. 7.____

8. The Town Council has just announced that the town is eligible for funding from a federal project designed to encourage the location of new businesses in the central districts of cities and towns. 8.____

Questions 9-18.

DIRECTIONS: Questions 9 through 18 are based on the following paragraph.

A proposal was put before the legislative body of a country to require air bags in all automobiles manufactured for domestic use in that country after 2019. The air bag, made of nylon or plastic, is designed to inflate automatically within a car at the impact of a collision, thus protecting front-seat occupants from being thrown forward. There has been much support of the measure from consumer groups, the insurance industry, key legislators, and the general public. The country's automobile manufacturers, who contend the new crash equipment would add up to $1,000 to car prices and provide no more protection than existing seat belts, are against the proposed legislation

CONCLUSION: On April 21, 2014, the legislation requiring air bags in all automobiles manufactured for domestic use in that country after 2019.

A. The statement proves the conclusion.
B. The statement supports the conclusion but does not prove it.
C. The statement disproves the conclusion.
D. The statement weakens the conclusion.
E. The statement is irrelevant to the conclusion.

9. A study has shown that 59% of car occupants do not use seat belts. 9.____

10. The country's Department of Transportation has estimated that the crash protection equipment would save up to 5,900 lives each year. 10.____

11. On April 27, 2013, Augusta Raneoni was named head of an advisory committee to gather and analyze data on the costs, benefits, and feasibility of the proposed legislation on air bags in automobiles. 11.____

12. Consumer groups and the insurance industry accuse the legislature of rejecting passage of the regulation for political reasons. 12.____

13. A study by the Committee on Imports and Exports projected that the sales of imported cars would rise dramatically in 2019 because imported cars do not have to include air bags, and can be sold more cheaply. 13.____

14. Research has shown that air bags, if produced on a large scale, would cost about $200 apiece, and would provide more reliable protection than any other type of seat belt. 14.____

15. Auto sales in 2011 increased 3% over the previous year. 15.____

16. A Department of Transportation report in July of 2020 credits a drop in automobile deaths of 4,100 to the use of air bags. 16.____

17. In June of 2014, the lobbyist of the largest insurance company receives a bonus for her work on the passage of the air bag legislation. 17.____

18. In 2020, the stock in crash protection equipment has risen three-fold over the previous year. 18.____

Questions 19-25.

DIRECTIONS: Questions 19 through 25 are based on the following paragraph.

On a national television talk show, Joan Rivera, a famous comedienne, has recently insulted the physical appearances of a famous actress and the dead wife of an ex-President. There has been a flurry of controversy over her comments, and much discussion of the incident has appeared in the press. Most of the comments have been negative. It appears that this tie she might have gone too far. There have been cancellations of two of her five scheduled performances in the two weeks since the show was televised, and Joan's been receiving a lot of negative mail. Because of the controversy, she has an interview with a national news magazine at the end of the week, and her press agent is strongly urging her to apologize publicly. She feels strongly that her comments were no worse than any other she has ever made, and that the whole incident will *blow over* soon. She respects her press agent's judgment, however, as his assessment of public sentiment tends to be very accurate.

CONCLUSION: Joan does not apologize publicly, and during the interview she challenges the actress to a weight-losing contest. For every pound the actress loses, Joan says she will donate $1 to the Cellulite Prevention League.

    A.   The statement proves the conclusion.
          B.   The statement supports the conclusion but does not prove it.
          C.   The statement disproves the conclusion.
          D.   The statement weakens the conclusion.
          E.   The statement is irrelevant to the conclusion.

19. Joan's mother, who she is very fond of, is very upset with Joan's comments.   19.____

20. Six months after the interview, Joan's income has doubled.   20.____

21. Joan's agent is pleased with the way Joan handles the interview.   21.____

22. Joan's sister has been appointed Treasurer of the Cellulite Prevention League   22.____
In her report, she states that Joan's $12 contribution is the only amount that
has been donated to the League in its first six months.

23. The magazine receives many letters commending Joan for the courage it   23.____
took for her to apologize publicly in the interview.

24. Immediately after the interview appears, another one of Joan's performances   24.____
is cancelled.

25. Due to a printers' strike, the article was not published until the following week.   25.____

Questions 26-30.

DIRECTIONS: Questions 25 through 30 are based on the following paragraph.

    The law-making body of Country X must decide what to do about the issue of recording television shows for home use. There is currently no law against recording shows directly from the TV as long as the DVDs are not used for commercial purposes. The increasing popularity of pay TV and satellite systems, combined with the increasing number of homes that own recording equipment, has caused a great deal of concern in some segments of the entertainment industry. Companies that own the rights to films, popular television shows, and sporting events feel that their copyright privileges are being violated, and they are seeking compensation or the banning of TV recording. Legislation has been introduced to make it illegal to record television programs for home use. Separate proposed legislation is also pending that would continue to allow recording of TV shows for home use, but would place a tax of 10% on each DVD that is purchased for home use. The income from that tax would then be proportionately distributed as royalties to those owning the rights to programs being aired. A weighted point system coupled with the averaging of several national viewing rating systems would be used to determine the royalties. There is a great deal of lobbying being done for both bills, as the manufacturers of DVDs and recording equipment are against the passage of the bills.

CONCLUSION: The legislature of Country X rejects both bills by a wide margin.

A. The statement proves the conclusion.
B. The statement supports the conclusion but does not prove it.
C. The statement disproves the conclusion.
D. The statement weakens the conclusion.
E. The statement is irrelevant to the conclusion.

26. Country X's Department of Taxation hires 500 new employees to handle the increased paperwork created by the new tax on DVDs.

27. A study conducted by the country's most prestigious accounting firm shows that the cost of implementing the proposed new DVD tax would be greater than the income expected from it.

28. It is estimated that 80% of all those working in the entertainment industry, excluding performers, own DVD recorders.

29. The head of Country X's law enforcement agency states that legislation banning the home recording of TV shows would be unenforceable.

30. Financial experts predict that unless a tax is placed on DVDs, several large companies in the entertainment industry will have to file for bankruptcy.

Questions 31-38.

DIRECTIONS: Questions 31 through 38 are variations on the type of question you just had. It is important that you read the question very carefully to determine exactly what is required.

31. In this question, select the choice that is MOST relevant to the conclusion.
  I. The Buffalo Bills football team is in second place in its division.
  II. The New England Patriots are in first place in the same division.
  III. There are two games left to play in the season, and the Bills will not play the Patriots again.
  IV. The New England Patriots won ten games and lost four games, and the Buffalo Bills have won eight games and lost six games.
  CONCLUSION: The Buffalo Bills win their division.
  A. The conclusion is proved by sentences I-IV.
  B. The conclusion is disproved by sentences I-IV.
  C. The facts are not sufficient to prove or disprove the conclusion.

32. In this question, select the choice that is MOST relevant to the conclusion.
    I. On the planet of Zeinon there are only two different eye colors and only two different hair colors.
    II. Half of those beings with purple hair have golden eyes.
    III. There are more inhabitants with purple hair than there are inhabitants with silver hair.
    IV. One-third of those with silver hair have green eyes.
    CONCLUSION: There are more golden-eyed beings on Zeinon than green-eyed ones.
    A. The conclusion is proved by sentences I-IV.
    B. The conclusion is disproved by sentences I-IV.
    C. The facts are not sufficient to prove or disprove the conclusion.

33. In this question, select the choice that is MOST relevant to the conclusion.
    John and Kevin are leaving Amaranth to go to school in Bethany. They've decided to rent a small truck to move their possessions. Joe's Truck Rental charges $100 plus 30¢ a mile. National Movers charges $50 more but gives free mileage for the first 100 miles. After the first 100 miles, they charge 25¢ a mile.
    CONCLUSION: John and Kevin rent their truck from National Movers because it is cheaper.
    A. The conclusion is proved by the facts in the above paragraph.
    B. The conclusion is disproved by the facts in the above paragraph.
    C. The facts are not sufficient to prove or disprove the conclusion.

34. For this question, select the choice that supports the information given in the passage.
    Municipalities in Country X are divided into villages, towns, and cities. A village has a population of 5,000 or less. The population of a town ranges from 5,001 to 15,000. In order to be incorporated as a city, the municipality must have a population over 15,000. If, after a village becomes a town, or a town becomes a city, the population drops below the minimum required (for example, the population of a city goes below 15,000), and stays below the minimum for more than ten years, it loses its current status, and drops to the next category. As soon as a municipality rises in population to the next category (village to town, for example), however, it is immediately reclassified to the next category.
    In the 2000 census, Plainfield had a population of 12,000. Between 2000 and 2010, Plainfield grew 10%, and between 2010 and 2020 Plainfield grew another 20%. The population of Springdale doubled from 2000 to 2010, and increased 25% from 2010 to 2020. The city of Smallville's population, 20,283, has not changed significantly in recent years. Granton had a population of 25,000 people in 1990, and has decreased 25% in each ten year period since then. Ellenville had a population of 4,283 in 1990, and grew 5% in each ten year period since 1990.

In 2020,
- A. Plainfield, Smallville, and Granton are cities.
- B. Smallville is a city, Granton is a town, and Ellenville is a village.
- C. Springdale, Granton, and Ellenville are towns.
- D. Plainfield and Smallville are cities, and Ellenville is a town.

35. For this question, select the choice that is MOST relevant to the conclusion.

    A study was done for a major food-distributing firm to determine if there is any difference in the kind of caffeine containing products used by people of different ages. A sample of one thousand people between the ages of twenty and fifty were drawn from selected areas in the country. They were divided equally into three groups.

    Those individuals who were 20-29 were designated Group A, those 30-39 were Group B, and those 40-50 were placed in Group C.

    It was found that on the average, Group A drank 1.8 cups of coffee, Group B 3.1, and Group C 2.5 cups of coffee daily. Group A drank 2.1 cups of tea, Group B drank 1.2, and Group C drank 2.6 cups of tea daily. Group A drank 3 1.8 ounces glasses of cola, Group B drank 1.9, and Group C drank 1.5 glasses of cola daily.

    CONCLUSION: According to the study, the average person in the 20-29 age group drinks less tea daily than the average person in the 40-50 age group, but drinks more coffee daily than the average person in the 30-39 age group drinks cola.
    - A. The conclusion is proved by the facts in the above paragraph.
    - B. The conclusion is disproved by the facts in the above paragraph.
    - C. The facts are not sufficient to prove or disprove the conclusion.

36. For this question, select the choice that is MOST relevant to the conclusion
    - I. Mary is taller than Jane but shorter than Dale.
    - II. Fred is taller than Mary but shorter than Steven.
    - III. Dale is shorter than Steven but taller than Elizabeth.
    - IV. Elizabeth is taller than Mary but not as tall as Fred.

    CONCLUSION: Dale is taller than Fred.
    - A. The conclusion is proved by sentences I-IV.
    - B. The conclusion is disproved by sentences I-IV.
    - C. The facts are not sufficient to prove or disprove the conclusion.

37. For this question, select the choice that is MOST relevant to the conclusion.
    - I. Main Street is between Spring Street and Glenn Blvd.
    - II. Hawley Avenue is one block south of Spring Street and three blocks north of Main Street.
    - III. Glenn Street is five blocks south of Elm and four blocks south of Main.
    - IV. All the streets mentioned are parallel to one another.

    CONCLUSION: Elm Street is between Hawley Avenue and Glenn Blvd.
    - A. The conclusion is proved by the facts in sentences I-IV.
    - B. The conclusion is disproved by the facts in sentences I-IV.
    - C. The facts are not sufficient to prove or disprove the conclusion.

38. For this question, select the choice that is MOST relevant to the conclusion. 38.____
    I. Train A leaves the town of Hampshire every day at 5:50 A.M. and arrives in New London at 6:42 A.M.
    II. Train A leaves New London at 7:00 A.M. and arrives in Kellogsville at 8:42 A.M.
    III. Train B leaves Kellogsville at 8:00 A.M. and arrives in Hampshire at 10:45 A.M.
    IV. Due to the need for repairs, there is just one railroad track between New London and Hampshire.
    CONCLUSION: It is impossible for Train A and Train B to follow these schedules without colliding.
    A. The conclusion is proved by the facts in sentences I-IV.
    B. The conclusion is disproved by the facts in sentences I-IV.
    C. The facts are not sufficient to prove or disprove the conclusion.

KEY (CORRECT ANSWERS)

1.	D	11.	C	21.	D	31.	C
2.	B	12.	C	22.	A	32.	A
3.	E	13.	D	23.	C	33.	C
4.	B	14.	B	24.	B	34.	B
5.	C	15.	E	25.	E	35.	B
6.	A	16.	B	26.	C	36.	C
7.	D	17.	A	27.	B	37.	A
8.	B	18.	B	28.	E	38.	B
9.	B	19.	D	29.	B		
10.	B	20.	E	30.	D		

SOLUTIONS TO QUESTIONS

1. The answer is D. This statement weakens the conclusion, but does not disprove it. If a new branch of the community college opened in September, it could possibly bring in new business for Mr. Bryant. Since it states in the conclusion that Mr. Bryant felt there would not be enough new business to support the additional stores, this would tend to disprove the conclusion. Choice C would not be correct because it's possible that he felt that the students would not have enough additional money to support his new venture, or would not be interested in his clothing styles. It's also possible that the majority of the students already live in the area, so that they wouldn't really be a new customer population. This type of question is tricky, and can initially be very confusing, so don't feel badly if you missed it. Most people need to practice with a few of these types of questions before they feel comfortable recognizing exactly what they're being asked to do.

2. The answer is B. It supports the conclusion because the closing of the factory would probably take money and customers out of the town, causing Mr. Bryant to lose some of his present business. It doesn't prove the conclusion, however, because we don't know how large the factory was. It's possible that only a small percentage of the population was employed there, or that they found other jobs.

3. The answer is E. The fact that the number of children per household dropped slightly nationwide in the decade is irrelevant. Statistics showing a drop nationwide doesn't mean that there was a drop in the number of children per household in Mr. Bryant's hometown. This is a tricky question, as choice B, supporting the conclusion but not proving it, may seem reasonable. If the number of children per household declined nationwide, then it may not seem unreasonable to feel that this would support Mr. Bryant's decision not to expand his business. However, we're preparing you for promotional exams, not "real life." One of the difficult things about taking exams is that sometimes you're forced to make a choice between two statements that both seem like they could be the possible answer. What you need to do in that case is choose the best choice. Becoming annoyed or frustrated with the question won't really help much. If there's a review of the exam, you can certainly appeal the question. There have been many cases where, after an appeal, two possible choices have been allowed as correct answers. We've included this question, however, to help you see what to do should you get a question like this. It's most important not to get rattled, and to select the BEST choice. In this case, the connection between the statistical information and Mr. Bryant's decision is pretty remote. If the question had said that the number of children in Mr. Bryant's town had decreased, then choice B would have been a more reasonable choice. It could also help in this situation to visualize the situation. Picture Mr. Bryant in his armchair reading that, nationwide, the average number of children per household has declined slightly. How likely would this be to influence his decision, especially since he sells men's and women's clothing? It would take a while for this decline in population to show up, and we're not even sure if it applies to Mr. Bryant's hometown. Don't feel badly if you missed this; it was tricky. The more of these you do, the more comfortable you'll feel.

4. The answer is B. If a new clothing boutique specializing in casual women's clothing were to open soon, this would lend support to Mr. Bryant's decision not to expand, but would not prove that he had actually made the decision to expand. A new women's clothing boutique would most likely be in competition with his existing business, thus making any possible expansion a riskier venture. We can't be sure from this, however, that he didn't go ahead and expand his business despite the increased competition. Choice A, proves the conclusion, would only be the answer if we could be absolutely sure from the statement that Mr. Bryant had actually not expanded his business.

5. The answer is C. This statement disproves the conclusion. In order for his sister to buy several items for her baby at Mr. Bryant's store, he would have to have changed his business to include children's clothing.

6. The answer is A. It definitely proves the conclusion. The passage states that Mr. Bryan's store had been in business since 1920. A pie baked in honor of his store's 100th anniversary would have to be presented sometime in 2020. The conclusion states that he made his decision not to expand on November 7, 2018. If, more than a year later Mrs. MacIntyre comments that his store has maintained the same look and feel over the years, it could not have been expanded, or otherwise significantly changed.

7. The answer is D. If Mr. Bryant's aunt lent him $50,000 in October, this would tend to weaken the conclusion, which took place in November. Because it was stated that Mr. Bryant would need to borrow money in order to expand his business, it would be logical to assume that if he borrowed money he had decided to expand his business, weakening the conclusion. The reason C, disproves the conclusion, is not the correct answer is because we can't be sure Mr. Bryant didn't borrow the money for another reason.

8. The answer is B. If Mr. Bryant's town is eligible for federal funds to encourage the location of new businesses in the central district, this would tend to support his decision not to expand his business. Funds to encourage new business would increase the likelihood of there being additional competition for Mr. Bryant's store to contend with. Since we can't say for sure that there would be direct competition from a new business, however, choice A would be incorrect. Note that this is also a tricky question. You might have thought that the new funds weakened the conclusion because it would mean that Mr. Bryant could easily get the money he needed. Mr. Bryant is expanding his present business, not creating a new business. Therefore, he is not eligible for the funding.

9. The answer is B. This is a very tricky question. It's stated that 59% of car occupants don't use seat belts. The legislature is considering the use of air bags because of safety issues. The advantage of air bags over seat belts is that they inflate upon impact, and don't require car occupants to do anything with them ahead of time. Since the population has strongly resisted using seat belts, the air bags could become even more important in saving lives. Since saving lives is the purpose of the proposed legislation, the information that a small percentage of people use seat belts could be helpful to the passage of the legislation. We can't be sure that this is reason enough for the legislature to vote for the legislation, however, so choice A in incorrect.

10. The answer is B, as the information that 5,900 lives could be saved would tend to support the conclusion. Saving that many lives through the use of air bags could be a very persuasive reason to vote for the legislation. Since we don't know for sure that it's enough of a compelling reason for the legislature to vote for the legislation, however, choice A could not be the answer.

11. The answer is C, disproves the conclusion. If the legislation had been passed as stated in the conclusion, there would be no reason to appoint someone head of an advisory committee six days later to analyze the "feasibility of the proposed legislation." The key word here is "proposed." If it has been proposed, it means it hasn't been passed. This contradicts the conclusion and, therefore, disproves it.

12. The answer is C, disproves the conclusion. If the legislation had passed, there would be no reason for supporters of the legislation to accuse the legislature of rejecting the legislation for political reasons. This question may have seemed so obvious that you might have thought there was a trick to it. Exams usually have a few obvious questions, which will trip you up if you begin reading too much into them.

13. The answer is D, as this would tend to disprove the conclusion. A projected dramatic rise in imported cars could be very harmful to the country's economy and could be a very good reason for some legislators to vote against the proposed legislation. It would be assuming too much to choose C, however, because we don't know if they actually did vote against it.

14. The answer is B. This information would tend to support the passage of the legislation. The estimate of the cost of the air bags is $800 less than the cost estimated by opponents, and it's stated that the protection would be more reliable than any other type of seat belt. Both of these would be good arguments in favor of passing the legislation. Since we don't know for sure, however, how persuasive they actually were, choice A would not be the correct choice.

15. The answer is E, as this is irrelevant information. It really doesn't matter whether auto sales in 2001 have increased slightly over the previous year. If the air bag legislation were to go into effect in 2004, that might make the information somehow more relevant. But the air bag legislation would not take effect until 2009, so the information is irrelevant, since it tells us nothing about the state of the auto industry then.

16. The answer is B, supports the conclusion. This is a tricky question. While at first it might seem to prove the conclusion, we can't be sure that the air bag legislation is responsible for the drop in automobile deaths. It's possible air bags came into popular use without the legislation, or with different legislation. There's no way we can be sure that it was the proposed legislation mandating the use of air bags that was responsible.

17. The answer is A. If, in June of 2009, the lobbyist received a bonus "for her work on the air bag legislation," we can be sure that the legislation passed. This proves the conclusion.

18. The answer is B. This is another tricky question. A three-fold stock increase would strongly suggest that the legislation had been passed, but it's possible that factors other than the air bag legislation caused the increase. Note that the stock is in "crash protection

equipment." Nowhere in the statement does it say air bags. Seat belts, motorcycle helmets, and collapsible bumpers are all crash protection equipment and could have contributed to the increase. This is just another reminder to read carefully because the questions are often designed to mislead you.

19. The answer is D. This would tend to weaken the conclusion because Joan is very fond of her mother and she would not want to upset her unnecessarily. It does not prove it, however, because if Joan strongly feels she is right, she probably wouldn't let her mother's opinion sway her. Choice E would also not be correct, because we cannot assume that Joan's mother's opinion is of so little importance to her as to be considered irrelevant.

20. The answer is E. The statement is irrelevant. We are told that Joan's income has doubled but we are not old why. The phrase "six months after the interview" can be misleading in that it leads us to assume that the increase and the interview are related. Her income could have doubled because she regained her popularity but it could also have come from stocks or some other business venture. Because we are not given any reason for her income doubling, it would be impossible to say whether or not this statement proves or disproves the conclusion. Choice E is the best choice of the five possible choices. One of the problems with promotional exams is that sometimes you need to select a choice you're not crazy about. In this case, "not having enough information to made a determination" would be the best choice. However, that's not an option, so you're forced to work with what you've got. On these exams it's sometimes like voting for President; you have to pick the "lesser of the two evils" or the least awful choice. In this case, the information is more irrelevant to the conclusion than it is anything else.

21. The answer is D, weakens the conclusion. We've been told that Joan's agent feels that she should apologize. If he is pleased with her interview, then it would tend to weaken the conclusion but not disprove it. We can't be sure that he hasn't had a change of heart, or that there weren't other parts of the interview he liked so much that they outweighed her unwillingness to apologize.

22. The answer is A. The conclusion states that Joan will donate $1 to the Cellulite Prevention League for every pound the actress loses. Joan's sister's financial report on the League's activities directly supports and proves the conclusion.

23. The answer is C, disproves the conclusion. If the magazine receives many letters commending Joan for her courage in apologizing, this directly contradicts the conclusion, which states that Joan didn't apologize.

24. The answer is B. It was stated in the passage that two of Joan's performances were cancelled after the controversy first occurred. The cancellation of another performance immediately after her interview was published would tend to support the conclusion that she refused to apologize. Because we can't be sure, however, that her performance wasn't cancelled for another reason, choice A would be incorrect.

25. The answer is E, as this information is irrelevant. Postponing the article an extra week does not affect Joan's decision or the public's reaction to it.

13 (#1)

26. The answer is C. If 500 new employees are hired to handle the "increased paperwork created by the new tax on DVDs," this would directly contradict the conclusion, which states that the legislature defeated both bills. (They should all be this easy.)

27. The answer is B. The results of the study would support the conclusion. If implementing the legislation was going to be so costly, it is likely that the legislature would vote against it. Choice A is not the answer, however, because we can't be sure that the legislature didn't pass it anyway.

28. The answer is E. It's irrelevant to the conclusion that 80% of all those working in the entertainment industry own DVD recorders. Sometimes if you're not sure about these, it can help a lot to try and visualize the situation. Why would someone voting on this legislation care about this fact? It doesn't seem to be the kind of information that would make any difference or impact upon the conclusion.

29. The answer is B. The head of the law enforcement agency's statement that the legislation would be unenforceable would support the conclusion. It's possible that many legislators would question why they should bother to pass legislation that would be impossible to enforce. Choice A would be incorrect, however, because we can't be sure that the legislation wasn't passed in spite of his statement.

30. The answer is D. This would tend to weaken the conclusion because the prospect of several large companies going bankrupt would seem to be a good argument in favor of the legislation. The possible loss of jobs and businesses would be a good reason for some people to vote for the legislation. We can't be sure, however, that this would be a competing enough reason to ensure passage of the legislation so choice C is incorrect.

This concludes our section on the "Validity of Conclusion" type of questions. We hope these weren't too horrible for you. It's important to keep in mind exactly what you've been given and exactly what they want you to do with it. It's also necessary to remember that you may have to choose between two possible answers. In that case, you must choose the one that seems the best. Sometimes you may think there is no good answer. You will probably be right, but you can't let that upset you. Just choose the one you dislike the least.

We want to repeat that it is unlikely that this exact format will appear on the exam. The skills required to answer these questions, however, are the same as those you'll need for the exam so we suggest that you review this section before taking the actual exam.

31. The answer is C. This next set of questions requires you to "switch gears" slightly, and get used to different formats. In this type of question, you have to decide whether the conclusion is proved by the facts give, disproved by the facts given, or neither because note enough information has been provided. Fortunately, unlike the previous questions, you don't have to decide whether particular facts support or don't support the conclusion. This type of question is more straight forward, but the reasoning behind it is the same. We are told that the Bills have won two games less than the Patriots, and that the Patriots are in first place and the Bills are in second place. We are also told that there are two games left to play, and that they won't play each other again. The conclusion states that the Bills won the division. Is there anything in the four statements that would prove this? We have

no idea what the outcome of the last two games of the season was. The Bills and Patriots could have ended up tied at the end of the season, or the Bills could have lost both or one of their last games while the Patriots did the same. There might even be another team tied for first or second place with the Bills or Patriots. Since we don't know for sure, Choice A is incorrect. Choice B is trickier. It might seem at first glance that the best the Bills could do would be to tie the Patriots if the Patriots lost their last two games and the Bills won their last two games. But it would be too much to assume that there is no procedure for a tiebreaker that wouldn't give the Bills the division championship. Since we don't know what the rules are in the event of a tie (for example, what if a tie was decided on the results of what happened when the two teams had played each other, or on the best record in the division, or on most points scored?), we can't say for sure that it would be impossible for the Bills to win their division. For this reason, choice C is the answer, as we don't have enough information to prove or disprove the conclusion. This question looked more difficult than it actually was. It's important to disregard any factors outside of the actual question, and to focus only on what you've been given. In this case, as on all of these types of questions, what you know or don't know about a subject is actually irrelevant. It's best to concentrate only on the actual facts given.

32. The answer is A. The conclusion is proved by the facts given.

In this type of problem, it is usually best to pull as many facts as possible from the sentences and then put them into a simpler form. The phrasing and the order of exam questions are designed to be confusing so you need to restate things as clearly as possible by eliminating the extras.

Sentence I tells us that there are only two possible colors for eyes and two for hair. Looking at the other sentences we learn that eyes are either green or gold and that hair is either silver or purple. If half the beings with purple hair have golden eyes, then the other half must have green eyes since it is the only other eye color. Likewise, if one-third of those with silver hair have green eyes, the other two-thirds must have golden eyes.

This information makes it clear that there are more golden-eyed beings on Zeinon than green-eyed ones. It doesn't matter that we don't know exactly how many are actually living on the planet. The number of those with gold eyes (1/2 plus 2/3) will always be greater than the number of those with green eyes (1/2 plus 1/3), no matter what the actual figures might be. Sentence III is totally irrelevant because even if there were more silver-haired inhabitants it would not affect the conclusion.

33. The answer is C. The conclusion is neither proved nor disproved by the facts because we don't know how many miles Bethany is from Amoranth.

With this type of question, if you're not sure how to approach it, you can always substitute in a range of "real numbers" to see what the result would be. If they were 200 miles apart, Joe's Truck Rental would be cheaper because they would charge a total of $160 while National Movers would charge $175.

Joe's - $100 plus .30 x 200 (or $60) = $160
National - $150 plus .25 x 100 (or $25) = $175

If the towns were 600 miles apart, however, National Movers would be cheaper. The cost of renting from National would be $275 compared to the $280 charged by Joe's Trucking.

Joe's - $100 plus .30 x 600 (or $180) = $280
National - $150 plus .25 x 500 (or $125) = $275

15 (#1)

34. The answer is B. We've varied the format once more, but the reasoning is similar. This is a tedious question that is more like a math question, but we wanted to give you some practice with this type, just in case. You won't be able to do this question if you've forgotten how to do percents. Many exams require this knowledge, so if you feel you need a review we suggest you read Booklets 1, 2 or 3 in this series.

The only way to attack this problem is to go through each choice until you find the one that is correct. Choice A states that Plainfield, Smallville, and Granton are cities. Let's begin with Plainfield. The passage states that in 1990 Plainfield had a population of 12,000, and that it grew 10% between 1990 and 2000, and another 20% between 2000 and 2010. Ten percent of 12,000 is 1200 (12,000 x .10 = 1200). Therefore, the population grew from 12,000 in 1990 to 12,000 + 1200 between 1990 and 2000. At the time of the 2000 Census, Plainfield's population was 13,200. It then grew another 20% between 2000 and 2010, so, 13,200 x .20 = 2640. 13,200 plus the additional increase of 2640 would make the population of Plainfield 15,840. This would qualify it as a city, since its population is over 15,000. Since a change upward in the population of a municipality is re-classified immediately, Plainfield would have become a city right away. So far, statement A is true. The passage states that Smallville's population has not changed significantly in the last twenty years. Since Smallville's population was 20,283, Smallville would still be a city. Granton had a population of 25,000 (what a coincidence that so any of these places have such nice, even numbers) in 1980. The population has decreased 25% in each ten year period since that time. So from 1980 to 1990, the population decreased 25%. 25,000 x .25 = 6,250. 25,000 minus 6,250 = 18,750. So the population of Granton in 1990 would have been 18,750. (Or, you could have saved a step and multiplied 25,000 by .75 to get 18,750.) The population from 1990 to 2000 decreased an additional 25%. So: 18,750 x .25 = 4,687.50. 18,750 minus 4,687.50 = 14,062.50. Or: 18,750 x .75 = 14,062.50. (Don't let the fact that a half of a person is involved confuse you; these are exam questions, not real life.) From 2000 to 2010 the population decreased an additional 25%. This would mean that Granton's population was below 15,000 for more than ten years, so it's status as a city would have changed to that of a town, which would make choice A incorrect.

Choice B states that Smallville is a city and Granton is a town, which we know to be true from the information above. Choice B is correct so far. We next need to determine if Ellenville is a village. Ellenville had a population of 4,283 in 1980, and increased 5% in each ten year period since 1980. 4,283 x .05 = 214.15. 4,283 plus 214.15 = 4,497.15, so Ellenville's population from 1980 to 1990 increased to 4,497.15. (Or: 4,283 x 1.05 – 4,497.15.) From 1990 to 2000 Ellenville's population increased another 5%: 4,497.15 x .05 = 224.86. 4,497.15 plus 224.86 = 4,772.01 (or: 4,497.15 x 1.05 = 4,722.01.) From 2000 to 2010, Ellenville's population increased another 5%: 4,722.01 x .05 = 236.10. 4,722.01 plus 236.10 = 4,958.11. (Or: 4,722.01 x 1.05 = 4,958.11.).

Ellenville's population is still under 5,000 in 2010, so it would continue to be classified as a village. Since all three statements in choice B are true, choice B must be the answer. However, we'll go through the other choices. Choice C states that Springdale is a town. The passage tells us that the population of Springdale doubled from 1990 to 2000, and increased 25% from 2000 to 2010. It doesn't give us any actual population figures, however, so it's impossible to know what the population of Springdale is, making choice C incorrect. Choice C also states that Granton is a town, which is true, and that Ellenville is a town, which is false (from choice B we know it's a village). Choice D states that Plainfield and Smallville are cities, which is information we already know is true, and that Ellenville is a town. Since Ellenville is a village, choice D is also incorrect.

This was a lot of work for just one question and we doubt you'll get one like this on this section of the exam, but we included it just in case. On an exam, you can always put a check mark next to a question like this and come back to it later, if you feel you're pressed for time and cold spend your time more productively on other, less time-consuming problems.

35. The answer is B. This question requires very careful reading. It's best to break the conclusion down into smaller parts in order to solve the problem. The first half of the conclusion states that the average person in the 20-29 age group (Group A) drinks less tea daily than the average person in the 40-50 age group (Group C). The average person in Group A drinks 2.1 cups of tea daily, while the average person in Group C drinks 2.6 cups of tea daily. Since 2.1 is less than 2.6, the conclusion is correct so far. The second half of the conclusion states that the average person in Group A drinks more coffee daily than the average person in the 30-39 age group (Group B) drinks cola. The average person in Group A drinks 1.8 cups of coffee daily, while the average person in Group B drinks 1.9 glasses of cola. This disproves the conclusion, which states that the average person in Group A drinks more coffee daily than the average person in Group B drinks cola.

36. The answer is C. The easiest way to approach a problem that deals with the relationship between a number of different people or things is to set up a diagram. This type of problem is usually too confusing to do in your head. For this particular problem, the "diagram" could be a line, one end of which would be labeled tall and the other end labeled short. Then, taking one sentence at a time, place the people on the line to see where they fall in relation to one another.

The diagram of the first sentence would look like this:

Mary is taller than Jane but shorter than Dale, so she would fall somewhere between the two of them. We have placed tall on the left and labeled it left just to make the explanation easier. You could just as easily have reversed the position.

The second sentence places Fred somewhere to the left of Mary because he is taller than she is. Steven would be to the left of Fred for the same reason. At this point we don't know whether Steven and Fred are taller or shorter than Dale. The new diagram would look like this:

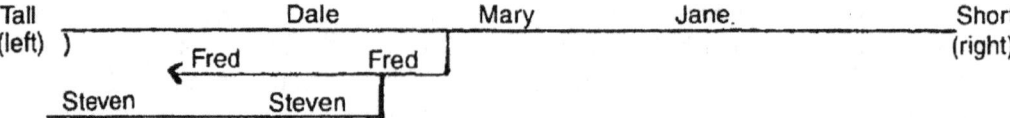

The third sentence introduces Elizabeth, presenting a new problem. Elizabeth can be anywhere to the right of Dale. Don't make the mistake of assuming she falls between Dale and Mary. At this point we don't know where she fits in relation to Mary, Jane, or even Fred.

We do get information about Steven, however. He is taller than Dale so he would be to the left of Dale. Since he is also taller than Fred (see sentence II), we know that Steven is the tallest person thus far. The diagram would now look like this:

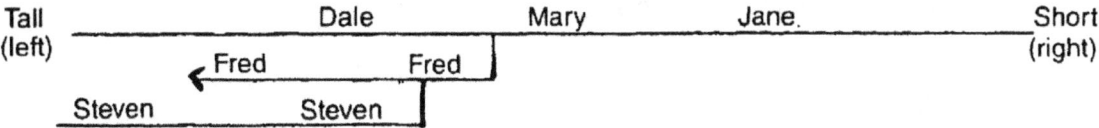

Fred's height is somewhere between Steven and Mary, Elizabeth's anywhere between Dale and the end of the line.

The fourth sentence tells us where Elizabeth stands, in relation to Fred and the others in the problem. The fact that she is taller than Mary means she is also taller than Jane. The final diagram would look like this:

| Tall | Steven | Dale | Elizabeth | Mary | Jane | Short |
| (left) | | Fred | | | | (right) |

We still don't know whether Dale or Fred is taller, however. Therefore, the conclusion that Dale is taller than Fred can't be proved. It also can't be disproved because we don't know for sure that he isn't. The answer has to be choice C, as the conclusion can't be proved or disproved.

37. The answer is A. This is another problem that is easiest for most people if they make a diagram. Sentence I states that Main Street is between Spring Street and Glenn Blvd. At this point we don't know if they are next to each other or if they are separated by a number of streets. Therefore, you should leave space between streets as you plot your first diagram.

The order of the streets could go either:

    Spring St.   or   Glenn Blvd.
    Main St.   Main St.
    Glenn Blvd.   Spring St.

Sentence II states that Hawley Street is one block south of Spring Street and 3 blocks north of Main Street. Because most people think in terms of north as above and south as below and because it was stated that Hawley is one block south of Spring Street and three blocks north of Main Street, the next diagram could look like this:

Spring
Hawley

————

Main
Glenn

The third sentence states that Glenn Street is five blocks south of Elm and four blocks south of Main. It could look like this:

Spring
Hawley

————

Elm
Main

————

————

Glenn

The conclusion states that Elm Street is between Hawley Avenue and Glenn Blvd. From the above diagram, we can see that this is the case.

38. The answer is B. For most people, the best way to do this problem is to draw a diagram, plotting the course of both trains. Sentence I states that Train A leaves Hampshire at 5:50 A.M. and reaches New London at 6:42. Your first diagram might look like this:

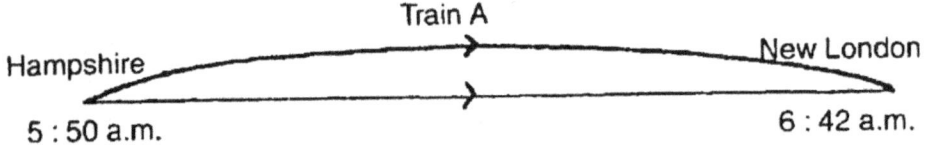

Sentence II states that the train leaves New London at 7:00 a.m. and arrives in Kellogsville at 8:42 a.m. The diagram might now look like this:

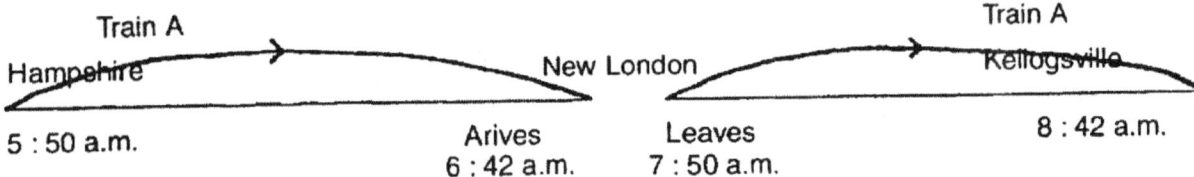

Sentence III gives us the rest of the information that must be included in the diagram. It introduces Train B, which moves in the opposite direction, leaving Kellogsville at 8:00 a.m. and arriving at Hampshire at 10:42 a.m. The final diagram might look like this:

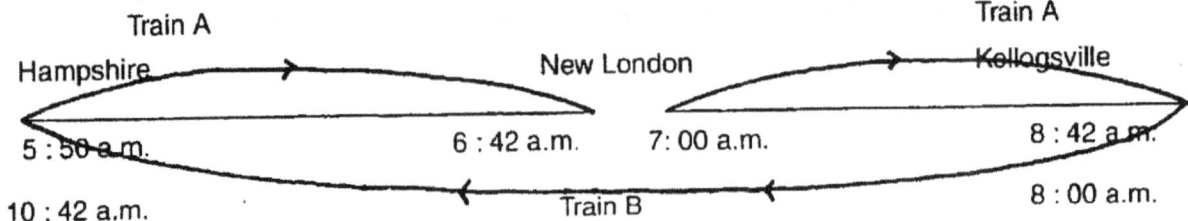

19 (#1)

As you can see from the diagram, the routes of the two trains will overlap somewhere between Kellogsville and New London. If you read sentence IV quickly and assumed that that was the section with only one track, you probably would have assumed that there would have had to be a collision. Sentence IV states, however, that there is only one railroad track between New London and Hampshire. That is the only section, then, where the two trains could collide. By the time Train B gets to that section, however, Train A will have passed it. The two trains will pass each other somewhere between New London and Kellogsville, not New London and Hampshire.

READING COMPREHENSION
UNDERSTANDING AND INTERPRETING WRITTEN MATERIAL
EXAMINATION SECTION
TEST 1

DIRECTIONS: Each question or incomplete statement is followed by several suggested answers or completions. Select the one that BEST answers the question or completes the statement. *PRINT THE LETTER OF THE CORRECT ANSWER IN THE SPACE AT THE RIGHT.*

1. The National Assessment of Educational Progress recently released the results of the first statistically valid national sampling of young adult reading skills in the United States. According to the survey, ninety-five percent of United States young adults (aged 21-25) can read at a fourth-grade level or better. This means they can read well enough to apply for a job, understand a movie guide or join the Army. This is a higher literacy rate than the eighty to eighty-five percent usually estimated for all adults. The study also found that ninety-nine percent can write their names, eighty percent can read a map or write a check for a bill, seventy percent can understand an appliance warranty or write a letter about a billing error, twenty-five percent can calculate the amount of a tip correctly, and fewer than ten percent can correctly figure the cost of a catalog or understand a complex bus schedule.
   Which statement about the study is BEST supported by the above passage?
   A. United States literacy rates among young adults are at an all-time high.
   B. Forty percent of young people in the United States cannot write a letter about a billing error.
   C. Twenty percent of United States teenagers cannot read a map,
   D. More than ninety percent of United States young adults cannot correctly calculate the cost of a catalog order.

   1.____

2. It is now widely recognized that salaries, benefits, and working conditions have more of an impact on job satisfaction than on motivation. If they aren't satisfactory, work performance and morale will suffer. But even when they are high, employees will not necessarily be motivated to work well. For example, THE WALL STREET JOURNAL recently reported that as many as forty or fifty percent of newly hired Wall Street lawyers (whose salaries start at upwards of $50,000) quit within the first three years, citing long hours, pressures, and monotony as the prime offenders. It seems there's just not enough of an intellectual challenge in their jobs. An up and coming money-market executive concluded: *Whether it was $1 million or $100 million, the procedure was the same. Except for the tension, a baboon could do my job.* When money and benefits are adequate, the most important additional determinants of job satisfaction are: more responsibility, a sense of achievement, recognition, and a chance to advance. All of these factors have a more significant influence on employee motivation and performance. As a footnote, several studies have found that the absence of these non-monetary factors can lead to serious stress-related illnesses.

   2.____

Which statement is BEST supported by the above passage?
A. A worker's motivation to perform well is most affected by salaries, benefits, and working conditions.
B. Low pay can lead to high levels of job stress.
C. Work performance will suffer if workers feel they are not paid well.
D. After satisfaction with pay and benefits, the next most important factor is more responsibility.

3. The establishment of joint labor-management production committees occurred in the United States during World War I and again during World War II. Their use was greatly encouraged by the National War Labor Board in World War I and the War Production Board in 1942. Because of the war, labor-management cooperation was especially desired to produce enough goods for the war effort, to reduce conflict, and to control inflation. The committees focused on how to achieve greater efficiency, and consulted on health and safety, training, absenteeism, and people issues in general. During the second world war, there were approximately five thousand labor-management committees in factories, affecting over six million workers. While research has found that only a few hundred committees made significant contributions to productivity, there were additional benefits in many cases. It became obvious to many that workers had ideas to contribute to the running of the organization, and that efficient enterprises could become even more so. Labor-management cooperation was also extended to industries that had never experienced it before. Directly after each war, however, few United States labor-management committees were in operation.
Which statement is BEST supported by the above passage?
A. The majority of United States labor-management committees during the second world war accomplished little.
B. A major goal of United States labor-management committees during the first and second world wars was to increase productivity.
C. There were more United States labor-management committees during the second world war than during the first world war.
D. There are few United States labor-management committees in operation today.

4. Studies have found that stress levels among employees who have a great deal of customer contact or a great deal of contact with the public can be very high. There are many reasons for this. Sometimes stress results when the employee is caught in the middle—an organization wants things done one way, but the customer wants them done another way. The situation becomes even worse for the employee's stress levels when he or she knows was to more effectively provide the service, but isn't allowed to, by the organization. An example is the bank teller who is required to ask a customer for two forms of identification before he or she can cash a check, even though the teller knows the customer well. If organizational mishaps occur or if there are problems with job design, the employee may be powerless to satisfy the customer, and also powerless to protect himself or herself from the customer's wrath. An example of this is the waitress who is forced to serve poorly prepared food. Studies have also found,

however, that if the organization and the employee design the positions and the service encounter well, and encourage the use of effective stress management techniques, stress can be reduced to levels that are well below average.
Which statement is BEST supported by the above passage?
- A. It is likely that knowledgeable employees will experience greater levels of job-related stress.
- B. The highest levels of occupational stress are found among those employees who have a great deal of customer contact.
- C. Organizations can contribute to the stress levels of their employees by poorly designing customer contact situations.
- D. Stress levels are generally higher in banks and restaurants.

5. It is estimated that approximately half of the United States population suffers from varying degrees of adrenal malfunction. When under stress for long periods of time, the adrenals produce extra cortisol and norepinephrine. By producing more hormones than they were designed to comfortably manufacture and secrete, the adrenals can *burn out* over time and then decrease their secretion. When this happens, the body loses its capacity to cope with stress, and the individual becomes sicker more easily and for longer periods of time. A result of adrenal malfunction may be a diminished output of cortisol. Symptoms of diminished cortisol output include any of the following: craving substances that will temporarily raise serum glucose levels such as caffeine, sweets, soda, juice, or tobacco; becoming dizzy when standing up too quickly; irritability; headaches; and erratic energy levels. Since cortisol is an anti-inflammatory hormone, a decreased output over extended periods of time can make one prone to inflammatory disease such ass arthritis, bursitis, colitis, and allergies. (Many food and pollen allergies disappear when adrenal function is restored to normal.) The patient will have no reserve energy, and infections can spread quickly. Excessive cortisol production, on the other hand, can decrease immunity, leading to frequent and prolonged illnesses.
Which statement is BEST supported by the above passage?
- A. Those who suffer from adrenal malfunction are most likely to be prone to inflammatory diseases such as arthritis and allergies.
- B. The majority of Americans suffer from varying degrees of adrenal malfunction.
- C. It is better for the health of the adrenals to drink juice instead of soda.
- D. Too much cortisol can inhibit the body's ability to resist disease.

5.____

6. Psychologist B.F. Skinner pointed out long ago that gambling is reinforced either by design or accidentally, by what he called a variable ratio schedule. A slot machine, for example, is cleverly designed to provide a payoff after it has been played a variable number of times. Although the person who plays it and wins while playing receives a great deal of monetary reinforcement, over the long run the machine will take in much more money than it pays out. Research on both animals and humans has consistently found that such variable reward schedules maintain a very high rate of repeat behavior, and that this behavior is particularly resistant to extinction.

6.____

Which statement is BEST supported by the above passage?
- A. Gambling, because it is reinforced by the variable ratio schedule, is more difficult to eliminate than most addictions.
- B. If someone is rewarded or wins consistently, even if it is not that often, he or she is likely to continue that behavior.
- C. Playing slot machines is the safest form of gambling because they are designed so that eventually the player will indeed win.
- D. A cat is likely to come when called if its owner has trained it correctly,

7. Paper entrepreneurialism is an offshoot of scientific management that has become so extreme that it has lost all connection to the actual workplace. It generates profits by cleverly manipulating rules and numbers that only in theory represent real products and real assets. At its worst, paper entrepreneurialism involves very little more than imposing losses on others for the sake of short-term profits. The others may be taxpayers, shareholders who end up indirectly subsidizing other shar holders, consumers, or investors. Paper entrepreneurialism has replaced product entrepreneurialism, is seriously threatening the United States economy, and is hurting our necessary attempts to transform the nation's industrial and productive economic base. An example is the United States company that complained loudly in 1979 that it did not have the $200 million needed to develop a video-cassette recorder, though demand for them had been very high. The company, however, did not hesitate to spend $1.2 billion that same year to buy a mediocre finance company. The video recorder market was handed over to other countries, who did not hesitate to manufacture them.

7.____

Which statement is BEST supported by the above passage?
- A. Paper entrepreneurialism involves very little more than imposing losses on others for the sake of short-term profits.
- B. Shareholders are likely to benefit most from paper entrepreneurialism.
- C. Paper entrepreneurialism is hurting the United States economy.
- D. The United States could have made better video-cassette recorders than the Japanese but we ceded the market to them in 1979.

8. The *prisoner's dilemma* is an almost 40-year-old game-theory model psychologists, biologists, economists, and political scientists use to try to understand the dynamics of competition and cooperation. Participants in the basic version of the experiment are told that they and their *accomplice* have been caught red-handed. Together, their best strategy is to cooperate by remaining silent. If they do this, each will get off with a 30-day sentence. But either person can do better for himself or herself. If you double-cross your partner, you will go scot free while he or she serves ten years. The problem is, if you each betray the other, you will both go to prison for eight years, not thirty days. No matter what your partner chooses, you are logically better off choosing betrayal. Unfortunately, your partner realizes this too, and so the odds are good that you will both get eight years. That's the dilemma. (The length of the prison sentences is always the same for each variation.) Participants at a recent symposium on behavioral economics at Harvard University discussed the many variations on the game that have been used

8.____

over the years. In one standard version, subjects are paired with a supervisor who pays them a dollar for each point they score. Over the long run, both subjects will do best if they cooperate every time. Yet in each round, there is a great temptation to betray the other because no one knows what the other will do. The best overall strategy for this variation was found to be *tit for tat*, doing unto your opponent as he or she has just done unto you. It is a simple strategy, but very effective. The partner can easily recognize it and respond. It is retaliatory enough not to be easily exploited, but forgiving enough to allow a pattern of mutual cooperation to develop.
Which statement is BEST supported by the above passage?
   A. The best strategy for playing *prisoner's dilemma* is to cooperate and remain silent.
   B. If you double-cross your partner, and he or she does not double-cross you, your partner will receive a sentence of eight years.
   C. When playing *prisoner's dilemma*, it is best to double-cross your partner.
   D. If you double-cross your partner, and he or she double-crosses you, you will receive an eight-year sentence.

9. After many years of experience as the vice president and general manager of a large company, I feel that I know what I'm looking for in a good manager. First, the manager has to be comfortable with himself or herself, and not be arrogant or defensive. Secondly, he or she has to have a genuine interest in people. There are some managers who love ideas—and that's fine—but to be a manager, you must love people, and you must make a hobby of understanding them, believing in them and trusting them. Third, I look for a willingness and a facility to manage conflict. Gandhi defined conflict as a way of getting at the truth. Each person brings his or her own grain of truth and the conflict washes away the illusion and fantasy. Finally, a manager has to have a vision, and the ability and charisma to articulate it. A manager should be seen as a little bit crazy. Some eccentricity is an asset. People don't want to follow vanilla leaders. They want to follow chocolate-fudge-ripple leaders.
Which statement is BEST supported by the above passage?
   A. It is very important that a good manager spend time studying people.
   B. It is critical for good managers to love ideas.
   C. Managers should try to minimize or avoid conflict.
   D. Managers should be familiar with people's reactions to different flavors of ice cream.

9.____

10. Most societies maintain a certain set of values and assumptions that make their members feel either good or bad about themselves, and either better or worse than other people. In most developed countries, these values are based on the assumption that we are all free to be what we want to be, and that differences in income, work, and education are a result of our own efforts. This may make us believe that people with more income work that is more skilled, more education, and more power are somehow *better* people. We may view their achievements as proof that they have more intelligence, more motivation, and more initiative than those with lower status. The myth tells us that power, income, and education are freely and equally available to all, and that our

10.____

failure to achieve them is due to our own personal inadequacy. This simply is not the case.

The possessions we own may also seem to point to our real worth as individuals. The more we own, the more worthy of respect we may feel we are. Or, the acquisition of possessions may be a way of trying to fulfill ourselves, to make up for the loss of community and/or purpose. It is a futile pursuit because lost community and purpose can never be compensated for by better cars or fancier houses. And too often, when these things fail to satisfy, we believe it is only because we don't have enough money to buy better quality items, or more items. We feel bad that we haven't been successful enough to get all that we think we need. No matter how much we do have, goods never really satisfy for long. There is always something else to acquire, and true satisfaction eludes many, many of us.
Which statement is BEST supported by the above passage?
  A. The author would agree with the theory of *survival of the fittest*.
  B. The possessions an individual owns are not a proper measure of his or her real worth.
  C. Many countries make a sincere attempt to ensure equal access to quality education for their citizens.
  D. The effect a society's value system has on the lives of its members is greatly exaggerated.

11. *De nihilo nihil* is Latin for *nothing comes from nothing*. In the first century, the Roman poet Persius advised that if anything is to be produced of value, effort must be expended. He also said, *In nihilum nil posse revorti*—anything once produced cannot become nothing again. It is thought that Persius was parodying Lucretius, who expounded the 500-year-old physical theories of Epicurus. *De nihilo nihil* can also be used as a cynical comment, to negatively comment on something that is of poor quality produced by a person of little talent. The implication here is: *What can you expect from such a source?*
Which statement is BEST supported by the above passage?
  A. *In nihilum nil posse revorti* can be interpreted as meaning, *If anything is to be produced of value, then effort must be expended.*
  B. *De nihilo nihil* can be understood in two different ways,
  C. Lucretius was a great physicist.
  D. Persius felt that Epicurus put in little effort while developing his theories.

12. A Cornell University study has found that less than one percent of the billion pounds of pesticides used in this country annually strike their intended targets. The study found that the pesticides, which are somewhat haphazardly applied to 370 million acres, or about sixteen percent of the nation's total land area, end up polluting the environment and contaminating almost all 200,000 species of plants and animals, including humans. While the effect of indirect contamination on human cancer rates was not estimated, the study found that approximately 45,000 human pesticide poisonings occur annually, including about 3,000 cases admitted to hospitals and approximately 200 fatalities.

Which statement is BEST supported by the above passage?
  A. It is likely that indirect pesticide contamination affects human health.
  B. Pesticides are applied to over one-quarter of the total United States land area.
  C. If pesticides were applied more carefully, fewer pesticide-resistant strains of pests would develop.
  D. Human cancer rates in this country would drop considerably if pesticide use was cut in half.

13. The new conservative philosophy presents a unified, coherent approach to the world. It offers to explain much of our experience since the turbulent 1960s, and it shows what we've learned since about the dangers of indulgence and permissiveness. But it also warns that the world has become more ruthless, and that as individuals and as a nation, we must struggle for survival. It is necessary to impose responsibility and discipline in order to defeat those forces that threaten us. This lesson is dramatically clear, and can be applied to a wide range of issues.
Which statement is BEST supported by the above passage?
  A. The 1970s were a time of permissiveness and indulgence.
  B. The new conservative philosophy may help in imposing discipline and a sense of responsibility in order to meet the difficult challenges facing this country.
  C. The world faced greater challenges during the second world war than it faces at the present time.
  D. More people identify themselves today as conservative in their political philosophy.

14. One of the most puzzling questions in management in recent years has been how usually honest, compassionate, intelligent managers can sometimes act in ways that are dishonest, uncaring, and unethical. How could top-level managers at the Manville Corporation, for example, suppress evidence for decades that proved beyond all doubt that asbestos inhalation was killing their own employees? What drove the managers of a Midwest bank to continue to act in a way that threatened to bankrupt the institution, ruin its reputation, and cost thousands of employees and investors their jobs and their savings? It's been estimated that about two out of three of America's five hundred largest corporations have been involved in some form of illegal behavior. There are, of course, some common rationalizations used to justify unethical conduct: believing that the activity is in the organization's or the individual's best interest, believing that the activity is not *really* immoral or illegal, believing that no one will ever know, or believing that the organization will sanction the behavior because it helps the organization. Ambition can distort one's sense of *duty*.
Which statement is BEST supported by the above passage?
  A. Top-level managers of corporations are currently involved in a plan to increase ethical behavior among their employees.
  B. There are many good reasons why a manager may act unethically.
  C. Some managers allow their ambitions to override their sense of ethics,
  D. In order to successfully compete, some organizations may have to indulge in unethical or illegal behavior from time to time.

15. Some managers and supervisors believe that they are leaders because they occupy positions of responsibility and authority. But leadership is more than holding a position. It is often defined in management literature as *the ability to influence the opinions, attitudes and behaviors of others.* Obviously, there are some managers that would not qualify as leaders, and some leaders that are not *technically* managers. Research has found that many people overrate their own leadership abilities. In one recent study, seventy percent of those surveyed rated themselves in the top quartile in leadership abilities, and only two percent felt they were below average as leaders.
Which statement is BEST supported by the above passage?
   A. In a recent study, the majority of people surveyed rated themselves in the top twenty-five percent in leadership abilities.
   B. Ninety-eight percent of the people surveyed in a recent study had average or above-average leadership skills.
   C. In order to be a leader, one should hold a management position.
   D. Leadership is best defined as the ability to be liked by those one must lead.

15.____

KEY (CORRECT ANSWERS)

1.	D	6.	B	11.	B
2.	C	7.	C	12.	A
3.	B	8.	D	13.	B
4.	C	9.	A	14.	C
5.	D	10.	B	15.	A

READING COMPREHENSION
UNDERSTANDING AND INTERPRETING WRITTEN MATERIAL
EXAMINATION SECTION

This exam section includes some passages and questions related to functions of the first computerized offices, which consisted of typewriters and other such manual office equipment.

TEST 1

DIRECTIONS: Each question or incomplete statement is followed by several suggested answers or completions. Select the one that BEST answers the question or completes the statement. *PRINT THE LETTER OF THE CORRECT ANSWER IN THE SPACE AT THE RIGHT.*

Questions 1-2.

DIRECTIONS: Questions 1 and 2 are to be answered SOLELY on the basis of the following passage.

The employees in a unit or division of a government agency may be referred to as a work group. Within a government agency which has existed for some time, the work groups will have evolved traditions of their own. The persons in these work groups acquire these traditions as part of the process of work adjustment within their groups. Usually, a work group in a large organization will contain *oldtimers*, *newcomers*, and *in-betweeners*. Like the supervisor of a group, who is not necessarily an oldtimer or the oldest member, oldtimers usually have great influence. They can recall events unknown to others and are a storehouse of information and advice about current problems in the light of past experience. They pass along the traditions of the group to the others who, in turn, become oldtimers themselves. Thus, the traditions of the group which have been honored and revered by long acceptance are continued.

1. According to the above passage, the traditions of a work group within a government agency are developed
    A. at the time the group is established
    B. over a considerable period of time
    C. in order to give recognition to oldtimers
    D. for the group before it is established

    1.____

2. According to the above passage, the oldtimers within a work group
    A. are the means by which long accepted practices and customs are perpetuated
    B. would best be able to settle current problems that arise
    C. are honored because of the changes they have made in the traditions
    D. have demonstrated that they have learned to do their work well

    2.____

Questions 3-4.

DIRECTIONS: Questions 3 and 4 are to be answered SOLELY on the following passage.

In public agencies, the success of a person assigned to perform first-line supervisory duties depends in large part upon the personal relations between him and his subordinate employees. The goal of supervising effort is something more than to obtain compliance with procedures established by some central office. The major objective is work accomplishment. In order for this goal to be attained, employees must want to attain it and must exercise initiative in their work. Only if employees are generally satisfied with the type of supervision which exists in an organization will they put forth their best efforts.

3. According to the above passage, in order for employees to try to do their work as well as they can, it is essential that
    A. they participate in determining their working conditions and rates of pay
    B. their supervisors support the employees' viewpoints in meetings with higher management
    C. they are content with the supervisory practices which are being used
    D. their supervisors make the changes in working procedures that the employees request

3._____

4. It can be inferred from the above passage that the goals of a unit in a public agency will not be reached unless the employees in the unit
    A. wish to reach them and are given the opportunity to make individual contributions to the work
    B. understand the relationship between the goals of the unit and goals of the agency
    C. have satisfactory personal relationships with employees of other units in the agency
    D. carefully follow the directions issued by higher authorities

4._____

Questions 5-9.

DIRECTIONS: Questions 5 through 9 are to be answered SOLELY on the basis of the following passage.

In an employee thinks he can save money, time, or material for the city or has an idea about how to do something better than it is being done, he shouldn't keep it to himself. He should send his ideas to the Employees' Suggestion Program, using the special form which is kept on hand in all departments. An employee may send in as many ideas as he wishes. To make sure that each idea is judged fairly, the name of the suggester is not made known until an award is made. The awards are certificate of merit or cash prizes ranging from $10 to $500.

5. According to the above passage, an employee who knows how to do a job in a better way should
    A. be sure it saves enough time to be worthwhile
    B. get paid the money he saves for the city
    C. keep it to himself to avoid being accused of causing a speed-up
    D. send his idea to the Employees' Suggestion Program

5._____

6. In order to send his idea to the Employees' Suggestion Program, an employee should
   A. ask the Department of Personnel for a special form
   B. get the special form in his own department
   C. mail the idea using Special Delivery
   D. send it on plain, white letter-size paper

7. An employee may send to the Employees' Suggestion Program
   A. as many ideas as he can think of
   B. no more than one idea each week
   C. no more than ten ideas in a month
   D. only one idea on each part of the job

8. The reason the name of an employee who makes a suggestion is not made known at first is to
   A. give the employee a larger award
   B. help the judges give more awards
   C. insure fairness in judging
   D. only one idea on each part of the job

9. An employee whose suggestion receives an award may be given a
   A. bonus once a year
   B. certificate for $10
   C. cash prize of up to $500
   D. salary increase of $500

Questions 10-12.

DIRECTIONS: Questions 10 through 12 are to be answered SOLELY on the basis of the following passage.

According to the rules of the Department of Personnel, the work of every permanent city employee is reviewed and rated by his supervisor at least once a year. The civil service rating system gives the employee and his supervisor a chance to talk about the progress made during the past year as well as about those parts of the job in which the employee needs to do better. In order to receive a pay increase each year, the employee must have a satisfactory service rating. Service ratings also count toward an employee's final mark on a promotion examination.

10. According to the above passage, a permanent city employee is rated AT LEAST once
    A. before his work is reviewed
    B. every six months
    C. yearly by his supervisor
    D. yearly by the Department of Personnel

11. According to the above passage, under the rating system the supervisor and the employee can discuss how
    A. much more work needs to be done next year
    B. the employee did his work last year
    C. the work can be made easier next year
    D. the work of the Department can be increased

12. According to the above passage, a permanent city employee will NOT receive a yearly pay increase
    A. if he received a pay increase the year before
    B. if he used his service rating for his mark on a promotion examination
    C. if his service rating is unsatisfactory
    D. unless he got some kind of a service rating

Questions 13-16.

DIRECTIONS: Questions 13 through 16 are to be answered SOLELY on the basis of the following passage.

It is an accepted fact that the rank and file employee can frequently advance worthwhile suggestions toward increasing efficiency. For this reason, an Employees' Suggestion System has been developed and put into operation. Suitable means have been provided at each departmental location for the confidential submission of suggestions. Numerous suggestions have been received thus far and, after study, about five percent of the ideas submitted are being translated into action. It is planned to set up, eventually, monetary awards for all worthwhile suggestions.

13. According to the above passage, a MAJOR reason why an Employees' Suggestion System was established is that
    A. an organized program of improvement is better than a haphazard one
    B. employees can often give good suggestions to increase efficiency
    C. once a fact is accepted, it is better to act on it than to do nothing
    D. the suggestions of rank and file employees were being neglected

14. According to the above passage, under the Employees' Suggestion System,
    A. a file of worthwhile suggestions will eventually be set up at each departmental location
    B. it is possible for employees to turn in suggestions without fellow employees knowing of it
    C. means have been provided for the regular and frequent collection of suggestions submitted
    D. provision has been made for the judging of worthwhile suggestions by an Employees' Suggestion Committee

15. According to the above passage, it is reasonable to assume that
    A. all suggestions must be turned in at a central office
    B. employees who make worthwhile suggestions will be promoted
    C. not all the prizes offered will be monetary ones
    D. prizes of money will be given for the best suggestions

16. According to the above passage, of the many suggestions made,
    A. all are first tested
    B. a small part are put into use
    C. most are very worthwhile
    D. samples are studied

Questions 17-20.

DIRECTIONS: Questions 17 through 20 are to be answered SOLELY on the basis of the following passage.

Employees may be granted leaves of absence without pay at the discretion of the Personnel Officer. Such a leave without pay shall begin on the first working day on which the employee does not report for duty and shall continue to the first day on which the employee returns to duty. The Personnel Division may vary the dates of the leave for the record so as to conform with payroll periods, but in no case shall an employee be off the payroll for a different number of calendar days than would have been the case if the actual dates mentioned above had been used. An employee who has vacation or overtime to his credit, which is available for normal use, may take time off immediately prior to beginning a leave of absence without pay, chargeable against all or part of such vacation or overtime.

17. According to the above passage, the Personnel Officer must 17.____
    A. decide if a leave of absence without pay should be granted
    B. require that a leave end on the last working day of a payroll period
    C. see to it that a leave of absence to conform with a payroll period
    D. vary the dates of a leave of absence to conform with a payroll period

18. According to the above passage, the exact dates of a leave of absence without 18.____
    pay may be varied provided that the
    A. calendar days an employee is off the payroll equal the actual leave granted
    B. leave conforms to an even number of payroll periods
    C. leave when granted made provision for variance to simplify payroll records
    D. Personnel Officer approves the variation

19. According to the above passage, a leave of absence without pay must extend 19.____
    from the
    A. first day of a calendar period to the first day the employee resumes work
    B. first day of a payroll period to the last calendar day of the leave
    C. first working day missed to the first day on which the employee resumes work
    D. last day on which an employee works through the first day he returns to work

20. According to the above passage, an employee may take extra time off just 20.____
    before the start of a leave of absence without pay if
    A. he charges this extra time against his leave
    B. he has a favorable balance of vacation or overtime which has been frozen
    C. the vacation or overtime that he would normally use for a leave without pay has not been charged in this way before
    D. there is time to his credit which he may use

Question 21.

DIRECTIONS: Question 21 is to be answered SOLELY on the basis of the following passage.

In considering those things which are motivators and incentives to work, it might be just as erroneous not to give sufficient weight to money as an incentive as it is to give too much weight. It is not a problem of establishing a rank-order of importance, but one of knowing that motivation is a blend or mixture rather than a pure element. It is simple to say that cultural factors count more than financial considerations, but this leads only to the conclusion that our society is financial-oriented.

21. Based on the above passage, in our society, cultural and social motivations to work are   21.____
    A. things which cannot be avoided
    B. melded to financial incentives
    C. of less consideration than high pay
    D. not balanced equally with economic or financial considerations

Question 22.

DIRECTIONS: Question 22 is to be answered SOLELY on the basis of the following passage.

A general principle of training and learning with respect to people is that they learn more readily if they receive *feedback*. Essential to maintaining proper motivational levels is knowledge of results which indicate level of progress. Feedback also assists the learning process by identifying mistakes. If this kind of information were not given to the learner, then improper or inappropriate job performance may be instilled.

22. Based on the above passage, which of the following is MOST accurate?   22.____
    A. Learning will not take place without feedback.
    B. In the absence of feedback, improper or inappropriate job performance will be learned.
    C. To properly motivate a learner, the learner must have his progress made known to him.
    D. Trainees should be told exactly what to do if they are to learn properly

Questions 23.

DIRECTIONS: Question 23 is to be answered SOLELY on the basis of the following passage.

In a democracy, the obligation of public officials is twofold. They must not only do an efficient and satisfactory job of administration, but also they must persuade the public that it is an efficient and satisfactory job. It is a burden which, if properly assumed, will make democracy work and perpetuate reform government.

23. The above passage means that   23.____
    A. public officials should try to please everybody

B. public opinion is instrumental if determining the policy of public officials
C. satisfactory performance of the job of administration will eliminate opposition to its work
D. frank and open procedure in a public agency will aid in maintaining progressive government

Question 24.

DIRECTIONS: Question 24 is to be answered SOLELY on the basis of the following passage.

Upon retirement for service, a member shall receive a retirement allowance which shall consist of an annuity which shall be the actuarial equivalent of his accumulated deductions at the time of his retirement and a pension, in addition to his annuity, which shall be equal to one service-fraction of his final compensation, multiplied by the number of years of service since he last became a member credited to him, and a pension which is the actuarial equivalent of the reserve-for-increased-take-home-pay to which he may then be entitled, if any.

24. According to the above passage, a retirement allowance shall consist of a(n) 24.____
    A. annuity, plus a pension, plus an actuarial equivalent
    B. annuity, plus a pension, plus reserve-for-increased-take-home-pay, if any
    C. annuity, plus reserve-for-increased-take-home-pay, if any, plus final compensation
    D. pension, plus reserve-for-increased-take-home-pay, if any, plus accumulated deductions

Question 25.

DIRECTIONS: Question 25 is to be answered SOLELY on the basis of the following passage.

Membership in the retirement system shall cease upon the occurrence of any one of the following conditions: when the time out of service of any member who has total service of less than 25 years, shall aggregate more than 5 years; when the time out of service of any member who has total service of 25 years or more, shall aggregate more than 10 years; when any member shall have withdrawn more than 50% of his accumulated deductions; or when any member shall have withdrawn the cash benefit provided by Section B3.35.0 of the Administrative Code.

25. According to the information in the above passage, membership in the 25.____
    retirement system shall cease when an employee
    A. with 17 years of service has been on a leave of absence for 3 years
    B. withdraws 50% of his accumulated deductions
    C. with 28 years of service has been out of service for 10 years
    D. withdraws his cash benefits

KEY (CORRECT ANSWERS)

1.	B	11.	B
2.	A	12.	C
3.	C	13.	B
4.	A	14.	B
5.	D	15.	D
6.	B	16.	B
7.	A	17.	A
8.	C	18.	A
9.	B	19.	C
10.	C	20.	D

21. B
22. C
23. D
24. B
25. D

TEST 2

DIRECTIONS: Each question or incomplete statement is followed by several suggested answers or completions. Select the one that BEST answers the question or completes the statement. *PRINT THE LETTER OF THE CORRECT ANSWER IN THE SPACE AT THE RIGHT.*

Questions 1-6.

DIRECTIONS: Questions 1 through 6 are to be answered SOLELY on the basis of the following passage.

Since almost every office has some contact with data-processed records, a stenographer should have some understanding of the basic operations of data processing. Data processing systems now handle a vast majority of all office paperwork. On coded forms and other specialized media, data are recorded before being fed into the computer for processing. The data written on the source document is converted in highly advanced ways in order to make the information accessible to the user. After data has been converted, it must be verified to guarantee absolute accuracy. In this manner, data becomes a permanent record which can be read by computers that compare, store, compute, and otherwise process data at high speeds.

One key person in a computer installation is a programmer, the man or woman who puts business and scientific problems into special symbolic languages that can be read by the computer. Jobs done by the computer range all the way from payroll operations to chemical process control, but most computer applications are directed toward management data. Most programmers employed by business come to their positions with college degrees; the rest are promoted to their positions from within the organization on the basis of demonstrated ability without regard to education.

1. Of the following, the BEST title for the above passage is
    A. The Stenographer As Data Processor
    B. The Relation of Data Input to Stenography
    C. Understanding Data Processing
    D. Permanent Office Records

1.____

2. According to the above passage, a stenographer should understand the basic operations of data processing because
    A. almost every office today has contact with data processed by computer
    B. any office worker may be asked to verify the accuracy of data
    C. most offices are involved in the production of permanent records
    D. data may be converted into computer language by specialized media

2.____

3. According to the above passage, data accuracy is reviewed during the _____ stage.
    A. processing
    B. verification
    C. programming
    D. stenographic

3.____

4. According to the above passage, computers are used MOST often to handle
   A. management data
   B. problems of higher education
   C. the control of chemical processes
   D. payroll operations

5. Computer programming is taught in many colleges and business schools. The above passage implies that programmers in industry
   A. must have professional training
   B. need professional training to advance
   C. must have at least a college education to do adequate programming tasks
   D. do not necessarily need college education to do programming work

6. According to the above passage, data to be processed by computer should be
   A. recent   B. basic   C. complete   D. verified

Questions 7-10.

DIRECTIONS: Questions 7 through 10 are to be answered SOLELY on the basis of the following passage.

There is nothing that will take the place of good sense on the part of the stenographer. You may be perfect in transcribing exactly what the dictator says and your speed may be adequate, but without an understanding of the dictator's intent as well as his words, you are likely to be a mediocre secretary.

A serious error that is made when taking dictation is putting down something that does not make sense. Most people who dictate material would rather be asked to repeat and explain than to receive transcribed material which has errors due to inattention or doubt. Many dictators request that their grammar be corrected by their secretaries, but unless specifically asked to do so, secretaries should not do it without first checking with the dictator. Secretaries should be aware that, in some cases, dictators may use incorrect grammar or slang expressions to create a particular effect.

Some people dictate commas, periods, and paragraphs, while others expect the stenographer to know when, where, and how to punctuate. A well-trained secretary should be able to indicate the proper punctuation by listening to the pauses and tones of the dictator's voice.

A stenographer who has taken dictation from the same person for a period of time should be able to understand him under most conditions. By increasing her tack, alertness, and efficiency, a secretary can become more competent.

7. According to the above passage, which of the following statements concerning the dictation of punctuation is CORRECT?
   A. Dictator may use incorrect punctuation to create a desired style.
   B. Dictator should indicate all punctuation.

C. Stenographer should know how to punctuate based on the pauses and tones of the dictator.
D. Stenographer should not type any punctuation if it has not been dictated to her.

8. According to the above passage, how should secretaries handle grammatical errors in a dictation?
Secretaries should
   A. *not correct* grammatical errors unless the dictator is aware that this is being done
   B. *correct* grammatical errors by having the dictator repeat the line with proper pauses
   C. *correct* grammatical errors if they have checked the correctness in a grammar book
   D. *correct* grammatical errors based on their own good sense

8.____

9. If a stenographer is confused about the method of spacing and indenting of a report which has just been dictated to her, she GENERALLY should
   A. do the best she can
   B. ask the dictator to explain what she should do
   C. try to improve her ability to understand dictated material
   D. accept the fact that her stenographic ability is not adequate

9.____

10. In the last line of the first paragraph, the word *mediocre* means MOST NEARLY
   A. superior   B. respected   C. disregarded   D. second-rate

10.____

Questions 11-12.

DIRECTIONS: Questions 11 and 12 are to be answered SOLELY on the basis of the following passage.

The number of legible carbon copies required to be produced determines the weight of the carbon paper to be used. When only one copy is made, heavy carbon paper is satisfactory. Most typists, however, use medium-weight carbon paper and find it serviceable for up to three or four copies. If five or more copies are to be made, it is wise to use light carbon paper. On the other hand, the finish of carbon paper to be used depends largely on the stroke of the typist and, in lesser degree, on the number of copies to be made and on whether the typewriter has pica or elite type. A soft-finish carbon paper should be used if the typist's touch is light or if a noiseless machine is used. It is desirable for the average typist to use medium-finish carbon paper for ordinary work, when only a few carbon copies are required. Elite type requires a harder carbon finish than pica type for the same number of copies.

11. According to the above passage, the lighter the carbon paper used, the
   A. softer the finish of the carbon paper will be
   B. greater the number of legible carbon copies that can be made
   C. greater the number of times the carbon paper can be used
   D. lighter the typist's touch should be

11.____

12. According to the above passage, the MOST important factor which determines whether the finish of carbon paper to be used in typing should be hard, medium, or soft is 12.____
    A. the touch of the typist
    B. the number of carbon copies required
    C. whether the type in the typewriter is pica or elite
    D. whether a machine with pica type will produce the same number of carbon copies as a machine with elite type

Questions 13-16.

DIRECTIONS: Questions 13 through 16 are to be answered SOLELY on the basis of the following passage.

Looking back at past developments in office work, advances were made at higher speeds and at greater efficiency thanks largely to the typewriter. The typewriter was a substitute for handwriting and, in the hands of a skilled typist, not only turned out letters and other documents at least three times faster than a penman, but turned out the greater volume more uniformly and legibly. With the use of carbon paper and onionskin paper, identical copies could be made at the same time.

The typewriter, besides its effect on the conduct of business and government, had a very important effect on the position of women. The typewriter did much to bring women into business and government, and in a short time span, women far outnumbered men as typists. Many women used the keys of the typewriter to climb the ladder to professional managerial positions.

The typewriter, as its name implies, employs type to make an ink impression on paper. For many years, the manual typewriter was the standard machine used. Eventually, the electric typewriter became dominant, leading to innovations in and widespread use of completely automatic electronic typewriters.

The mechanism of the office manual typewriter includes a set of keys arranged systematically in rows; a semicircular frame of type, connected to the keys by levers; the carriage, or paper carrier; a rubber roller, called a platen, against which the type strikes; and an inked ribbon which makes the impression of the type character when the key strikes it.

13. The above passage mentions a number of good features of the combination of a skilled typist and a typewriter. 13.____
    Of the following the feature which is NOT mentioned in the passage is
    A. speed   B. reliability   C. uniformity   D. legibility

14. According to the above passage, a skilled typist can 14.____
    A. turn out at least five carbon copies of typed matter
    B. type at least three times faster than a penman can write
    C. type more than 80 words in a minute
    D. readily move into a managerial position

15. According to the above passage, which of the following is NOT part of the mechanism of a manual typewriter?
    A. Carbon paper
    B. Platen
    C. Paper carrier
    D. Inked ribbon

    15._____

16. According to the above passage, the typewriter helped
    A. men more than women in business
    B. women in career advancement into management
    C. men and women equally, but women have taken better advantage of it
    D. more women than men, because men generally dislike routine typing work

    16._____

Questions 17-21.

DIRECTIONS: Questions 17 through 21 are to be answered SOLELY on the basis of the following passage.

The recipient gains an impression of a typewritten letter before he begins to read the message. Factors which provide for a good first impression include margins and spacing that are visually pleasing, formal parts of the letter which are correctly placed according to the style of the letter, copy which is free of obvious erasures and over-strikes, and transcript that is even and clear. The problem for the typist is that of how to produce that first, positive impression of her work.

There are several general rules which a typist can follow when she wishes to prepare a properly spaced letter on a sheet of letterhead. Ordinarily, the width of a letter should not be less than four inches nor more than six inches. The side margins should also have a desirable relation to the bottom margin and the space between the letterhead and the body of the letter. Usually the most appealing arrangement is when the side margins are even and the bottom margin is slightly wider than the side margins. In some offices, however, standard line length is used for all business letter, and the secretary then varies the spacing between the date line and the inside address according to the length of the letter.

17. The BEST title for the above passage would be
    A. Writing Office Letters
    B. Making Good First Impressions
    C. Judging Well-Typed Letters
    D. Good Placing and Spacing for Office Letters

    17._____

18. According to the above passage, which of the following might be considered the way in which people very quickly judge the quality of work which has been typed? By
    A. measuring the margins to see if they are correct
    B. looking at the spacing and cleanliness of the typescript
    C. scanning the body of the letter for meaning
    D. reading the date line and address for errors

    18._____

19. What, according to the above passage, would be definitely UNDESIRABLE as the average line length of a typed letter?   19.____
    A. 4"   B. 6"   C. 5"   D. 7"

20. According to the above passage, when the line length is kept standard, the secretary   20.____
    A. does not have to vary the spacing at all since this also is standard
    B. adjusts the spacing between the date line and inside address for different lengths of letters
    C. uses the longest line as a guidance for spacing between the date line and inside address
    D. varies the number of spaces between the lines

21. According to the above passage, side margins are MOST pleasing when they   21.____
    A. are even and somewhat smaller than the bottom margin
    B. are slightly wider than the bottom margin
    C. vary with the length of the letter
    D. are figured independently from the letterhead and the body of the letter

Questions 22-25.

DIRECTIONS: Questions 22 through 25 are to be answered SOLELY on the basis of the following passage.

Typed pages can reflect the simplicity of modern art in a machine age. Lightness and evenness can be achieved by proper layout and balance of typed lines and white space. Instead of solid, cramped masses of uneven, crowded typing, there should be a pleasing balance up and down as well as horizontal.

To have real balance, your page must have a center. The eyes see the center of the sheet slightly above the real center. This is the way both you and the reader see it. Try imagining a line down the center of the page that divides the paper in equal halves. On either side of your paper, white space and blocks of typing need to be similar in size and shape. Although left and right margins should be equal, top and bottom margins need not be as exact. It looks better to hold a bottom border wider than a top margin, so that your typing rests upon a cushion of white space. To add interest to the appearance of the page, try making one paragraph between one-half and two-thirds the size of an adjacent paragraph.

Thus, by taking full advantage of your typewriter, the pages that you type will not only be accurate but will also be attractive.

22. It can be inferred from the above passage that the basic importance of proper balancing on a typed page is that proper balancing   22.____
    A. makes a typed page a work of modern art
    B. provides exercise in proper positioning of a typewriter
    C. increases the amount of typed copy on the paper
    D. draws greater attention and interest to the page

23. A reader will tend to see the center of a typed page
    A. somewhat higher than the true center
    B. somewhat lower than the true center
    C. on either side of the true center
    D. about two-thirds of an inch above the true center

24. Which of the following suggestions is NOT given by the above passage?
    A. Bottom margins may be wider than top borders.
    B. Keep all paragraphs approximately the same size.
    C. Divide your page with an imaginary line down the middle.
    D. Side margins should be equalized.

25. Of the following, the BEST title for the above passage is
    A. Increasing the Accuracy of the Typed Page
    B. Determination of Margins for Typed Copy
    C. Layout and Balance of the Typed Page
    D. How to Take Full Advantage of the Typewriter

KEY (CORRECT ANSWERS)

1.	C		11.	B
2.	A		12.	A
3.	B		13.	B
4.	A		14.	B
5.	D		15.	A
6.	D		16.	B
7.	C		17.	D
8.	A		18.	B
9.	B		19.	D
10.	D		20.	B

21. A
22. D
23. A
24. B
25. C

TEST 3

DIRECTIONS: Each question or incomplete statement is followed by several suggested answers or completions. Select the one that BEST answers the question or completes the statement. *PRINT THE LETTER OF THE CORRECT ANSWER IN THE SPACE AT THE RIGHT.*

Questions 1-5.

DIRECTIONS: Questions 1 through 5 are to be answered SOLELY on the basis of the following passage.

    A written report is a communication of information from one person to another. It is an account of some matter especially investigated, however routine that matter may be. The ultimate basis of any good written report is facts, which become known through observation and verification. Good written reports may seem to be no more than general ideas and opinions. However, in such cases, the facts leading too these opinions were gathered, verified, and reported earlier, and the opinions are dependent upon these facts. Good style, proper form, and emphasis cannot make a good written report out of unreliable information and bad judgment; but on the other hand, solid investigation and brilliant thinking are not likely to become very useful until they are effectively communicated to others. If a person's work calls for written reports, then his work is often no better than his written reports.

1. Based on the information in the above passage, it can be concluded that opinions expressed in a report should be
    A. based on facts which are gathered and reported
    B. emphasized repeatedly when they result from a special investigation
    C. kept to a minimum
    D. separated from the body of the report

    1.____

2. In the above passage, the one of the following which is mentioned as a way of establishing facts is
    A. authority
    B. reporting
    C. communication
    D. verification

    2.____

3. According to the above passage, the characteristic shared by ALL written reports is that they are
    A. accounts of routine matters
    B. transmissions of information
    C. reliable and logical
    D. written in proper form

    3.____

4. Which of the following conclusions can logically be drawn from the information given in the above passage?
    A. Brilliant thinking can make up for unreliable information in a report.
    B. One method of judging an individual's work is the quality of the written reports he is required to submit.
    C. Proper form and emphasis can make a good report out of unreliable information.
    D. Good written reports that seem to be no more than general ideas should be rewritten.

    4.____

5. Which of the following suggested titles would be MOST appropriate for the above passage?
    A. Gathering and Organizing Facts
    B. Techniques of Observation
    C. Nature and Purpose of Reports
    D. Reports and Opinions: Differences and Similarities

5.____

Questions 6-8.

DIRECTIONS: Questions 6 through 8 are to be answered SOLELY on the basis of the following passage.

    The most important unit of the mimeograph machine is a perforated metal drum over which is stretched a cloth ink pad. A reservoir inside the drum contains the ink which flows through the perforations and saturates the ink pad. To operate the machine, the operator first removes from the machine the protective sheet, which keeps the ink from drying while the machine is not in use. He then hooks the stencil face down on the drum, draws the stencil smoothly over the drum, and fastens the stencil at the bottom. The speed with which the drum turns determines the blackness of the copies printed. Slow turning gives heavy, black copies; fast turning gives light, clear-cut reproductions. If reproductions are run on other than porous paper, slip-sheeting is necessary to prevent smearing. Often, the printed copy fails to drop readily as it comes from the machine. This may be due to static electricity. To remedy this difficulty, the operator fastens a strip of tinsel from side to side near the impression roller so that the printed copy just touches the soft stems of the tinsel as it is ejected from the machine, thus grounding the static electricity to the frame of the machine.

6. According to the above passage,
    A. turning the drum fast produces light copies
    B. stencils should be placed face up on the drum
    C. ink pads should be changed daily
    D. slip-sheeting is necessary when porous paper is being used

6.____

7. According to the above passage, when a mimeograph machine is not in use, the
    A. ink should be drained from the drum
    B. ink pad should be removed
    C. machine should be covered with a protective sheet
    D. counter should be set at zero

7.____

8. According to the above passage, static electricity is grounded to the frame of the mimeograph machine by means of
    A. a slip-sheeting device
    B. a strip of tinsel
    C. an impression roller
    D. hooks located at the top of the drum

8.____

Questions 9-10.

DIRECTIONS: Questions 9 and 10 are to be answered SOLELY on the basis of the following passage.

The proofreading of material typed from copy is performed more accurately and more speedily when two persons perform this work as a team. The person who did not do the typing should read aloud the original copy while the person who did the typing should check the reading against the typed copy. The reader should speak very slowly and repeat the figures, using a different grouping of number when repeating the figures. For example, in reading 1967, the reader may say *one-nine-six-seven* on first reading the figure and *nineteen-sixty-seven* on repeating the figure. The reader should read all punctuation marks, taking nothing for granted. Since mistakes can occur anywhere, everything typed should be proofread. To avoid confusion, the proofreading team should use the standard proofreading marks, which are given in most dictionaries.

9. According to the above passage, the
   A. person who holds the typed copy is called the reader
   B. two members of a proofreading team should take turns in reading the typed copy aloud
   C. typed copy should be checked by the person who did the typing
   D. person who did not do the typing should read aloud from the typed copy

10. According to the above passage,
    A. it is unnecessary to read the period at the end of a sentence
    B. typographical errors should be noted on the original copy
    C. each person should develop his own set of proofreading marks
    D. figures should be read twice

Questions 11-16.

DIRECTIONS: Questions 11 through 16 are to be answered SOLELY on the basis of the following passage.

Basic to every office is the need for proper lighting. Inadequate lighting is a familiar cause of fatigue and serves to create a somewhat dismal atmosphere in the office. One requirement of proper lighting is that it be of an appropriate intensity. Intensity is measured in foot-candles. According to the Illuminating Engineering Society of New York, for casual seeing tasks such as in reception rooms, inactive file rooms, and other service areas, it is recommending that the amount of light be 30 foot-candle. For ordinary seeing tasks such as reading, work in active file rooms, and in mailrooms, the recommended lighting is 100 foot-candles. For very difficult seeing tasks such as accounting, transcribing, and business machine use, the recommended lighting is 150 foot-candles.

Lighting intensity is only one requirement. Shadows and glare are to be avoided. For example, the larger the proportion of a ceiling filled with lighting units, the more glare-free and comfortable the lighting will be. Natural lighting from window is not too dependable because on dark wintry days, windows yield little usable light, and on sunny afternoons, the glare from windows may be very distracting. Desks should not face the windows. Finally, the main lighting source ought to be overhead and to the left of the user.

11. According to the above passage, insufficient light in the office may cause 11.____
    A. glare   B. tiredness   C. shadows   D. distraction

12. Based on the above passage, which of the following must be considered when planning lighting arrangements? The 12.____
    A. amount of natural light present
    B. amount of work to be done
    C. level of difficulty of work to be done
    D. type of activity to be carried out

13. It can be inferred from the above passage that a well-coordinated lighting scheme is LIKELY to result in 13.____
    A. greater employee productivity   B. elimination of light reflection
    C. lower lighting cost   D. more use of natural light

14. Of the following, the BEST title for the above passage is 14.____
    A. Characteristics of Light
    B. Light Measurement Devices
    C. Factors to Consider When Planning Lighting Systems
    D. comfort vs. Cost When Devising Lighting Arrangements

15. According to the above passage, a foot-candle is a measurement of the 15.____
    A. number of bulbs used
    B. strength of the light
    C. contrast between glare and shadow
    D. proportion of the ceiling filled with lighting units

16. According to the above passage, the number of foot-candles of light that would be needed to copy figures onto a payroll is _____ foot-candles. 16.____
    A. less than 30   B. 100   C. 30   D. 140

Questions 17-23.

DIRECTIONS: Questions 17 through 23 are to be answered SOLELY on the basis of the following passage.

<u>FEE SCHEDULE</u>

1. A candidate for any baccalaureate degree is not required to pay tuition fees for undergraduate courses until he exceeds 128 credits. Candidates exceeding 128 credits in undergraduate courses are charged at the rate of $100 a credit for each credit of undergraduate course work in excess of 128. Candidates for a baccalaureate degree who are taking graduate courses must pay the same fee as any other student taking graduate courses.

B. Non-degree students and college graduates are charged tuition fees for courses, whether undergraduate or graduate, at the rate of $180 a credit. For such students, there is an additional charge of $150 for each class hour per week in excess of the number of course credits. For example, if a three-credit course meets five hours a week, there is an additional charge for the extra two hours. Graduate courses are shown with a (G) before the course number.

C. All students are required to pay the laboratory fees indicated after the number of credits given for that course.

D. All students must pay a $250 general fee each semester.

E. Candidates for a baccalaureate degree are charged a $150 medical insurance fee for each semester. All other students are charged a $100 medical insurance fee each semester.

17. Miss Burton is not a candidate for a degree. She registers for the following courses in the spring semester: Economics 12, 4 hours a week, 3 credits; History (G 23, 4 hours a week, 3 credits; English 1, 2 hours a week, 2 credits. The TOTAL amount in fees that Miss Burton must pay is
    A. less than $2,000
    B. at least $2,000 but less than $2,100
    C. at least $2,100 but less than $2,200
    D. $2,200 or over

17.____

18. Miss Gray is not a candidate for a degree. She registers for the following courses in the fall semester: History 3, 3 hours a week, 3 credits; English 5, 3 hours a week, 2 credits; Physics 5, 6 hours a week, 3 credits, laboratory fee $60; Mathematics 7, 4 hours a week, 3 credits.
    The TOTAL amount in fees that Miss Gray must pay is
    A. less than $3,150
    B. at least $3,150 but less than $3,250
    C. at least $3,250 but less than $3,350
    D. $3,350 or over

18.____

19. Mr. Wall is a candidate for the Bachelor of Arts degree and has completed 126 credits. He registers for the following courses in the spring semester, his final semester at college; French 4, 3 hours a week, 3 credits; Physics (G) 15, 6 hours a week, 3 credits, laboratory fee $80; History (G) 33, 4 hours a week, 3 credits.
    The TOTAL amount in fees that this candidate must pay is
    A. less than $2,100
    B. at least $2,100 but less than $2,300
    C. at least $2,300 but less than $2,500
    D. $2,500

19.____

6 (#3)

20. Mr. Tindall, a candidate for the B.A. degree, has completed 122 credits of undergraduate courses. He registers for the following courses in his final semester: English 31, 3 hours a week, 3 credits; Philosophy 12, 4 hours a week, 4 credits; Anthropology 15, 3 hours a week, 3 credits; Economics (G) 68, 3 hours a week, 3 credits.
The TOTAL amount in fees that Mr. Tindall must pay in his final semester is
   A. less than $1,200
   B. at least $1,200 but less than $1,400
   C. at least $1,400 but less than $1,600
   D. $1,600

20.____

21. Mr. Cantrell, who was graduated from the college a year ago, registers for graduate courses in the fall semester. Each course for which he register carries the same number of credits as the number of hours a week it meets. If he pays a total of $1,530, including a $100 laboratory fee, the number of credits for which he is registered is
   A. 4   B. 5   C. 6   D. 7

21.____

22. Miss Jayson, who is not a candidate for a degree, has registered for several courses including a lecture course in History. She withdraws from the course in History for which she had paid the required course fee of $690.
The number of hours that this course is scheduled to meet is
   A. 4   B. 5   C. 2   D. 3

22.____

23. Mr. Van Arsdale, a graduate of a college in Iowa, registers for the following courses in one semester: Chemistry 35, 5 hours a week, 3 credits; Biology 14, 4 hours a week, 3 credits, laboratory fee $150; Mathematics (G) 179, 3 hours a week, 3 credits.
The TOTAL amount in fees that Mr. Van Arsdale must pay is
   A. less than $2,400
   B. at least $2,400 but less than $2,500
   C. at least $2,500 but less than $2,600
   D. at least $2,600 or over

23.____

Questions 24-25.

DIRECTIONS: Questions 24 and 25 are to be answered SOLELY on the basis of the following passage.

A duplex envelope is an envelope composed of two sections securely fastened together so that they become one mailing piece. This type of envelope makes it possible for a first class letter to be delivered simultaneously with third or fourth class matter and yet not require payment of the much higher first class postage rate on the entire mailing. First class postage is paid only on the letter which goes in the small compartment, third or fourth class postage being paid on the contents of the larger compartment. The larger compartment generally has an ungummed flap or clasp for sealing. The first class or smaller compartment has a gummed flap for sealing. Postal regulations require that the exact amount of postage applicable to each compartment be separately attached to it.

24. On the basis of the above passage, it is MOST accurate to state that 24.____
    A. the smaller compartment is placed inside the larger compartment before mailing
    B. the two compartments may be detached and mailed separately
    C. two classes of mailing matter may be mailed as a unit at two different postage rates
    D. the more expensive postage rate is paid on the matter in the larger compartment

25. When a duplex envelope is used, the 25.____
    A. first class compartment may be sealed with a clasp
    B. correct amount of postage must be placed on each compartment
    C. compartment containing third or fourth class mail requires a gummed flap for sealing
    D. full amount of postage for both compartments may be placed on the larger compartment

KEY (CORRECT ANSWERS)

1.	A		11.	C
2.	D		12.	D
3.	B		13.	A
4.	B		14.	C
5.	C		15.	B
6.	A		16.	D
7.	C		17.	B
8.	B		18.	A
9.	C		19.	B
10.	D		20.	B

21. C
22. A
23. C
24. C
25. B

READING COMPREHENSION
UNDERSTANDING AND INTERPRETING WRITTEN MATERIAL
EXAMINATION SECTION
TEST 1

DIRECTIONS: Each question or incomplete statement is followed by several suggested answers or completions. Select the one that BEST answers the question or completes the statement. *PRINT THE LETTER OF THE CORRECT ANSWER IN THE SPACE AT THE RIGHT.*

Questions 1-4.

DIRECTIONS: Questions 1 through 4 are to be answered SOLELY on the basis of the information contained in the following passage.

After conducting and completing an interview, the interviewer is faced with the responsibility of recording it in some manner. Very considerable amounts of staff time and agency finances are absorbed in recording. Time and cost studies of agency expenditures indicate that, for every dollar spent on interviewing, three dollars are spent on recording. In addition to actual time spent by the worker in recording, such expense involves clerical transcribing time, filing time and space, and time in reading records.

Recording insures a continuity of client-agency contact that transcends the client's contact with any individual social worker. The case record also implements the agency's accountability to the community. It provides a permanent, documented account of services to clients. The interviewer about to record the interview faces the essential question, what should be recorded and how should the recording be organized? Just as purpose guides interview interaction, so it guides selection of material for recording. Traditionally, social work recording has been designed to meet a number of different purposes. We record to achieve more effective practice, to provide material for in-service training and teaching, and for research purposes. There is no consensus on the principal purpose of social work recording. Consequently, recording has served these various purposes with limited effectiveness, and has served no one purpose well.

1. According to the above passage, the relationship between recording and interviewing costs for social work purposes is such that

    A. recording is three times more expensive than interviewing
    B. recording is one-third as expensive as interviewing
    C. recording is four times more expensive than interviewing
    D. interviewing is much more expensive than recording

2. The one of the following that is SPECIFICALLY mentioned as a purpose of case recording is

    A. saving time   B. economy
    C. research   D. convenience

1.____

2.____

3. Of the following, according to the above passage, a MAJOR contributing factor to the expense of case recording is

    A. supervision
    B. in-service training
    C. research
    D. record reading time

4. It can be concluded that the author's opinion regarding the capacity of social work recording to achieve its various purposes is

    A. enthusiastic
    B. guarded
    C. neutral
    D. confused

Questions 5-7.

DIRECTIONS: Questions 5 through 7 are to be answered SOLELY on the basis of the information in the following passage.

It is important that interviewers understand to some degree the manner in which stereotyped thinking operates. Stereotypes are commonly held, but predominantly false, preoccupations about the appearance and traits of individuals of different racial, religious, ethnic, and subcultural groups. Distinct traits, physical and mental, are associated with each group, and membership in a particular group is enough, in the mind of a person holding the stereotype, to assure that these traits will be perceived in individuals who are members of that group. Conversely, possession of the particular stereotyped trait by an individual usually indicates to the holder of the stereotype that the individual is a group member. Linked to the formation of stereotypes is the fact that mental traits, either positive or negative, such as honesty, laziness, avariciousness, and other characteristics are associated with particular stereotypes. Either kind of stereotype, if held by an interviewer, can seriously damage the results of an interview. In general, stereotypes can be particularly dangerous when they are part of the belief patterns of administrators, interviewers, and supervisors, who are in a position to affect the lives of others and to stimulate or retard the development of human potential. The holding of a stereotype by an interviewer, for example, diverts his attention from significant essential facts and information upon which really valid assessments may be made. Unfortunately, it is the rare interviewer who is completely conscious of the real basis upon which he is making his evaluation of the people he is interviewing. The specific reasons given by an interviewer for a negative evaluation, even though apparently logical and based upon what, in the mind of the interviewer, are very good reasons, may not be the truly motivating factors. This is why the careful selection and training of interviewers is such an important responsibility of an agency which is attempting to help a great diversity of human beings.

5. Of the following, the BEST title for the above paragraph is

    A. POSITIVE AND NEGATIVE EFFECTS OF STEREOTYPED THINKING
    B. THE RELATIONSHIP OF STEREOTYPES TO INTERVIEWING
    C. AN AGENCY'S RESPONSIBILITY IN INTERVIEWING
    D. THE IMPACT OF STEREOTYPED THINKING ON PROFESSIONAL FUNCTIONS

6. According to the above passage, MOST interviewers

   A. compensate for stereotyped beliefs to avoid negatively affecting the results of their interviews
   B. are influenced by stereotypes they hold, but put greater stress on factual information developed during the interview
   C. are seldom aware of their real motives when evaluating interviewees
   D. give logical and good reasons for negative evaluations of interviewees

7. According to the above passage, which of the following is NOT a characteristic of stereotypes?

   A. Stereotypes influence estimates of personality traits of people.
   B. Positive stereotypes can damage the results of an interview.
   C. Physical traits associated with stereotypes seldom really exist.
   D. Stereotypes sometimes are a basis upon which valid personality assessments can be made.

Questions 8-12.

DIRECTIONS: Questions 8 through 12 are to be answered SOLELY on the basis of the following passage.

At one time, people thought that in the interview designed primarily to obtain information, the interviewer had to resort to clever and subtle lines of questioning in order to accomplish his ends. Some people still believe that this is necessary, but it is not so. An example of the *tricky* approach may be seen in the work of a recent study. The study deals with materials likely to be buried beneath deep defenses. Interviewers utilized methods of questioning which, in effect, trapped the interviewee and destroyed his defenses. Doubtless, these methods succeeded in bringing out items of information which straightforward questions would have missed. Whether they missed more information than they obtained and whether they obtained the most important facts must remain unanswered questions. In defense of the *clever* approach, it is often said that, in many situations, the interviewee is motivated to conceal information or to distort what he chooses to report.

Technically, it is likely that a highly skilled interviewer can, given the time and the inclination, penetrate the interviewee's defenses and get information which the latter intended to keep hidden. It is unlikely that the interviewer can successfully elicit all of the information that might be relevant. If, for example, he found that an applicant for financial assistance was heavily in debt to gamblers, he might not care about getting any other information. There are situations in which one item, if answered in the *wrong* way, is enough. Ordinarily, this is not true. The usual situation is that there are many considerations and that the plus and minus features must be weighed before a decision may be made. It is, therefore, important to obtain complete information.

8. According to the above passage, it was GENERALLY believed that an interviewer would have difficulty in obtaining the information he sought from a person if he

   A. were tricky in his methods
   B. were open and frank in his approach

C. were clever in his questioning
D. utilized carefully prepared questions

9. The passage does NOT reveal whether the type of questions used 9.____

   A. trapped those being interviewed
   B. elicited facts which an open method of questioning might miss
   C. elicited the most important facts that were sought
   D. covered matters which those interviewed were reluctant to talk about openly

10. An argument in favor of the *tricky* or *clever* interviewing technique is that, unless this approach is used, the person interviewed will NOT 10.____

    A. offer to furnish all pertinent information
    B. answer questions concerning routine data
    C. clearly understand what is being sought
    D. want to continue the interview

11. According to the above passage, in favorable circumstances, a talented interviewer would be able to obtain from the person interviewed information 11.____

    A. which the person regards as irrelevant
    B. which the person intends to conceal
    C. about the person's family background
    D. which the person would normally have forgotten

12. According to the above passage, a highly skilled interviewer should concentrate, in most cases, on getting 12.____

    A. one outstanding fact about the interviewee which would do away with the need for prolonged questioning
    B. facts which the interviewee wanted to conceal because these would be the most relevant in making a decision
    C. all the facts so that he can consider their relative values before reaching any conclusion
    D. information about any bad habits of the interviewee, such as gambling, which would make further questioning

Questions 13-14.

DIRECTIONS: Questions 13 and 14 are to be answered SOLELY on the basis of the information given below.

The ability to interview rests not on any single trait, but on a vast complex of them. Habits, skills, techniques, and attitudes are all involved. Competence in interviewing is acquired only after careful and diligent study, prolonged practice (preferably under supervision), and a good bit of trial and error; for interviewing is not an exact science, it is an art. Like many other arts, however, it can and must draw on science in several of its aspects.

There is always a place for individual initiative, for imaginative innovations, and for new combinations of old approaches. The skilled interviewer cannot be bound by a set of rules. Likewise, there is not a set of rules which can guarantee to the novice that his interviewing will be successful. There are, however, some accepted, general guideposts which may help the beginner to avoid mistakes, learn how to conserve his efforts, and establish effective working relationships with interviewees; to accomplish, in short, what he sets out to do.

13. According to the above passage, rules and standard techniques for interviewing are 13.____

    A. helpful for the beginner, but useless for the experienced, innovative interviewer
    B. destructive of the innovation and initiative needed for a good interviewer
    C. useful for even the experienced interviewer who may, however, sometimes go beyond them
    D. the means by which nearly anybody can become an effective interviewer

14. According to the above passage, the one of the following which is a prerequisite to competent interviewing is 14.____

    A. avoiding mistakes
    B. study and practice
    C. imaginative innovation
    D. natural aptitude

Questions 15-17.

DIRECTIONS: Questions 15 through 17 are to be answered SOLELY on the basis of the following paragraph.

The physical setting of the interview may determine its entire potentiality. Some degree of privacy and a comfortable relaxed atmosphere are important. The interviewee is not encouraged to give much more than his name and address if the interviewer seems busy with other things, if people are rushing about, if there are distracting noises. He has a right to feel that, whether the interview lasts five minutes or an hour, he has, for that time, the undivided attention of the interviewer. If the interviewee has waited in a crowded room for what seems to him an interminably long period, he is naturally in no mood to sit down and discuss what is on his mind. Indeed, by that time the primary thing on his mind may be his irritation at being kept waiting, and he frequently feels it would be impolite to express this. If a wait or interruptions have been unavoidable, it is always helpful to give the client some recognition that these are disturbing and that we can naturally understand that they make it more difficult for him to proceed. At the same time, if he protests that they have not troubled him, the interviewer can best accept his statements at their face value, as further insistence that they must have been disturbing may be interpreted by his as accusing, and he may conclude that the interviewer has been personally hurt by his irritation.

15. Distraction during an interview may tend to limit the client's responses. 15.____
    In a case where an interruption has occurred, it would be BEST for the investigator to

    A. terminate this interview and have it rescheduled for another time period
    B. ignore the interruption since it is not continuous
    C. express his understanding that the distraction can cause the client to feel disturbed
    D. accept the client's protests that he has been troubled by the interruption

16. To maximize the rapport that can be established with the client, an appropriate physical setting is necessary. At the very least, some privacy would be necessary.
In addition, the interviewer should

   A. always appear to be busy in order to impress the client
   B. focus his attention only on the client
   C. accept all the client's statements as being valid
   D. stress the importance of the interview to the client

17. Clients who have been waiting quite some time for their interview may, justifiably, become upset.
However, a client may INITIALLY attempt to mask these feelings because he may

   A. personally hurt the interviewer
   B. want to be civil
   C. feel that the wait was unavoidable
   D. fear the consequences of his statement

Questions 18-20.

DIRECTIONS: Questions 18 through 20 are to be answered SOLELY on the basis of information given in the passage below.

A personnel interviewer, selecting job applicants, may find that he reacts badly to some people even on first contact. This reaction cannot usually be explained by things that the interviewee has done or said. Most of us have had the experience of liking or disliking, of feeling comfortable or uncomfortable with people on first acquaintance, long before we have had a chance to make a conscious, rational decision about them. Often, too, our liking or disliking is transmitted to the other person by subtle processes such as gestures, posture, voice intonations, or choice of words. The point to be kept in mind is this: the relations between people are complex and occur at several levels, from the conscious to the unconscious. This is true whether the relationship is brief or long, formal or informal.

Some of the major dynamics of personality which operate on the unconscious level are projection, sublimation, rationalization, and repression. Encountering these for the first time, one is apt to think of them as representing pathological states. In the extreme, they undoubtedly are, but they exist so universally that we must consider them also to be parts of normal personality.

Without necessarily subscribing to any of the numerous theories of personality, it is possible to describe personality in terms of certain important aspects or elements. We are all aware of ourselves as thinking organisms.

This aspect of personality, the conscious part, is important for understanding human behavior, but it is not enough. Many find it hard to accept the notion that each person also has an unconscious. The existence of the unconscious is no longer a matter of debate. It is not possible to estimate at all precisely what proportion of our total psychological life is conscious, what proportion unconscious. Everyone who has studied the problem, however, agrees that consciousness is the smaller part of personality. Most of what we are and do is a result of unconscious processes. To ignore this is to risk mistakes.

18. The above passage suggests that an interviewer can be MOST effective if he   18._____

    A. learns how to determine other peoples' unconscious motivations
    B. learns how to repress his own unconsciously motivated mannerisms and behavior
    C. can keep others from feeling that he either likes or dislikes them
    D. gains an understanding of how the unconscious operates in himself and in others

19. It may be inferred from the above passage that the *subtle processes such as gestures,*   19._____
    posture, voice intonation, or choice of words referred to in the first paragraph are USU-
    ALLY

    A. in the complete control of an expert investigator
    B. the determining factors in the friendships a person establishes
    C. controlled by a person's unconscious
    D. not capable of being consciously controlled

20. The above passage implies that various different personality theories are USUALLY   20._____

    A. so numerous and different as to be valueless to an investigator
    B. in basic agreement about the importance of the unconscious
    C. understood by the investigator who strives to be effective
    D. in agreement that personality factors such as projection and repression are patho-
       logical

Questions 21-25.

DIRECTIONS: Questions 21 through 25 are to be answered SOLELY on the basis of the infor-
             mation given in the following paragraph.

The nature of the interview varies with the aim or the use to which it is put. While these uses vary widely, interviews are basically of three types: fact-finding, informing, and motivating. One of these purposes usually predominates in an interview, but not to the exclusion of the other two. If the main purpose is fact-finding, for example, the interviewer must often motivate the interviewee to cooperate in revealing the facts. A major factor in the interview is the interaction of the personalities of the interviewer and the interviewee. The interviewee may not wish to reveal the facts sought, or even though willing enough to impart them, he may not be able to do so because of a lack of clear understanding as to what is wanted or because of lack of ability to put into words the information he has to give. On the other hand, the interviewer may not be able to grasp and report accurately the facts which the one being interviewed is trying to convey. Also, the interviewer's prejudice may make him not want to get at the real facts or make him unable to recognize the truth.

21. According to the above paragraph, the purpose of an interview   21._____

    A. determines the nature of the interview
    B. is usually the same for the three basic types of interviews
    C. is predominantly motivation of the interviewee
    D. is usually to check on the accuracy of facts previously obtained

22. In discussing the use or purpose of an interview, the above paragraph points out that

    A. a good interview should have only one purpose
    B. an interview usually has several uses that are equally important
    C. fact-finding should be the main purpose of an interview
    D. the interview usually has one main purpose

23. According to the above paragraph, an obstacle to the successful interview sometimes attributable to the interviewee is

    A. a lack of understanding of how to conduct an interview
    B. an inability to express himself
    C. prejudice toward the interviewer
    D. too great a desire to please

24. According to the above paragraph, one way in which the interviewer may help the interviewee to reveal the facts sought is to

    A. make him willing to impart the facts by stating clearly the consequences of false information
    B. make sure he understands what information is wanted
    C. motivate him by telling him how important he is in the investigation
    D. tell him what words to use to convey the information wanted

25. According to the above paragraph, bias on the part of the interviewer could

    A. be due to inability to understand the facts being imparted
    B. lead him to report the facts accurately
    C. make the interviewee unwilling to impart the truth
    D. prevent him from determining the facts

KEY (CORRECT ANSWERS)

1. A		11. B	
2. C		12. C	
3. D		13. C	
4. B		14. B	
5. B		15. C	
6. C		16. B	
7. D		17. B	
8. B		18. D	
9. C		19. C	
10. A		20. B	

21. A
22. D
23. B
24. B
25. D

REPORT WRITING
EXAMINATION SECTION
TEST 1

DIRECTIONS: Each question or incomplete statement is followed by several suggested answers or completions. Select the one that BEST answers the question or completes the statement. *PRINT THE LETTER OF THE CORRECT ANSWER IN THE SPACE AT THE RIGHT.*

Questions 1-4.

DIRECTIONS: Answer Questions 1 through 4 on the basis of the following report which was prepared by a supervisor for inclusion in his agency's annual report.

```
Line #
1    On Oct. 13, I was assigned to study the salaries paid.
2    to clerical employees in various titles by the city and by
3    private industry in the area.
4    In order to get the data I needed, I called Mr. Johnson at
5    the Bureau of the Budget and the payroll officers at X Corp.—
6    a brokerage house, Y Co. —an insurance company, and Z Inc. —
7    a publishing firm. None of them was available and I had to call
8    all of them again the next day.
9    When I finally got the information I needed, I drew up a
10   chart, which is attached. Note that not all of the companies I
11   contacted employed people at all the different levels used in the
12   city service.
13   The conclusions I draw from analyzing this information is
14   as follows: The city's entry-level salary is about average for
15   the region; middle-level salaries are generally higher in the
16   city government plan than in private industry; but salaries at the
17   highest levels in private industry are better than city em-
18   ployees' pay.
```

1. Which of the following criticisms about the style in which this report is written is MOST valid?
   A. It is too informal.
   B. It is too concise.
   C. It is too choppy.
   D. The syntax is too complex.

   1.____

2. Judging from the statements made in the report, the method followed by this employee in performing his research was
   A. *good*; he contacted a representative sample of businesses in the area
   B. *poor*; he should have drawn more definite conclusions
   C. *good*; he was persistent in collecting information
   D. *poor*; he did not make a thorough study

   2.____

3. One sentence in this report contains a grammatical error. This sentence begins on line number
   A. 4   B. 7   C. 10   D. 14

4. The type of information given in this report which should be presented in footnotes or in an appendix is the
   A. purpose of the study
   B. specifics about the businesses contacted
   C. reference to the chart
   D. conclusions drawn by the author

5. The use of a graph to show statistical data in a report is SUPERIOR to a table because it
   A. features approximations
   B. emphasizes facts and relationships more dramatically
   C. presents data more accurately
   D. is easily understood by the average reader

6. Of the following, the degree of formality required of a written report in tone is MOST likely to depend on the
   A. subject matter of the report
   B. frequency of its occurrence
   C. amount of time available for its preparation
   D. audience for whom the report is intended

7. Of the following, a distinguishing characteristic of a written report intended for the head of your agency as compared to a report prepared for a lower-echelon staff member is that the report for the agency head should USUALLY include
   A. considerably more detail, especially statistical data
   B. the essential details in an abbreviated form
   C. all available source material
   D. an annotated bibliography

8. Assume that you are asked to write a lengthy report for use by the administrator of your agency, the subject of which is "The Impact of Proposed New Data Processing Operation on Line Personnel" in your agency. You decide that the *most* appropriate type of report for you to prepare is an analytical report, including recommendations.
   The MAIN reason for your decision is that
   A. the subject of the report is extremely complex
   B. large sums of money are involved
   C. the report is being prepared for the administrator
   D. you intend to include charts and graphs

9. Assume that you are preparing a report based on a survey dealing with the attitudes of employees in Division X regarding proposed new changes in compensating employees for working overtime. Three percent of the respondents to the survey voluntarily offer an unfavorable opinion on the method of assigning overtime work, a question not specifically asked of the employees.
   On the basis of this information, the MOST appropriate and significant of the following comments for you to make in the report with regard to employees' attitudes on assigning overtime work is that
   A. an insignificant percentage of employees dislike the method of assigning overtime work
   B. three percent of the employees in Division X dislike the method of assigning overtime work
   C. three percent of the sample selected for the survey voiced an unfavorable opinion on the method of assigning overtime work
   D. some employees voluntarily voiced negative feelings about the method of assigning overtime work, making it impossible to determine the extent of this attitude

10. A supervisor should be able to prepare a report that is well-written and unambiguous.
    Of the following sentences that might appear in a report, select the one which communicates MOST clearly the intent of its author.
    A. When your subordinates speak to a group of people, they should be well-informed.
    B. When he asked him to leave, SanMan King told him that he would refuse the request.
    C. Because he is a good worker, Foreman Jefferson assigned Assistant Foreman D'Agostino to replace him.
    D. Each of us is responsible for the actions of our subordinates.

11. In some reports, especially longer ones, a list of the resources (books, papers, magazines, etc.) used to prepare it is included. This list is called the
    A. accreditation   B. bibliography
    C. summary   D. glossary

12. Reports are usually divided into several sections, some of which are more necessary than others.
    Of the following, the section which is ABSOLUTELY necessary to include in a report is
    A. a table of contents   B. the body
    C. an index   D. a bibliography

13. Suppose you are writing a report on an interview you have just completed with a particularly hostile applicant.
    Which of the following BEST describes what you should include in this report?
    A. What you think caused the applicant's hostile attitude during the interview
    B. Specific examples of the applicant's hostile remarks and behavior
    C. The relevant information uncovered during the interview
    D. A recommendation that the applicant's request be denied because of his hostility

13.____

14. When including recommendations in a report to your supervisor, which of the following is MOST important for you to do?
    A. Provide several alternative courses of action for each recommendation
    B. First present the supporting evidence, then the recommendations
    C. First present the recommendations, then the supporting evidence
    D. Make sure the recommendations arise logically out of the information in the report

14.____

15. It is often necessary that the writer of a report present facts and sufficient arguments to gain acceptance of the points, conclusions, or recommendations set forth in the report.
    Of the following, the LEAST advisable step to take in organizing a report, when such argumentation is the important factor, is a(n)
    A. elaborate expression of personal belief
    B. businesslike discussion of the problem as a whole
    C. orderly arrangement of convincing data
    D. reasonable explanation of the primary issues

15.____

16. In some types of reports, visual aids add interest, meaning, and support. They also provide an essential means of effectively communicating the message of the report.
    Of the following, the selection of the suitable visual aids to use with a report is LEAST dependent on the
    A. nature and scope of the report
    B. way in which the aid is to be used
    C. aid used in other reports
    D. prospective readers of the report

16.____

17. Visual aids used in a report may be placed either in the text material or in the appendix.
    Deciding where to put a chart, table, or any such aid should depend on the
    A. title of the report   B. purpose of the visual aid
    C. title of the visual aid   D. length of the report

17.____

18. A report is often revised several times before final preparation and distribution in an effort to make certain the report meets the needs of the situation for which it is designed.
    Which of the following is the BEST way for the author to be sure that a report covers the areas he intended?

18.____

    A. Obtain a coworker's opinion
    B. Compare it with a content checklist
    C. Test it on a subordinate
    D. Check his bibliography

19. In which of the following situations is an oral report preferable to a written report? When a(n)
    A. recommendation is being made for a future plan of action
    B. department head requests immediate information
    C. long-standing policy change is made
    D. analysis of complicated statistical data is involved

20. When an applicant is approved, the supervisor must fill in standard forms with certain information.
    The GREATEST advantage of using standard forms in this situation rather than having the supervisor write the report as he sees fit is that
    A. the report can be acted on quickly
    B. the report can be written without directions from a supervisor
    C. needed information is less likely to be left out of the report
    D. information that is written up this way is more likely to be verified

21. Assume that it is part of your job to prepare a monthly report for your unit head that eventually goes to the director. The report contains information on the number of applicants you have interviewed that have been approved and the number of applicants you have interviewed that have been turned down.
    Errors on such reports are serious because
    A. you are expected to be able to prove how many applicants you have interviewed each month
    B. accurate statistics are needed for effective management of the department
    C. they may not be discovered before the report is transmitted to the director
    D. they may result in loss to the applicants left out of the report

22. The frequency with which job reports are submitted should depend MAINLY on
    A. how comprehensive the report has to be
    B. the amount of information in the report
    C. the availability of an experienced man to write the report
    D. the importance of changes in the information included in the report

23. The CHIEF purpose in preparing an outline for a report is usually to insure that
    A. the report will be grammatically correct
    B. every point will be given equal emphasis
    C. principal and secondary points will be properly integrated
    D. the language of the report will be of the same level and include the same technical terms

24. The MAIN reason for requiring written job reports is to
    A. avoid the necessity of oral orders
    B. develop better methods of doing the work
    C. provide a permanent record of what was done
    D. increase the amount of work that can be done

25. Assume you are recommending in a report to your supervisor that a radical change in a standard maintenance procedure should be adopted.
    Of the following, the MOST important information to be included in this report is
    A. a list of the reasons for making this change
    B. the names of others who favor the change
    C. a complete description of the present procedure
    D. amount of training time needed for the new procedure

KEY (CORRECT ANSWERS)

1.	A		11.	B
2.	D		12.	B
3.	D		13.	C
4.	B		14.	D
5.	B		15.	A
6.	D		16.	C
7.	B		17.	B
8.	A		18.	B
9.	D		19.	B
10.	D		20.	C

21. B
22. D
23. C
24. C
25. A

TEST 2

DIRECTIONS: Each question or incomplete statement is followed by several suggested answers or completions. Select the one that BEST answers the question or completes the statement. *PRINT THE LETTER OF THE CORRECT ANSWER IN THE SPACE AT THE RIGHT.*

1. It is often necessary that the writer of a report present facts and sufficient arguments to gain acceptance of the points, conclusions, or recommendations set forth in the report.
   Of the following, the LEAST advisable step to take in organizing a report, when such argumentation is the important factor, is a(n)
   A. elaborate expression of personal belief
   B. businesslike discussion of the problem as a whole
   C. orderly arrangement of convincing data
   D. reasonable explanation of the primary issues

   1.____

2. Of the following, the factor which is generally considered to be LEAST characteristic of a good control report is that it
   A. stresses performance that adheres to standard rather than emphasizing the exception
   B. supplies information intended to serve as the basis for corrective action
   C. provides feedback for the planning process
   D. includes data that reflect trends as well as current status

   2.____

3. An administrative assistant has been asked by his superior to write a concise, factual report with objective conclusions and recommendations based on facts assembled by other researchers.
   Of the following factors, the administrative assistant should give LEAST consideration to
   A. the educational level of the person or persons for whom the report is being prepared
   B. the use to be made of the report
   C. the complexity of the problem
   D. his own feelings about the importance of the problem

   3.____

4. When making a written report, it is often recommended that the findings or conclusions be presented near the beginning of the report.
   Of the following, the MOST important reason for doing this is that it
   A. facilitates organizing the material clearly
   B. assures that all the topics will be covered
   C. avoids unnecessary repetition of ideas
   D. prepares the reader for the facts that will follow

   4.____

5. You have been asked to write a report on methods of hiring and training new employees. Your report is going to be about ten pages long.
For the convenience of your readers, a brief summary of your findings should
   A. appear at the beginning of your report
   B. be appended to the report as a postscript
   C. be circulated in a separate memo
   D. be inserted in tabular form in the middle of your report

6. In preparing a report, the MAIN reason for writing an outline is usually to
   A. help organize thoughts in a logical sequence
   B. provide a guide for the typing of the report
   C. allow the ultimate user to review the report in advance
   D. ensure that the report is being prepared on schedule

7. The one of the following which is MOST appropriate as a reason for including footnotes in a report is to
   A. correct capitalization
   B. delete passages
   C. improve punctuation
   D. cite references

8. A completed formal report may contain all of the following EXCEPT
   A. a synopsis
   B. a preface
   C. marginal notes
   D. bibliographical references

9. Of the following, the MAIN use of proofreaders' marks is to
   A. explain corrections to be made
   B. indicate that a manuscript has been read and approved
   C. let the reader know who proofread the report
   D. indicate the format of the report

10. Informative, readable, and concise reports have been found to observe the following rules:
    Rule I. Keep the report short and easy to understand
    Rule II. Vary the length of sentences.
    Rule III. Vary the style of sentences so that, for example, they are not all just subject-verb, subject-verb.
    Consider this hospital laboratory report: The experiment was started in January. The apparatus was put together in six weeks. At that time, the synthesizing process was begun. The synthetic chemicals were separated. Then they were used in tests on patients.
    Which one of the following choices MOST accurately classifies the above rules into those which are violated by this report ad those which are not?
    A. II is violated, but I and III are not.
    B. III is violated, but I and II are not.
    C. II and III are violated, but I is not.
    D. I, II, and III are violated,

Questions 11-13.

DIRECTIONS: Questions 11 through 13 are based on the following example of a report. The report consists of eight numbered sentences, some of which are not consistent with the principles of good report writing.

(1) I interviewed Mrs. Loretta Crawford in Room 424 of County Hospital. (2) She had collapsed on the street and been brought into emergency. (3) She is an attractive woman with many friends judging by the cards she had received. (4) She did not know what her husband's last job had been, or what their present income was. (5) The first thing that Mrs. Crawford said was that she had never worked and that her husband was presently unemployed. (6) She did not know if they had any medical coverage or if they could pay the bill. (7) She said that her husband could not be reached by telephone but that he would be in to see her that afternoon. (8) I left word at the nursing station to be called when he arrived.

11. A good report should be arranged in logical order.
    Which of the following sentences from the report does NOT appear in its proper sequence in the report?
    A. 1   B. 4   C. 7   D. 8

12. Only material that is relevant to the main thought of a report should be included.
    Which of the following sentences from the report contains material which is LEAST relevant to this report? Sentence
    A. 3   B. 4   C. 6   D. 8

13. Reports should include all essential information.
    Of the following, the MOST important fact that is missing from this report is:
    A. Who was involved in the interview
    B. What was discovered at the interview
    C. When the interview took place
    D. Where the interview took place

Questions 14-15.

DIRECTIONS: Each of Questions 14 and 15 consists of four numbered sentences which constitute a paragraph in a report. They are not in the right order. Choose the numbered arrangement appearing after letter A, B, C, or D which is MOST logical and which BEST expresses the thought of the paragraph.

14. I. Congress made the commitment explicit in the Housing Act of 1949, establishing as a national goal the realization of a decent home and suitable environment for every American family.
    II. The result has been that the goal of decent home and suitable environment is still as far distant as ever for the disadvantaged urban family
    III. In spite of this action by Congress, federal housing programs have continued to be fragmented and grossly under-funded.
    IV. The passage of the National Housing Act signaled a new federal commitment to provide housing for the nation's citizens.

4 (#2)

The CORRECT answer is:
A. I, IV, III, II   B. IV, I, III, II   C. IV, I, III, II   D. II, IV, I, III

15.
I. The greater expense does not necessarily involve "exploitation," but it is often perceived as exploitative and unfair by those who are aware of the price differences involved, but unaware of operating costs.
II. Ghetto residents believe they are "exploited" by local merchants, and evidence substantiates some of these beliefs.
III. However, stores in low-income areas were more likely to be small independents, which could not achieve the economies available to supermarket chains and were, therefore, more likely to charge higher prices, and the customers were more likely to buy smaller-sized packages which are more expensive per unit of measure.
IV. A study conducted in one city showed that distinctly higher prices were charged for goods sold in ghetto stores than in other areas.

The CORRECT answer is:
A. IV, II, I, III   B. IV, I, III, II   C. II, IV, III, I   D. II, III, IV, I

15.____

16. In organizing data to be presented in a formal report, the FIRST of the following steps should be
   A. determining the conclusions to be drawn
   B. establishing the time sequence of the data
   C. sorting and arranging like data into groups
   D. evaluating how consistently the data support the recommendations

16.____

17. All reports should be prepared with at least one copy so that
   A. there is one copy for your file
   B. there is a copy for your supervisor
   C. the report can be sent to more than one person
   D. the person getting the report can forward a copy to someone else

17.____

18. Before turning in a report of an investigation he has made, a supervisor discovers some additional information he did not include in this report. Whether he rewrites this report to include this additional information should PRIMARILY depend on the
   A. importance of the report itself
   B. number of people who will eventually review this report
   C. established policy covering the subject matter of the report
   D. bearing this new information has on the conclusions of the report

18.____

KEY (CORRECT ANSWERS)

1.	A	11.	B
2.	A	12.	A
3.	D	13.	C
4.	D	14.	B
5.	A	15.	C
6.	A	16.	C
7.	D	17.	A
8.	C	18.	D
9.	A		
10.	C		

EXAMINATION SECTION
TEST 1

DIRECTIONS: Each question or incomplete statement is followed by several suggested answers or completions. Select the one that BEST answers the question or completes the statement. *PRINT THE LETTER OF THE CORRECT ANSWER IN THE SPACE AT THE RIGHT.*

Questions 1-25.

DIRECTIONS: Select the word with the MOST appropriate meaning for the italicized word in each of Questions 1 through 25.

1. The directions were *explicit*. 1.____
   - A. petulant
   - B. satiric
   - C. awkward
   - D. unequivocal
   - E. foreign

2. The teacher explained *mutability*. 2.____
   - A. change
   - B. harmony
   - C. annihilation
   - D. ethics
   - E. candor

3. He was a *secular* man. 3.____
   - A. holy
   - B. evil
   - C. worldly
   - D. superior
   - E. small

4. They submitted a list of their *progeny*. 4.____
   - A. experiments
   - B. books
   - C. holdings
   - D. theories
   - E. offspring

5. She admired his *sententious* replies. 5.____
   - A. simple
   - B. pithy
   - C. coherent
   - D. lucid
   - E. inane

6. He believed in the ancient *dogma*. 6.____
   - A. priest
   - B. prophet
   - C. seer
   - D. doctrine
   - E. ruler

7. They studied a Grecian *archetype*. 7.____
   - A. model
   - B. urn
   - C. epic
   - D. ode
   - E. play

8. The *insurrection* was described on the front page. 8.____
   - A. surgery
   - B. pageant
   - C. ceremony
   - D. game
   - E. revolt

9. He was known for his *procrastination*. 9.____
   - A. justification
   - B. learning
   - C. delay
   - D. ambition
   - E. background

10. The doctor analyzed the *toxic* ingredients.   10._____
    A. poisonous   B. anemic   C. trivial
    D. obscure   E. distinct

11. It was a *portentous* occurrence.   11._____
    A. pleasant   B. decisive   C. ominous
    D. monetary   E. hearty

12. His *espousal* of the plan was applauded.   12._____
    A. explanation   B. rejection   C. ridicule
    D. adoption   E. revision

13. Her condition was *lachrymose*.   13._____
    A. improved   B. tearful   C. hopeful
    D. precocious   E. tenuous

14. It was a *precarious* situation.   14._____
    A. uncomplicated   B. peaceful   C. precise
    D. uncertain   E. precipitous

15. He was lost in a *reverie*.   15._____
    A. chancery   B. dream   C. forest
    D. cavern   E. tarn

16. The hero was a young *gallant*.   16._____
    A. suitor   B. fool   C. gull
    D. lawyer   E. executive

17. Their practices were *nefarious*.   17._____
    A. unprofitable   B. ignorant   C. multifarious
    D. wicked   E. wishful

18. He insisted upon the *proviso*.   18._____
    A. stipulation   B. pronunciation   C. examination
    D. supply   E. equipment

19. The spirit came from the *nether* regions.   19._____
    A. frozen   B. lower   C. lost
    D. bright   E. mysterious

20. His actions were *malevolent*.   20._____
    A. unassuming   B. silent   C. evil
    D. peaceful   E. constructive

21. He had a *florid* complexion.   21._____
    A. sanguine   B. pallid   C. fair
    D. sickly   E. normal

22. The lawyer explained the legal *parlance*. 22.____
    A. action B. maneuver C. situation
    D. language E. procedure

23. They were present at the *interment*. 23.____
    A. concert B. trial C. embarkation
    D. burial E. performance

24. He made a *moot* point. 24.____
    A. definite B. sensible C. debatable
    D. strong E. correct

25. They carefully examined the *cryptic* message. 25.____
    A. occult B. legible C. valid
    D. familiar E. warning

Questions 26-40.

DIRECTIONS: Indicate the number of syllables in each of the following words.

26. vicissitude 26.____

27. blown 27.____

28. maintenance 28.____

29. symbolization 29.____

30. athletics 30.____

31. actually 31.____

32. friend 32.____

33. perseverance 33.____

34. physiology 34.____

35. pronunciation 35.____

36. vacuum 36.____

37. sophomore 37.____

38. opportunity 38.____

39. hungry 39.____

40. temperament 40.____

Questions 41-60.

DIRECTIONS: Indicate the one misspelled work in each of the following Questions 41 through 60 by indicating the letter of the misspelled word in the space at the right.

41. A. holiday B. noticeable C. fourty 41.____
    D. miniature E. yeast

42. A. grievance B. murmur C. occurance 42.____
    D. business E. captain

43. A. succeed B. vegatable C. pleasant 43.____
    D. picnicking E. shepherd

44. A. psychology B. plebian C. exercise 44.____
    D. fiery E. concise

45. A. ninety B. optimistic C. professor 45.____
    D. repitition E. siege

46. A. tarriff B. absence C. grammar 46.____
    D. license E. balloon

47. A. dissipation B. ecstasy C. prarie 47.____
    D. marriage E. consistent

48. A. supersede B. twelfth C. vacillate 48.____
    D. playright E. expense

49. A. fundamental B. government C. accomodate 49.____
    D. cafeteria E. surely

50. A. cemetary B. indispensable C. dormitory 50.____
    D. environment E. divine

51. A. irritible B. permissible C. irresistible 51.____
    D. rhythmical E. source

52. A. interprete B. opinion C. guard 52.____
    D. familiar E. possible

53. A. conscience B. existence C. loneliness 53.____
    D. leisure E. exhileration

54. A. villian B. weird C. seize 54.____
    D. tragedy E. crystal

55. A. develop B. bachelor C. dilemma 55.____
    D. operate E. synonym

56. A. university   B. connoiseur   C. aisle   56.____
    D. transferred   E. division

57. A. zoology   B. conscious   C. aptitude   57.____
    D. restaurant   E. sacriligious

58. A. tendency   B. vital   C. analyze   58.____
    D. consistant   E. proceed

59. A. proceedure   B. surround   C. disastrous   59.____
    D. beginning   E. arrival

60. A. encrease   B. pursuing   C. necessary   50.____
    D. tyranny   E. strength

Questions 61-80.

DIRECTIONS: Indicate the part of speech for each italicized word in the following sentences by selecting the letter of the part of speech from the key above each set of questions.

    A. Noun
    B. Pronoun
    C. Verb
    D. Adjective
    E. Adverb

61. You are entirely *wrong*.   61.____

62. On *Sunday*, we will attend church.   62.____

63. *That* is the main problem.   63.____

64. He was invited to the party, *Saturday*.   64.____

65. I shall introduce a *technical* term.   65.____

66. It was a *novel* turn of events.   66.____

67. He wanted *that* gift for himself.   67.____

68. A few definitions will help *us* to understand.   68.____

69. He let them reach their own *conclusions*.   69.____

70. I must ask *you* to remain silent.   70.____

A. Preposition
B. Conjunction
C. Pronoun
D. Adverb
E. Adjective

71. *This* is a stupid answer. 71._____

72. He solved the mystery *without* the police. 72._____

73. She felt *secure* in his protection. 73._____

74. He believed in the *scientific* method. 74._____

75. Do not destroy their *traditional* beliefs. 75._____

76. They chartered the bus, *but* they did not go. 76._____

77. The young men are *quiet* with fear. 77._____

78. She talked *cheerfully* to the visitors. 78._____

79. The candidate was *certain* of victory. 79._____

80. I hope you will take *that* with you. 80._____

Questions 81-100.

DIRECTIONS: Indicate the use of each italicized word in the following sentences by choosing the letter of the CORRECT usage from the key above each set of questions.

A. Subject of Verb
B. Predicate Nominative or Subjective Complement
C. Predicate Adjective
D. Direct Object of Verb
E. Indirect Object of Verb

81. They made *him* president of the club. 81._____

82. There was nothing *odd* about the situation. 82._____

83. Give them *time* enough for thought. 83._____

84. He supervised the *work* himself. 84._____

85. Will you do *me* a favor? 85._____

86. The salad dressing tasted *good*. 86._____

87. In the crash, the *body* was thrown forward.   87.____

88. On a bench in the park was a single *man*.   88.____

89. There were two *men* who carried the trunk.   89.____

90. I am older than *you*.   90.____

      A. Object of Preposition
      B. Subject of Infinitive
      C. Direct Object of Verb
      D. Indirect Object of Verb
      E. Predicate Nominative or Subjective Complement

91. Let *them* suffer the consequences.   91.____

92. Offer *them* the key to the apartment.   92.____

93. He heard the *bell* ring.   93.____

94. Let *us* try another solution.   94.____

95. No one except *John* had volunteered.   95.____

96. Show *us* one example of your style.   96.____

97. Will you send *her* the flowers?   97.____

98. I want *you* to take her home.   98.____

99. He told his *father* that he would obey.   99.____

100. Do not write on the second *page*.   100.____

Questions 101-115.

DIRECTIONS: Indicate the kind of verbal italicized in the following sentences by choosing the appropriate letter from the key below.

      A. Gerund
      B. Participle
      C. Infinitive

101. The manuscript, *corrected* and typed, was on the desk.   101.____

102. He heard the bullet *ricochet*.   102.____

103. *Finding* the answer is a difficult task.   103.____

104. The animal, *hidden* from view, was trembling.   104.____

105. *Pretending* to be asleep, he listened attentively.   105.____

106. The professor, a *qualified* lecturer, entered the room.   106.____

107. They enjoyed *camping* at the lake.   107.____

108. Let them *come* to me.   108.____

109. He was annoyed by the *buzzing* sound.   109.____

110. It was a *stimulating* performance.   110.____

111. He had an accident while *returning* to the city.   111.____

112. *Encouraged* to study, the class opened the books.   112.____

113. He heard the gun *explode*.   113.____

114. They called him the *forgotten* man.   114.____

115. *Realizing* his mistake, he apologized.   115.____

Questions 116-130.

DIRECTIONS: Indicate the CORRECT punctuation for the following sentences by choosing the letter of the correct punctuation from the key below where brackets appear.

      A.   Comma
      B.   Semicolon
      C.   Colon
      D.   Dash
      E.   No punctuation

116. He explained [ ] that he could not attend.   116.____

117. The executive [ ] prepared for the interview and entered the room.   117.____

118. She admitted [ ] that the suggestion was wrong.   118.____

119. He did not object [ ] to dealing with him.   119.____

120. The chairman disagreed [ ] the members did not.   120.____

121. You must report to duty on November 10 [ ] 2022.   121.____

122. The father [ ] and two sons went fishing.   122.____

123. Act on the following problems [ ] administration, supervision, and policy. 123.____

124. This is excellent [ ] it has insight. 124.____

125. "I will take the car [ ]" he said. 125.____

126. I will do it [ ] however, you must help me. 126.____

127. When the show ended [ ] he returned home. 127.____

128. Stop [ ] making all of that noise. 128.____

129. Be firm [ ] exercise your authority. 129.____

130. The first example is poor [ ] the second is good. 130.____

Questions 131-150.

DIRECTIONS: Place a *C* in the space at the right if the sentence is correctly punctuated and a *W* in the space at the right if the sentence is incorrectly punctuated.

131. Its later than you think. 131.____

132. While I was eating the toast burned. 132.____

133. The fire started at ten o'clock in the morning. 133.____

134. She asked, "Did you say, 'I will go?" 134.____

135. Richards handling of the question warranted praise. 135.____

136. July 4 is a holiday. 136.____

137. Oh perhaps you are right. 137.____

138. Will you answer the door, John? 138.____

139. While he was bathing the dog came in. 139.____

140. He was a calm gentle person. 140.____

141. He wore a new bow tie. 141.____

142. The shout "Block that kick" echoed upon the field. 142.____

143. Ladies and gentlemen take your seats. 143.____

144. However you must do your work. 144.____

10 (#1)

145. My brothers are: John, Bill, and Charles. 145.____

146. While I was painting the neighbor opened the door. 146.____

147. One should fight for honor: not fame. 147.____

148. "Will you sing" he asked? 148.____

149. He played tennis, and then bowled. 149.____

150. On Monday April 5, we leave for Europe. 150.____

KEY (CORRECT ANSWERS)

1. D	31. 4	61. D	91. C	121. A
2. A	32. 1	62. A	92. D	122. E
3. C	33. 4	63. B	93. C	123. C
4. E	34. 5	64. A	94. C	124. D
5. B	35. 5	65. D	95. A	125. A
6. D	36. 2	66. D	96. C	126. B
7. A	37. 3	67. D	97. C	127. A
8. E	38. 5	68. B	98. C	128. E
9. C	39. 2	69. A	99. C	129. B
10. A	40. 3	70. B	100. A	130. B
11. C	41. C	71. C	101. B	131. W
12. D	42. C	72. A	102. B	132. W
13. B	43. B	73. D	103. A	133. C
14. D	44. B	74. E	104. B	134. W
15. B	45. D	75. E	105. A	135. W
16. A	46. A	76. B	106. B	136. C
17. D	47. C	77. E	107. A	137. W
18. A	48. D	78. D	108. C	138. C
19. B	49. C	79. E	109. B	139. W
20. C	50. A	80. C	110. B	140. W
21. A	51. A	81. D	111. A	141. C
22. D	52. A	82. C	112. B	142. W
23. D	53. E	83. D	113. C	143. W
24. C	54. A	84. D	114. B	144. W
25. A	55. C	85. E	115. A	145. W
26. 3	56. B	86. C	116. E	143. W
27. 1	57. E	87. A	117. E	147. W
28. 3	58. D	88. B	118. E	148. W
29. 5	59. A	89. A	119. E	149. W
30. 3	60. A	90. C	120. B	150. W

BASIC FUNDAMENTALS OF WRITTEN COMMUNICATION

CONTENTS	Page
INSTRUCTIONAL OBJECTIVES	1
CONTENT	1
Introduction	1
1. Business Writing	1
Letters	
Selet the letter type	
Select the Right Format	
Know the Letter Elements	
Be Breef	
Use Concrete Nouns	
Use Active Verbs	
Use a Natural Tone	
Forms	4
Memoranda	5
Minutes of meetings	5
Short Reports	6
News Releases	8
2. Reporting on a Topic	9
Preparation for the Report	9
What is the Purpose of the Report?	
What Questions Should it Answer?	
Where Can the Relevant information be obtained?	
The Text of the Report	10
What Are the Answers to the Questions?	
Organizing the Report	
The Writer's Responsibilities	11
Conclusions and Recommendations	11
3. Persuasive Writing	11
General Guidelines for Writing	11
Persuasively	
Know the Source Credibility	
Avoid Overemotional Appeal	
Consider the Other Man's Point of wiew	
Interpersonal Communications	12
Conditions of Persuading	
The Persuassion campain	
4. Instructional Writing	13
Advances Organizers	
Practice	
Errorless Learning	
Feedback	
STUDENT LEARNING ACTIVITIES	16
TEACHERS MANAGEMENT ACTIVTIES	17
EVALUATION QUESTIONS	19

BASIC FUNDAMENTALS OF WRITTEN COMMUNICATION

INSTRUCTIONAL OBJECTIVES
1. Ability to write legibly.
2. Ability to fill out forms and applications correctly.
3. Ability to take messages and notes accurately.
4. Ability to write letters effectively.
5. Ability to write directions and instructions clearly.
6. Ability to outline written and spoken information.
7. Ability to persuade or teach others through written communication.
8. Ability to write effective overviews and summaries.
9. Ability to make smooth transitions within written communications.
10. Ability to use language forms appropriate for the reader.
11. Ability to prepare effective informational reports.

CONTENT

INTRODUCTION

Public-service employees are required to prepare written communications for a variety of purposes. Written communication is a fundamental tool, not only for the public-service occupations, but throughout the world of work. Many public-service occupations require written communication with ordinary citizens of diverse backgrounds, so the trainee should develop the ability to write in simple, nontechnical language that the ordinary citizen will understand.

This unit is designed to develop the student's ability to communicate effectively in writing for a number of different purposes and in a number of different formats. Whatever the particular purpose or format, how-- ever, effective writing will require the writer:

- to have a clear idea of his purpose and his audience;
- to organize his thoughts and information in an orderly way;
- to express himself concisely, accurately, and concretely;
- to report relevant facts;
- to explain and summarize ideas clearly; and
- to evaluate the effectiveness of his communication.

1. ## BUSINESS WRITING
   Several forms of written communication tend to recur frequently in most public-service agencies, including:
   - letters
   - forms
   - memoranda
   - minutes of meetings
   - short reports
   - telegrams and cables
   - news releases
   - and many others

   The public-service employee should be familiar with the principles of writing in these forms, and should be able to apply them in preparing effective communications.

   ### Letters

   Every letter sent from a public-service agency should be considered an ambassador of goodwill. The impression it creates may mean the difference between favorable public attitudes or unfavorable ones. It may mean the difference between creating a friend or an enemy for the agency. Every public-service employee has a responsibility to serve the public effectively and to provide services in an efficient and courteous manner. The letters an agency sends out reflect its attitudes toward the public.

The impression a letter creates depends upon both its appearance and its tone. A letter which shows erasures and pen written corrections gives an impression that the sending agency is slovenly. Similarly, a rude or impersonal letter creates the impression that the agency is insensitive or unfeeling. In preparing letters, the employee should apply principles of style and tone which will serve to create the most favorable impression.

<u>Select the Letter Type</u>. The two most common types of business letters are letters of inquiry and letters of response - that is, "asking" letters and "answering" letters. Whichever type of letter the employee is asked to write, the following guidelines will simplify the task and help to achieve a style and tone which will create a favorable impression on the reader.

<u>Select the Right Format</u>. Several styles of letter format are in common use today, including:

- the indented format,
- the block format, and
- the semi-block format.

Modified forms of these are also in use in some offices. The student should become familiar with the formats preferred for usage in his office, and be able to use whichever form the employer requests.

<u>Know the Letter Elements</u>. Every letter includes certain basic elements, such as:

- the letterhead, which identifies the name and address of the sender.
- the date on which the letter was transmitted.
- the inside address, with the name, street, city, and state of the addressee.
- the salutation, greeting the addressee.
- the body, containing the message.
- the complimentary close, the "good-bye" of the business letter.
- the signature, handwritten by the sender.
- the typed signature, the typewritten name and title of the sender.

In addition, several other elements are occasionally found in business letters:

- the *attention line,* directing the letter to the attention of a particular individual or his representative.
- the *subject line,* informing the reader at a glance of the subject of the letter.

- the *enclosure notation,* noting items enclosed with the letter.
- the *copy notation,* listing other persons who receive copies of the letter.
- the *postscript,* an afterthought sometimes (but not normally) added following the last typed line of the letter.

Be <u>*Brief.*</u> Use only the words which help to say what is needed in a clear and straightforward manner. Do not repeat information already known to the reader, or contained elsewhere in the letter. Likewise, do not repeat information contained in the letter being answered. Rather than repeat the content of a previous letter, one can say something like, "Please refer to our letter dated March 5:"

An employee can shorten his letters by using single words that serve the same function as longer phrases. Many commonly used phrases can be replaced by single words. For example,

Phrase	Single word
in order to	to
in reference to in	about
the amount of	for, of
in a number of cases	some
in view of	because
with regard to	about, in

Similarly, avoid the use of adjectives and nouns that are formed from verbs. If the root verbs are used instead, the writing will be more concise and more vivid. For example,

Noun form	Verb form
We made an adjustment on our books	We adjusted our books
We are sorry we cannot make a replacement of	We are sorry we cannot replace
Please make a correction in our order	Please correct our order

Be on the lookout for unnecessary adjectives and adverbs which tend to clutter letters without adding information or improving style. Such unnecessary words tend to distract the reader and make it more difficult for him to grasp the main points. Observe how the superfluous words, italicized in the following example, obscure the meaning: "You may be *very much* disappointed to learn that the *excessively large* demand for our *highly popular recent* publication, 'Your Income Taxes,' has led to an *unexpected* shortage of this *attractive* publication and we *sadly* expect they will not be replenished until *quite* late this year."

Summarizing, then, a *good letter is simple and clear, with short, simple words, sentences, and paragraphs. Related parts* of *sentences and paragraphs are kept together and placed in an order which makes it easy for the reader to follow the main thoughts.*

Be Natural. Whenever possible, use a human touch. Use names and personal pronouns to let the reader know the letter was written by a person, not an institution. Instead of saying, "It is the policy of this agency to contact its clients once each year to confirm their status," try this: "Our policy, Mr. Jones, is to confirm your status once each year."

Use Concrete Nouns. Avoid using abstract words and generalizations. Use names of objects, places, and persons rather than abstractions.

Use Active verbs. The passive voice gives a motionless, weak tone to most writing. Instead of "The minutes were taken by Mrs. Smith," say, "Mrs. Smith took the minutes." Instead of "The plans were prepared by the banquet committee," say, "The banquet committee prepared the plans."

Use a Natural Tone. Many people tend to become hard, cold, and unnatural the moment they write a letter. *Communicating by letter should have the same natural tone of conversation used in everyday speech.* One way to achieve a natural and personal tone in the majority of letters is through the use of personal pronouns. Instead of saying, "Referring to your letter of March 5, reporting the non-receipt of goods ordered last February 15, please be advised that the goods were shipped as requested," say, "I am sorry to hear that you failed to receive the items you ordered last February 15. We shipped them the same day we received your letter."

Forms

In most businesses and public service agencies, repetitive work is simplified by the use of *forms*. Forms exist for nearly every purpose imaginable: for ordering supplies, preparing invoices, applying for jobs, applying for insurance, paying taxes, recording inventories, and so on. While the forms encountered in different agencies may differ widely, several principles should be applied in completing any form:

- *Legibility.* Entries on forms should be clear and legible. Print or type wherever possible. When space provided is insufficient, attach a supplementary sheet to the form.

- *Completeness.* Make an entry in every space provided on the form. If a particular space does not apply to the applicant, enter there the term "N/A" (for "not applicable"). The reader of the completed form will then know that the applicant did not simply overlook that space.

- *Conciseness.* Forms are intended to elicit a maximum amount of information in the least possible space. When completing a form, it is usually not necessary to write complete sentences. Provide the necessary information in the least possible words.

- *Accuracy.* Be sure the information provided on the form is accurate. If the entry is a number, such as a social security number or an address, double-check the correctness of the number. Be sure of the spelling of names, No one appreciates receiving a communication in which his name is misspelled.

Memoranda

The written communications passing between offices or departments are usually transmitted in a form known as *"interoffice memorandum."* The headings most often used on such "memos" are:

- TO: identifying the addressee,
- FROM: identifying the sender or the originating office,
- SUBJECT: identifying briefly the subject of the memo,
- DATE: identifying the date the memo was prepared.

Larger agencies may also use headings such as FILE or REFERENCE NO. to aid in filing and retrieving memoranda.

In writing a memo, many of the same rules for letter-writing may be applied. Both the appearance and tone of the memo should create a pleasing impression. The format should be neat and follow the standards set by the originating office. The tone should be friendly, courteous, and considerate. The language should be clear, concise, and complete.

Memos usually dispense with salutations, complimentary closings, and signatures of the writers. In most other respects, however, the memorandum will follow the rules of good letter-writing.

Minutes of Meetings

Most formal public-service organization conduct meetings from time to time at which group decisions are made about agency policies, procedures, and work assignments. The records of such meetings are called *minutes*.

Minutes should be written as clearly and simply as possible, summarizing only the essential facts and decisions made at the meeting. While some issue may have been discussed at great length, only the final decision or resolution made of it should be recorded in the minutes. Information of this sort is usually included:

- Time and place of the call to order,
- Presiding officer and secretary,
- Voting members present (with names, if a small organization),

- Approval and corrections of previous minutes,
- Urgent business,
- Old business,
- New business,
- Time of adjournment,
- Signature of recorder.

Minutes should be written in a factual and objective style. The opinions of the recorder should not be in evidence. Every item of business coming up before a meeting should be included in the minutes, together with its disposition. For example:

- "M/S/P (Moved, seconded, passed) that Mr. Thomas Jones take responsibility for rewriting the personnel procedures manual."
- "Discussion of the summer vacation schedule was tabled until the next meeting."
- "M/S/P, a resolution that no client of the agency should be kept waiting more than 20 minutes for an interview."

Note that considerable discussion may have surrounded each of the above items in the minutes, but that only the topic and its resolution are recorded.

Short Reports

The public-service employee often is called upon to prepare a short report gathering and interpreting information on a single topic. Reports of this kind are sometimes prepared so that all the relevant information may be assembled in one place to aid the organization in making certain decisions. Such reports may be read primarily by the staff of the organization or by others closely related to the decision-making process.

Reports may be prepared at other times for distribution to the public or to other agencies and institutions. These reports may serve the purpose of informing public opinion or persuading others on matters of public policy.

Whatever the purpose of the short report, its physical appearance and style of presentation should be designed to create a favorable impression on the reader. Even if the report is distributed only within the writer's own unit, an attractive, clear, thorough report will reflect the writer's dedication to his assignment and the pride he takes in his work.

Some guidelines which will assist the trainee in preparation of effective short reports include use of the following:

- A good quality paper;
- Wide and even margins, allowing binding room;

- An accepted standard style of typing;
- A title page;
- A table of contents (for more lengthy reports only);
- A graphic numbering or outlining system, if needed for clarity;
- Graphics and photos to clarify meaning when useful;
- Footnotes, used sparingly, and only when they contribute to the report;
- A bibliography of sources, using a standard citation style.

A discussion of the organization of content for informational reports follows later in this document.

News Releases

From time to time, the public-service employees may be called upon to prepare a news release for his agency. Whenever the activities of the agency are newsworthy or of interest to the public, the agency has an obligation to report such activities to the press. The most common means for such reporting is by using the press release. Most newspapers and broadcasting stations are initially informed of agencies' activities by news releases distributed by the agencies themselves. Thus, the news release is a basic tool for communicating with the public served by the agency.

The news release is written in news style, with these basic characteristics:

- Sentences are short and simple.

- Paragraphs are short (one or two sentences) and relate to a single item of information.

- Paragraphs are arranged in *inverted order* — the most important in information appears first.

- The first or *lead* paragraph summarizes the entire story. If the reader went no further, he would have the essential information.

- Subsequent paragraphs provide further details, the most important occurring first.

- Reported information is attributed to sources; that is, the source of the news is reported in the story.

- The expression of the writer's opinions is scrupulously avoided.

- The 5 W's (who, what, why, where, when) are included.

News releases should be typed double spaced on standard 8 1/2 x 11 paper, with generous margins and at least 2" of open space above the lead paragraph. Do not write headlines - that is the editor's job. At the top of the first page of the release include the name of the agency releasing the story and the name and phone number of the person to contact if more information is needed. If the release runs more than one page, end each page with the word "-more-" to indicate that more copy follows. End the release with the symbols "###" to indicate that the copy ends at that point.

Accuracy and physical appearance are essential characteristics of the news release. Typographical errors, or errors of fact, such as misspelled names, lead editors to doubt the reliability of the story. Great care should be taken to assure the accuracy and reliability of a news release.

2. REPORTING ON A TOPIC

At one time or another, most public-service employees will be asked to prepare a report on some topic. Usually the need for the report grows out of some policy decision contemplated by the agency for which full information must be considered. For example:

- Should the agency undertake some new project or service?
- Should working conditions be changed?
- Are new specialists needed on the staff?
- Or should a branch office be opened up?

Or any of a hundred other such decisions which the agency must make from time to time.

When called upon to prepare such a report, the employee should have a model to follow which will guide his collection of information and will help him to prepare an effective and useful report.

As with other forms of written communication, both the physical appearance and content of the report are important to create a favorable impression and to engender confidence. The physical appearance of such reports has been discussed earlier; additional suggestions for reports are given in Unit 3. Basic guidelines follow below for organizing and preparing the content.

Preparation for the Report

What is the Purpose of the Report? The preparer of the report should have clearly in mind why the report is needed:

- What is the decision being contemplated by the agency?
- To what use will the report be put?

Before beginning to prepare the report, the writer should discuss its purpose fully with the decision-making staff to articulate the purpose the report is intended to serve. If the employee is himself initiating the report, it would be well to discuss its purpose with colleagues to assure that its purpose is clear in his own mind.

What Questions Should the Report Answer? Once the purpose of the report is clear, the questions the report must answer may begin to become clear. For example, if the decision faced by the agency is whether or not to offer a new service, questions may be asked such as these:

- What persons would be served by the new service?

- What would the new service cost?
- What new staff would be needed?
- What new equipment and facilities would be needed?
- What alternative ways exist for offering the service?
- How might the new service be administered?

And so on. Unless the purpose of the report is clear, it is difficult to decide what specific questions need to be answered. Once the purpose is clear, these questions can be specified.

Where Can the Relevant Information be Obtained? Once the questions are clear in the writer's mind, he can identify the information he will need to answer them. Information may usually be obtained from two general sources:

- *Relevant documents.* Records, publications, and other reports are often useful in locating the information needed to answer particular questions. These may be in the files of the writer's own agency, in other agencies, or in libraries.

- *Personal contacts.* Persons in a position to know the needed information may be contacted in person, by phone, or by letter. Such contacts are especially important in obtaining firsthand accounts of previous experience.

The Text of the Report

What are the Answers to the Questions? Once the relevant information is in hand, the answers to the questions may be assembled.

- What does the information reveal? This activity amounts to summarizing the information obtained. It often helps to organize this summary around the specific questions asked by the report. For example, if the report asks in one part, "What are the costs of the new service likely to be?" one section of the report should summarize the information gathered to answer this question.

Organizing the Report. The organization of a report into main and subsections depends upon the nature of the report. Reports will differ widely in their organization and treatment. In general, however, the report should generally follow the pattern previously discussed. That is, reports which generally include the following subjects in order will be found to be clear in their intent and to communicate effectively:

- *Description of problem or purpose.* Example: "One problem facing our agency is whether or not we should extend our hours of operation to better serve the public. This report is intended to examine the problem and make recommendations."

- *Questions to be answered.* Example: "In examining this problem, answers were sought to the following questions: What persons would be served? What would it cost? What staff would be needed?"

- *Information sources.* Example: "To answer these questions, letters of complaint for the past three years were examined. Interviews with clients were conducted by phone and in person, phone interviews were conducted with the agency directors in Memphis, Philadelphia, and Chicago."

- *Summary of findings.* Example: "At least 25 percent of the agency's clients would be served better by evening or Saturday service. The costs of operating eight hours of extended service would be negligible, since the service could be provided by rescheduling work assignments. The present staff report they would be inconvenienced by evening and Saturday work assignments."

<u>The Writer's Responsibilities.</u> It is the writer's responsibility to address finally the original purpose of the report. Once the questions have been answered, an informed judgment can be made as to the decision facing the agency. It is at this stage that the writer attempts to draw conclusions from the information he has gathered and summarized. For example, if the original purpose of the report was to help make a decision about whether or not the agency should offer a new service, the writer should draw conclusions from the information and recommend either for or against the new service.

<u>Conclusions and Recommendations.</u> Example: "It appears that operating during extended hours would better serve a significant number of clients. The writer recommends that the agency offer this new service. The present staff should be given temporary assignments to cover the extended hours. As new staff are hired to replace separating persons, they should be hired specifically to cover the extended hours."

3. <u>PERSUASIVE WRITING</u>

Often in life, people are called upon to persuade individuals and groups to adopt ideas believed to be good, or attitudes favorable to ideas thought to be worthwhile or behavior believed to be beneficial. The public service employee may find he must persuade the staff of his own agency, his superiors, the clients of the agency, or the general public in his community.

Persuading others by means of written and other forms of communication is a difficult task and requires much practice. Some principles have emerged from the study of persuasion which may provide some guidelines for developing a model for persuasive writing.

General Guidelines for Writing Persuasively

Know the Credibility of the Source. People are more likely to be persuaded by a message they perceive originates from a trustworthy source. Their trust is enhanced if the source is seen as authoritative, or knowledgeable on the issue discussed in the message. Their trust is increased also if the source appears to have nothing to gain either way, has no vested interest in the final decision. Then, the assertions made in persuasive writing should be backed up by referencing trustworthy and disinterested information sources.

Avoid Overemotional Appeals. Appealing to the common emotions of man—love, hate, tear, sex, etc.—can have a favorable effect on the outcome of a persuasive message. But care should be taken because, if the appeal is too strong, it can lead to a reverse effect. For example, if an agency wanted to persuade the public to get chest X-rays, it would have much greater chance of success if it adopted a positive and helpful attitude rather than trying to frighten them into this action. For instance, appealing mildly to the sense of well-being which accompanies knowledge of one's own good health, instead of shocking the public by showing horror pictures of patients who died from lack of timely X-rays.

Consider the Other Man's Point of View. To persuade another to one's own point of view, should the writer include information and arguments contrary to his own position? Or should he argue only for his own side?

Generally, it depends on where most of the audience stand in the first place. If most of the audience already favor the position being advocated, then the writer will probably do better including only information favorable to his position. However, if the greater part of the audience are likely to oppose this position, then the writer would probably be better off including their arguments also. In this case, he may be helping his cause by rebutting the opposing arguments as he introduces them into the writing.

An example of this technique might occur in arguing for such an idea as a four-day, forty-hour workweek. Thus: "Many people feel that the ten-hour day is too long and that they would arrive home too late for their regular dinner hour. But think! If you have dinner a littler later each night, you'll have a three-day weekend every week. More days free to go fishing, or camping. More days with your wife and children." That is good persuasive writing!

Interpersonal Communications

The important role of interpersonal communication in persuading others—face-to-face and person-to-person communications—has been well documented. Mass mailings or printed messages will likely have less effect than personal letters and conversations between persons already known to each other. In any persuasion campaign the personal touch is very important.

An individual in persuading a large number of persons will likely be more effective if he can organize a letter-writing campaign of persuasive messages written by persons favorable to his position to their friends and acquaintances, than if his campaign is based upon sending out a mass mailing of a printed message.

Conditions for Persuading. In order for an audience of one or many to be persuaded in the manner desired, these conditions must be met:

- the audience must be *exposed* to the message,
- members of the audience must *perceive* the intent of the message,
- they must *remember* the message afterwards,
- each member must *decide* whether or not to adopt the ideas.

Each member of the audience will respond to a message differently. While every person may receive the message, not everyone will read it. Even among those who read it, not everyone will perceive it in the same way. Some will remember it longer than others. Not everyone will decide to adopt the ideas. These effects are called *selective exposure, selective perception, selective retention,* and *selective decision*.

The Persuasion Campaign. How can one counteract these selective effects in persuading others? One thing that is known is that *people tend to be influenced by persuasive messages which they are already predisposed to accept*. This means a person is more likely to persuade people a little than to persuade them a lot.

In planning a persuasion campaign, therefore, the messages should be tailored to the audiences. Success will be more likely if one starts with people who believe *almost* as the writer wants to persuade them to believe—people who are most likely to agree with the position advocated.

The writer also wants to use arguments based on values the particular audience already accepts. For example, in advocating a new teenage job program, he might argue with business men that the program will help business; with parents, that it will build character; with teachers, that it is educational; with taxpayers, that it will reduce future taxes; and so on.

The idea is to find some way to make sure that each member of the particular audiences reached can see an advantage for himself, and for the writer to then tailor the messages for those audiences.

4. INSTRUCTIONAL WRITING

Another task that the public-service employee may expect to face from time to time is the instruction of some other person in the performance of a task. This may sometimes involve preparing written instructions to other employees in the unit, or preparing a training manual for new employees.

It may sometimes involve preparing instructional manuals for clients of the unit, such as "How to Apply for a Real Estate License," "How to Bathe your Baby," or "How to Recognize the Symptoms of Heart Disease."

Whatever the purpose or the audience, certain principles of instruction may be applied which will help make more effective these instructional or training communications. These are: *advance organizers, practice, errorless learning,* and *feedback.*

Advance Organizers

At or near the beginning of an instructional communication, it helps the learner if he is provided with what can be called an "advance organizer." This element of the communication performs two functions:

- it provides a framework or "map" for the leader to organize the information he will encounter,
- it helps the learner perceive his purpose in learning the tasks which will follow.

The first paragraphs in this section, for example, serve together as an advance organizer. The trainee is informed that he may be called upon to perform these tasks in his job *(perceived purpose),* and that he will be instructed in advance organizers, practice, errorless learning, and feedback *(framework, or "map").*

Practice

The notion of *practice makes perfect* is a sound instructional principle. When trying to teach someone to perform a task by means of written communication, the writer should build in many opportunities for practicing the task, or parts of it. This built-in practice should be both appropriate and active:

- *Appropriate practice* is practice which is directly related to learning the tasks at hand.

- *Active practice* is practice in actually performing the task at hand or parts of it, rather than simply reading about the task, or thinking about it.

By inserting questions into the text of the communication, by giving practice quizzes, exercises, or field work, one can build into his instructional communication the kind of practice necessary for the reader to readily learn the task.

Errorless Learning

The practice given learners should be easy to do. That is, they should not be asked to practice a task if they are likely to make a lot of mistakes. When a mistake is practiced it is likely to recur again and again, like spelling "demons," which have been spelled wrong so often it's difficult to recall the way they should be spelled. Because it is better to practice a task right from the first, it is important that learners do not make errors in practice.

- One method for encouraging correct practice is to give the reader hints, or *prompts,* to help him practice correctly.

- Another method is to instruct him in a logical sequence a little bit at a time. Don't try to teach everything at once. Break the task down into small parts and teach each part of the task in order. Then give the learner practice in each part of the task before giving him practice in the whole thing.

- A third way of encouraging errorless learning is to build in practice and review throughout the communication. The learner may forget part of the task if the teacher doesn't review it with him from time to time.

Remember, people primarily learn from what they do, so build in to the instructional communication many opportunities for the learner to practice correctly all of the parts of the task required for learning, first separately and then all together.

Feedback

The reader, or learner, can't judge how well he is learning the task unless he is informed of it. In a classroom situation, the teacher usually confirms that the learner has been successful, or points out the errors he made, and provides additional instruction. An instructional communication can also help learners in the same way, by providing *feedback* to the learner.

Following practice, the writer should include in his instructional communication information which will let the reader know whether he performed the task correctly. In case he didn't, the writer should also include some further information which will help the reader perform it correctly next time. This feedback, then, performs two functions:

- it helps the learner confirm that his practice was done correctly, and

- it helps him correct his performance of the task in case he made any errors.

Feedback will be most helpful to the learner if it occurs immediately following practice. The learner should be brought to know of his success or his errors just as soon as possible after practice.

STUDENT LEARNING ACTIVITIES

- Write "asking" and "answering" letters, and answer a letter of complaint, using the format assigned by the teacher.

- Write memoranda to other "offices" in a fictitious organization. Plan a field trip using only memos to communicate with other students in the class.

- Take minutes of a small group meeting. Or attend a meeting of the school board and take minutes.

- Write a short report on a public service occupation of special interest to you.

- Write a 15-word telegram reserving a single room at a hotel and asking to be picked up at the airport.

- Write a news release announcing a new service offered to the public by your agency.

- Based upon hearing a reading or pretaping of a report, summarize the report in news style.

- View films on effective communication, for example, *Getting the Facts, Words that Don't Inform,* and *A Message to No One.*

- For a given problem or purpose, compile a list of specific questions you would need to answer to write a report on the topic.

- For a given list of questions, discuss and compile a list of information sources relevant to the questions.

- As a member of a group, consider the problem of "What field trip should the class take to help students learn how to write an effective news release?" What questions will you need to answer? Where will you obtain your information?

- As a member of a group, gather the information and prepare a short report based on it for presentation to the class.

- Write a report on a problem assigned by your teacher.

- Write a brief persuasive letter to a friend on a given topic. Assume he does not already agree with you. Apply principles of source credibility, emotional appeals, and one or both sides of the issue to persuade him.

- Plan a persuasive campaign to persuade a given segment of your community to take some given action.

- Write a short instructional communication on a verbal learning task assigned by your teacher.

- Write a short instructional communication on a learning task which involves the operation of equipment.

- Try your instructional communications with a fellow student to check for errors during practice.

TEACHER MANAGEMENT ACTIVITIES

- Have students practice letter writing. Assign letters of "asking" and "answering." Read them a letter of complaint and ask them to write an answering letter. Establish common rules of format and style for each assignment. Change the rules from time to time to give practice in several styles.

- Have small groups plan an event, such as a field trip, assigning the various tasks to one another using only memoranda. Evaluate the effectiveness of each group's memo writing by the speed and completeness of their planning.

- Have the class attend a public meeting. Assign each the task of taking the minutes. Evaluate the minutes for brevity and completeness.

- Encourage each student to prepare a short report on a public service occupation of special interest to himself.

- Give the students practice in writing 15-word telegrams.

- Have the students prepare a news release announcing some new service offered to the public, such as "Taxpayers can now obtain help from the Internal Revenue Service in completing their income tax forms as a result of a new service now being offered by the agency."

- Give the students practice in summarizing and writing leads by giving them the facts of a news event and asking them to write a one or two-sentence lead summarizing the significant facts of the event.

- Read a speech or a story. Have students write a summary and a report of the speech or story in news style.

- Show films on effective communication, for example, *Getting the Facts, Words that Don't Inform,* and *A Message to No One.*

- State a general problem and have each student prepare a list of the specific questions implied by the problem.

- State a list of specific questions and discuss with the class the sources of information which might bear upon each of the questions.

- Have small groups consider and write short reports jointly on the general problem, "What field trip should the class take to help students learn how to write an effective news release?" Have each group identify the specific questions to be answered, with sources for needed information.

- Have each student identify and prepare a short report on a general problem of interest.

- Assign students to work in groups of three or four to draft a letter to a friend to persuade him to make a contribution to establish a new city art museum.

- Assign the students to groups of five or six, each group to map out a persuasive campaign on a given topic. Some topics are "Give Blood," "Get Chest X-Ray," "Quit Smoking," "Don't Litter," "Inspect Your House Wiring," etc.

- Have each student identify a simple verbal learning task and prepare an instructional communication to teach that task to another student not familiar with the task.

- Have each student prepare an instructional manual designed to train someone to operate some simple piece of equipment, such as an adding machine, a slide projector, a tape recorder, or something of similar complexity.

- Have each student try his instructional communication out on another student, unfamiliar with the task. He should observe the activities and responses of the trial student to identify errors made in practice. He should revise the communication, adding practice, review, and prompts wherever needed to reduce errors in practice.

EVALUATION QUESTIONS

Written Communications

1. Which type of letter would be correct for a public service worker to send?   1.____

    A. A letter containing erasures
    B. A letter reflecting goodwill
    C. A rude letter
    D. An impersonal letter

2. Memos usually leave out: 2.____

    A. Complimentary closings
    B. The name of the sender
    C. The name of the addressee
    D. The date the memo was sent

3. A good business letter would not contain: 3.____

    A. Short, simple words, sentences, and paragraphs
    B. Information contained in the letter being answered
    C. Concrete nouns and active verbs
    D. Orderly placed paragraphs

4. In writing business letters it is important to: 4.____

    A. Use a conversational tone
    B. Use a hard, cold tone
    C. Use abstract words
    D. Use a passive tone

5. Messages between departments in an agency are usually sent by: 5.____

    A. Letter
    B. Memo
    C. Telegram
    D. Long reports

6. Repetitive work can be simplified by the use of: 6.____

    A. Memos
    B. Telegrams
    C. Forms
    D. Reports

7. In filling out forms and applications, it is important to be: 7.____

    A. Legible
    B. Complete
    C. Accurate
    D. All of the above

8. Memos should be: 8.___

    A. Clear
    B. Brief
    C. Complete
    D. All of the above

9. Minutes of meetings should not include: 9.___

    A. The opinions of the recorder
    B. The approval of previous minutes
    C. The corrections of previous minutes
    D. The voting members present

10. Reports are written by public service workers to: 10.___

    A. Assemble information in one place
    B. Aid the organization in making decisions
    C. Inform the public and other agencies
    D. All of the above

11. News releases should include: 11.___

    A. A lead paragraph summarizing the story
    B. Long paragraphs about many topics
    C. The writer's opinion
    D. All of the above

12. Readers of news releases and reports are influenced by the: 12.___

    A. Content of the material
    B. Accuracy of the material
    C. Physical appearance of the material
    D. All of the above

13. The contents of a report should include: 13.___

    A. A description of the problem
    B. The questions to be answered
    C. Unimportant information
    D. A summary of findings

14. People tend to be influenced easier if: 14.___

    A. They can see something in the position that would be advantageous to them
    B. They are almost ready to agree anyhow
    C. The appeal to the emotions is not overly strong
    D. All of the above

KEY (CORRECT ANSWERS)

1. B
2. A
3. B
4. A
5. B

6. C
7. D
8. D
9. A
10. D

11. A
12. D
13. C
14. D

ESSAY WRITING

THE WRITING PROCESS

Under ideal conditions, writing involves a series of steps:

1. Pre-writing activities which facilitate understanding the purpose and the audience for a particular piece of writing and which might include generating ideas through brainstorming, notes, reflection, research, or discussion;

2. Focusing the material generated in step one by framing a thesis (controlling idea) and a direction (organization);

3. Getting the first draft on paper, using standard grammar, correct mechanics, and accurate spelling;

4. Assessing the success of the first draft by yourself or in consultation with a reliable reader;

5. Revising the draft by clarifying the thesis, topic sentences, supporting detail, and word choice; and

6. Proofreading for mistakes in grammar and spelling.

Ideal conditions do not always exist in the real world. Often you have to write under pressure and produce a clear statement. This is the case in a test situation. You must streamline the writing process to compose an acceptable essay in approximately one hour. This section will help you to practice necessary strategies by describing how you might do the following:

1. Turn the directions into a purpose statement.
2. Brainstorm for material to put in the essay.
3. Group and focus your ideas.
4. Compose your essay with clear signals for the reader.
5. Proofread for word choice, grammar, and mechanics.

TURN DIRECTIONS INTO PURPOSE STATEMENTS

For each of the following sets of essays, the directions specify a topic, an audience, and some possible ways to develop the essay. You have some choice about how to develop the essay, but you must stick to the topic given and a style appropriate to the audience. The directions consist of four sentences which give

1. an indication of audience,
2. a description of audience,
3. suggestions for development, and
4. a restatement of the topic.

You can distinguish the sentences that suggest development because they contain words which give options rather than commands; for example, the sentences that give you commands about the topic will look like this:

In writing, tell the panel why you are considering teaching as a career.

On the other hand, sentences that suggest development will look like this:
The reasons may include...
You might want to consider...
The experiences could be...

Your first step, then, is to sort out the essential commands in the directions and convert them into a clear purpose statement such as *I will explain my reasons for choosing teaching as a career*. The purpose statement must cover all the essential parts of the assignment.

EXERCISE B

For each of the following sets of directions, underline the sentences that give you commands about the topic and write a purpose statement, using your own words if possible.

Prompt 1
A committee of teachers and administrators is reviewing your qualifications for a scholarship. In writing, tell the committee about a special activity you engage in, either in school or outside of school. It could be a job, an organization you belong to, a hobby or sport you participate in, or something you do with your family. Tell the committee what your special activity is and explain why this activity is important to you.

Prompt 2
A superintendent of schools has reviewed your application for a teaching position. Before holding a formal interview with you, the superintendent wants you to provide a writing sample that tells what motivated you to choose teaching as a profession. You might want to discuss a special learning experience you had or your interest in a chosen field or subject. Tell the superintendent what your motivation is and explain why your learning experience or your interest in a special field or subject is important to you.

Prompt 3
Your college advisor has just notified you that the college has instituted an open curriculum. As a result, you may choose any three courses or activities you wish to take next semester. You will be given equal course credit for academic subjects and activities such as sports, cultural

activities (music, theater, art), school newspaper or literary magazine activities, fraternities, sororities, community projects, or any other activity whose importance you can justify. In writing, indicate what three courses you would select and how each one would make you a better person.

Prompt 4
You have just been given the opportunity to write a letter of application to the Director of Admissions at the college of your choice. Imagine that cost is not a concern to you; you may choose a college that offers a traditional liberal arts curriculum or one that allows you to study only those courses that relate to your field of interest. In your essay, tell the Director of Admissions the type of college you are choosing and identify the reasons for your choice.

Prompt 5
A committee of teachers is reviewing your application for admission into the teacher education program of your choice. The committee has asked you to write an essay that describes a book that made the most lasting impression on you or from which you believe you learned some valuable lesson. The book may be on any subject, fiction or nonfiction, that is meaningful to you. The book need not be something you read for a course. Explain to the committee what your impression or lesson is and why it is important to you.

BRAINSTORM FOR MATERIAL TO PUT IN THE ESSAY

The directions on the subtest often contains suggestions for areas to explore. The sample directions which ask for an essay on your reasons for choosing a teaching career suggest that you consider *examples set by other people, benefits you expect from a teaching career, or the challenges you think teaching offers.* Remember that these suggestions are only suggestions. Before you respond to them, you should think about how you would accomplish the writing task if the suggestions had not been made. To be convincing, the material in your essay must come from your own experiences and knowledge. Brainstorming can help you accomplish this.

There are different ways to brainstorm. Some people prefer to write freely for 5-10 minutes. Others like to make lists or sketches. Others mull over ideas and ask themselves questions before jotting down a few key words. If you have a method that works for you, stick with it. If you don't, try one of the three approaches just mentioned.

EXERCISE C

1. Think about your reasons for wanting to teach and jot down a list of those reasons.

2. Compare your list with the suggestions given for considering teaching as a career: (examples, benefits, and challenges).

3. Which reasons fit the category of the rewards of teaching?

4. Which reasons could be labeled challenges of teaching?

5. Which reasons are related to examples set by other people?

6. What labels or categories do your other reasons fall under?

7. Are some of your reasons related to experiences that you have had as a learner or teacher (e.g., sports, scouting, 4-H, religious classes)?

8. Are some of your reasons related to your interest in a particular subject such as mathematics or art?

9. Are some of your reasons related to particular qualities you possess such as patience, enthusiasm, or tolerance?

LISTEN TO YOUR INNER VOICE

The purpose of brainstorming is to come up with enough detail or elaboration to satisfy the evaluation requirements. You should aim to produce enough material for an introduction and at least three additional paragraphs. Once you list a few initial ideas, the best way to generate more detail is to imagine a voice saying, *Tell me more about that.* Let's suppose that your initial list of reasons for wanting to teach looked like this.

- I like kids.
- Summers off.
- Make a contribution to society.
- Encouragement from teachers.

Responding to that imaginary voice saying, *Tell me more*, might help you elaborate the first reason as follows:

I like kids…
because they all have some undeveloped potential.
because their responses aren't always predictable.
because they get so excited when they learn something new.

Another way to elaborate on the first reason is through examples:

- The two boys I used to babysit.
- The girl I helped to get over her fear of water.
- The special education student who was my *little brother.*

Imagine the voice asking for more information until you believe you have enough for a satisfactory essay. Not every statement will give you as much room for development as others, but you can expand upon all of the statements. Each time you elaborate, your writing becomes more specific. Including specific detail makes your ideas concrete and your writing more convincing. Specific detail is one of the criteria for evaluating your essay.

EXERCISE D

1. Go back to the list of purpose statements that you developed in Exercise C, and brainstorm for material you might include in an essay.

2. Go back to your list of reasons for wanting to teach and elaborate as much as you can on each one.

GROUP AND FOCUS YOUR IDEAS

A good essay is unified by a controlling idea or thesis which dictates a pattern of organization. The thesis should be stated in one or two sentences. The words you choose to write the thesis statement should repeat or echo the directions for the essay. This strategy will ensure that you state the topic clearly. One way to write a thesis is to do one of the following:

1. Look at your purpose statement.
    Example 1: I must explain my reasons for choosing teaching as a career.
    Example 2: I must explain how a learning experience motivated me to go into teaching.

2. Look at the list of ideas you generated by brainstorming and try to sum up the ideas in a sentence or two:
    Sample Thesis 1: I have chosen teaching as a career because I enjoy young children, particularly those who have a learning disability. Teaching is a career that will enable me to make a contribution to society.
    Sample Thesis 2: The experience that I had as a *big brother* to a special education student helped me to realize that everyone has the potential to learn. This experience strengthened my interest in teaching as a career.

The thesis prepares the reader for what is to follow. It is a promise that you will discuss certain ideas and not others.

You will not always use all the material you generated during the brainstorming step. In the sample that we have been discussing, you might have decided not to use material related to summers off or the encouragement of teachers. However, if you decide that there is some material you want to include in the body of your essay material which is not indicated by the thesis, you need to revise the thesis. Suppose you decide to include the information about summers off and the encouragement of teachers, how could you revise the thesis? Here is one possibility:

Revised Thesis: There are many reasons why I have chosen teaching as a career. The pleasure of working with children, the opportunity to make a contribution to society, the encouragement of teachers, and time during the summer to continue my own education and interests are a few of them.

You should understand that it is not necessary or advisable to give every reason why you would like to teach. Be selective. Choose reasons on which you can elaborate and ones you feel strongly about. This will make a more convincing essay.

OUTLINING

There are different ways of grouping brainstorming ideas. The traditional format is the outline. Here is one example, based on the thesis we have been discussing.

Thesis: There are many reasons why I have chosen teaching as a career; some of them are the pleasure of working with children, the opportunity to make a contribution to society, the encouragement of teachers, and time during the summer to continue my own education and interests.

I. I enjoy working with children.
   A. All children have potential.
   B. Their responses are unpredictable.
   C. They are excited when they learn something.

II. I will make a contribution to society.
   A. Many jobs have questionable social value even if they have high salaries.
   B. Teachers can help children develop a good self-image and give them necessary skills.

III. Teachers have encouraged me.
   A. They say I can express myself clearly.
   B. They see that I am enthusiastic about learning.

IV. Summers will be time to continue my education and interests.
   A. Teachers must be lifelong learners.
   B. Intensity of teaching requires time for pursuing other interests.

CLUSTERING

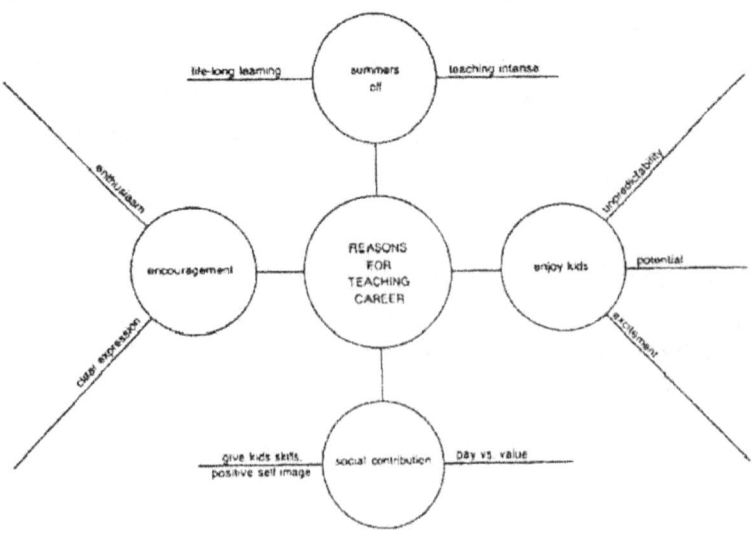

FLOW CHARTS

Still another way to map ideas is with the help of a flow chart. The main idea is placed in a box at the top, and other categories branch off below.

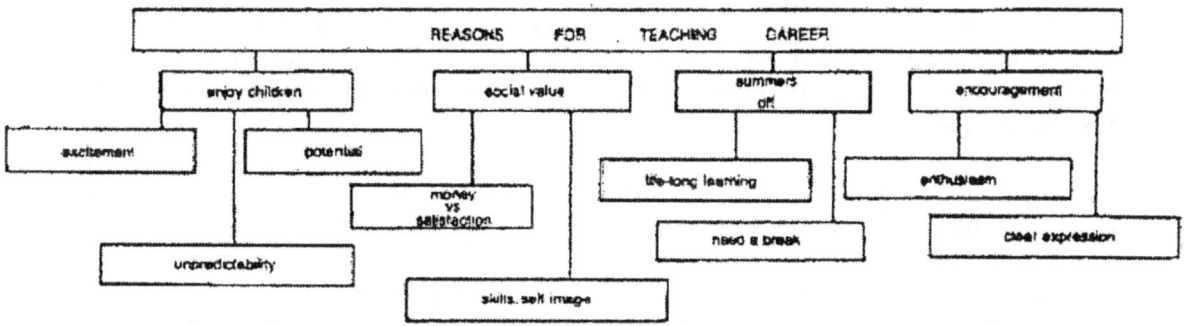

INFORMAL LISTS

An informal list is an easy way to group ideas.

My Reasons:

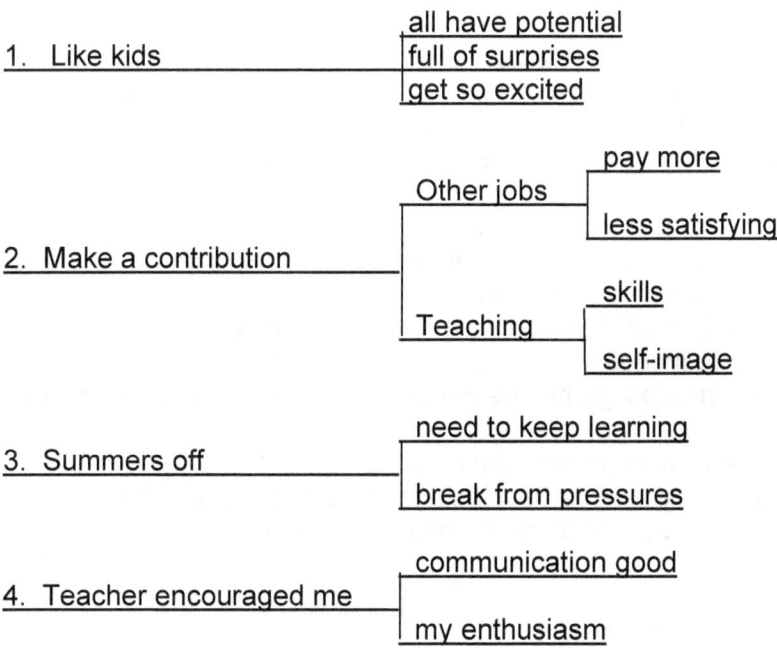

Regardless of which method you use to group your ideas, the goal is to pull together related bits of information and sketch the paragraph structure for your essay before you actually start writing your essay in the test booklet.

EXERCISE E

1. Go back to the material that you produced through brainstorming in Exercise D.2 and group the ideas by using one of the formulas illustrated.

2. Using one of the strategies mentioned previously, group the ideas given below in each set. For each set, read through the ideas in the set and identify or create a thesis statement; group related sentences; and find or create a sentence or phrase that will hold each group of sentences together.

    SET A.
    1. TV cartoons show characters recovering quickly from serious injury.
    2. Mr. Rogers never loses his temper.
    3. Ads associate happiness and good times with possession of a product.
    4. The ads show cereal boxes opening by themselves and dancing on the table.
    5. TV gives children a distorted sense of reality.
    6. Mr. Rogers always takes off his shoes when he comes inside.
    7. A character falls off a mountain top, shakes his head, and gets up.
    8. Positive role models, like Mr. Rogers, are unlike any real-life adult.
    9. Mr. Rogers never raises his voice.
    10. The ads are deceptive and manipulative.
    11. Characters who smash into walls are never badly hurt.

    SET B.
    1. I felt welcome when I went to see my math teacher during his office hours.
    2. The activity fair during orientation week had something to offer everyone.
    3. The counselors were helpful.
    4. Many teachers ask if students need help rather than wait for the students to get in trouble.
    5. The counselors helped with course selection.
    6. Resident advisors counsel students about adjustment problems.
    7. The counselors provided placement testing.
    8. Teachers talk to students after class rather than just rushing off.
    9. Students on campus are friendly.
    10. My experience at Winona College has been good, and I would recommend it to others.
    11. Teachers go over sample tests before you take the first test.
    12. The dorm council plans activities and projects to bring students together.
    13. The counselors offer minicourses on taking notes and tests.

    SET C.
    1. I don't belong to any organizations.
    2. I'm not involved in any special activities.
    3. I go to classes, work at the store, and see my friends on weekends.
    4. My job isn't special.
    5. I work at a supermarket.
    6. I need the job for spending money and college expenses.

7. I have learned some things from working.
8. It's not like school.
9. You have to be there to get paid.
10. The boss isn't always fair.
11. Sometimes she is impatient.
12. As a lowly clerk, you don't get any respect.
13. The boss seemed annoyed when I brought back the shopping carts.
14. There were long lines at the registers.
15. She told me to help bag groceries.
16. There's a pecking order in most companies.
17. My boss is under pressure from the manager.
18. I'm trying to stay on top of the situation rather than just reacting.
19. I ask the boss how things have been going.
20. I try to anticipate what she'll ask me to do and offer to do it first.
21. Sometimes I feel frustrated about being low on the totem pole.
22. The manager doesn't even know who I am.
23. There's not much incentive to do good work.
24. You can always be replaced by another minimum wage worker.

SET D.
1. DEATH OF A SALESMAN is a book that influenced me because of the connections between the play and my own life.
2. Each time I had a different reaction.
3. I read the play once in high school, again in college, and then saw it on TV.
4. In high school, Biff was a good-looking football hero.
5. The play is about a salesman named Willy, his wife, and two sons, Biff and Happy.
6. Happy was just an ordinary kid, living in his brother's shadow.
7. When Biff learned that his father was not perfect, he began to drift around.
8. I realized I was only hurting myself.
9. I had an older brother who was a star.
10. I was always trying to get my parents' attention.
11. I even tried to get their attention by doing poorly in school.
12. At first, I identified with Happy.
13. Biff had a big ego because of all the attention he received.
14. Biff became a bum because of all the attention he received as a teenager.
15. When I read the play in college, I sympathized with Willy.
16. He never received any respect from his boss.
17. I have been working at a supermarket.
18. Clerks are a dime a dozen, just like salespeople.
19. I want a career where a paycheck is not the only satisfaction you receive.
20. The TV version made me admire the mother.
21. She held the family together.
22. She was completely loyal to Willy.
23. We all want someone to stick by us like she did.

SET E.
1. Earning credit for my choice of courses and activities will give me a chance to integrate course work and real experience.
2. Reading Methods is a required course.
3. I'll learn how to assess a student's reading level.
4. I'll learn about various methods for teaching reading skills.
5. I plan to work as a literacy volunteer.
6. I want to know why people don't learn to read.
7. I'll learn about methods for teaching adults.
8. I'll learn how illiteracy affects a person's life.
9. I'll realize what's at stake if the education system fails.
10. I want to take either an advanced composition course or an independent study in composition.
11. I would like to keep a journal of my experience as a literacy volunteer.
12. I would like to write about the connections I see between the methods course and my tutoring experience.
13. I would like to write some feature stories about illiteracy for the college newspaper.

COMPOSE YOUR ESSAY WITH CLEAR SIGNALS FOR THE READER

Your essay is judged on how well the essay communicates a whole message. If you keep the reader in mind, your essay is likely to communicate more effectively. The most important signals to use are topic sentences to state the main idea of each paragraph and transitions to link sentences within the paragraphs. One basic pattern you might use in composing your paragraphs is the five paragraph essay. Here is one example of such an essay written in response to Prompt 1, Exercise B. Study the way in which the topic sentences give the reader a preview of what will be discussed.

Paragraph I. Lead and thesis statement.

Lead Some students may have time for sports, clubs, or volunteer organizations. Unfortunately, my schedule of classes and part-time work does not give me much time to devote to other activities. However, my job has been quite a learning experience.

Thesis <u>Although I am just a supermarket clerk, I have gained insight into the demands of a job, the behavior of supervisors, and my ability to influence a situation,</u>

Paragraph II Topic sentence developed with sufficient detail.

Topic Sentence <u>I realized that the demands of a job re not always like the demands of school.</u> Maybe that is something that other people know from the start, but it did not work that way for me. In fact, I can remember how the equation between work and pay dawned on me; if I missed an afternoon of work, I missed an equivalent amount of money in my paycheck. The connection between work and rewards is not quite so clear in school. A student can study hard for a test and do poorly. On the other hand, a student can sometimes bluff through a test and get a good grade.

Paragraph III.	Another topic sentence with supporting detail.
Topic Sentence	<u>I did not work for very long before I also realized that bosses can be difficult.</u> At first, my supervisor seemed like a nice enough person. However, I had a look at her other side one day when I returned to the store, pushing a long line of shopping carts which she had told me to gather from the parking lot. Lines had formed at all the registers, and she snapped at me to bag for one of the cashiers. It was as if it my fault that she had sent two of the cashiers out for supper just as it was getting busy in the store.
Paragraph IV.	Another topic sentence followed by detail.
Topic sentence	<u>After my initial anger at the boss's behavior, I decided to try to influence the situation rather than just reacting to it.</u> I realized this approach might work as I was bagging groceries. I saw the store manager peering down at my box from her office window. My boss had a boss who had a boss who had a boss. She was part of the pecking order just like me. Now I try to make small talk with her, ask how things have been going, and so forth. Also, I try to anticipate what she might ask me to do and then offer to do it first. This gives me the feeling that I can be an actor rather than just a puppet.
Paragraph V.	Conclusion with restatement of thesis.
Thesis Restated	Sometimes I still get frustrated at work. As a lowly clerk, I do not get much respect in a large, impersonal company. <u>However, my job has shown me that even the most ordinary parts of my life can give me an opportunity to learn something about myself and other people.</u>

Topic sentences do not always occur at the beginning of paragraphs. In fact, at times it seems stilted to put the topic sentence at the start of a paragraph. You may need a sentence or two that makes a bridge with the preceding paragraph. For example, the fourth paragraph in the sample essay above might have been written more chronologically, following the sequence of events more closely.

Example:	After my initial anger, I noticed the store manager peering down at my boss from the upstairs office window. I realized that my boss had a boss who had a boss;
Thesis Statement	She was just a part of the pecking order like me. <u>I decided to try to influence the situation instead of just reacting to it.</u>

Placing the topic sentence at the start of a paragraph gives the clearest signal to a reader, but it is not always essential to place the topic sentence at the beginning. It is important, however, to have a sentence that holds the rest of the paragraph together. It can come at the beginning, the middle, or the end of the paragraph. Here is a paragraph without a topic sentence:

Ms. Rodriquez always had a word of encouragement on each test she handed back. Furthermore, she taught me the difference between an intelligent mistake and a dumb one. An intelligent mistake occurs when a learner applies a rule or procedure to a special situation where it does not apply. For example, if a young child says, "I taked the book," she is applying the rule to use a "d" sound for a past action. Ms. Rodriguez also had a way of making math problems exciting mysteries. We watched her solve equations on the board like Sherlock Holmes in pursuit of a suspect. The work was never easy, but she always made us feel that it was possible to succeed if we put in enough time.

One way to phrase a topic sentence for the paragraph above would be:
Ms. Rodriguez was one of the best teachers I ever had.

Even if you think that the point of the paragraph is perfectly clear without a topic sentence, put one in. You are now writing this essay for a sophisticated magazine; you are taking a test to show that you can get an idea across clearly to a reader.

EXERCISE F.

1. Each paragraph below lacks a topic sentence. Create a topic sentence for each paragraph and decide where best to place it.

    a. I would be happy if I could make some difference in the lives of the students I will teach. It might just mean making them more curious about the world or more accepting of themselves. I realize that it is difficult to reach each student, but that does not mean that I will not try.
    b. Mr. Wright began every class by putting the homework on the board. Then he would announce what we were going to do that day. Usually, we went over the homework problems first. Students were asked to put their solutions on the board. After discussing them and making necessary corrections, Mr. Wright would turn to the new material. Using three or four pieces of colored chalk, he illustrated and commented on the examples in the book. Finally, if we finished all of the scheduled lesson, there was time at the end of class to start on the homework.
    c. Every teacher spends a minimum of 35 hours in school. In addition, teachers must often supervise activities such as the drama club or school newspaper. Conferences with parents, staff meetings, and required professional development activities also add to the total hours required. A teacher usually has three different course-related preparations, each of which may take an hour or more, depending on the teacher's experience. English teachers who have 25 to 30 students per class may assign a short piece of writing each week, and may spend 4 to 5 minutes reading each paper. This may add 13 hours of additional work per week.

2. Go back to the material that you brainstormed and organized in Exercise D. Pick at least one batch of material and turn it into an essay following the pattern of the five-paragraph essay described previously.

TRANSITIONS

Transitions are signals to your reader about how your ideas are connected. Certain words and phrases prepare the reader for what is to follow. Examples of important transitions to use in your essay are:

1. Words that indicate sequence of events or ideas: first, second (etc.), finally, last, ultimately, eventually, later, meanwhile, afterwards;

2. Words that indicate examples: for instance, for example, specifically, in particular;

3. Words that indicate addition of similar ideas: and, also, furthermore, moreover, similarly, equally important, another;

4. Words that indicate addition of contrasting ideas: however, but, on the other hand, on the contrary, still, yet, in contrast, nevertheless.

Transitions between sentences can also be achieved by repeating key words, using synonyms, or using pronouns.

1. Example of a repeated key word: *Literacy* is not just a matter of learning the ABC's, *Literacy* means having sufficient control of the language to function in one's society.

2. Example of use of a synonym: *Literacy* is not just a matter of learning the ABC's. One's ability to read and write must be equal to the demands of one's society.

3. Example use of a pronoun: *Literacy* is not just a matter of learning the ABC's. It means having sufficient control of the language to function in your society.

EXERCISE G.

1. Look at the paragraphs you wrote in Exercise F and underline all the transitions.

2. Go back to the essay you wrote in Exercise F. Underline any transitions you used. Find places where you might insert additional transitions.

PROOFREAD FOR WORD CHOICE, GRAMMAR, AND MECHANICS

Under ideal conditions, you would complete a first draft and then evaluate it for content and structure. However, a subtest, lasting approximately one hour, does not allow time for true revision. You may want to think of your brainstorming as a type of first draft and your focusing as a type of revision. As you focus and compose your essay, you will do a certain amount of revision, deciding to change the order of paragraphs, inserting or deleting details, trying out sentences in your head before you put them down on paper. Once you have completed the essay, you need to proofread to make sure you have used words correctly and avoid errors that will detract from your essay and subsequently from the score you receive for your essay.

WORD CHOICE

In choosing words to express your ideas, keep in mind that the directions on the examination writing subtest are likely to specify an audience that requires you to use a professional tone. You should avoid slang and cliches. On the other hand, don't go overboard and complicate your essay with fancy terms and inflated language. Aim for a clear and direct expression of your ideas.

Here are a few examples of the kinds of words and expressions to avoid:

1. One activity that I've really *gotten into* lately is sailing. (Substitute *became involved in, become interested in, become enthusiastic about*).

2. The person sitting behind me talked *a lot* during the class. (Try to be as specific as possible about what *a lot* means in the sentence where you are tempted to use it. Here, you might use *continuously* or *incessantly*, but at other times, you might want to substitute *a great deal* or *often*.)

3. My first class was *awful*. (General words such as *awful, perfect, beautiful*, etc. are acceptable if you are going to follow up with more specific description. However, it is almost always better to use specific language. In what respect was the experience or the person awful, perfect, or beautiful? In the example above, was the class dull, disorganized, too demanding?)

4. I was faced with a *number of alternatives*. (Strictly defined, an alternative is a choice between two things. If you mean more than two, use *options* or *choices*.)

5. Computers are a *new innovation* in the classroom. (Innovation means *new*; therefore, the phrase is redundant. The same would be true of expressions such as *personal friend* and *advance planning*.)

Our language is constantly changing. At any period in history, some words and expressions are considered suitable for formal writing while others are considered colloquial and appropriate only for informal settings. As you prepare for the writing subtest, you might want to use a dictionary or a glossary of usage in a handbook. These references will provide guidance in currently acceptable choices. You might also want to keep in mind that no references will be available during the test. Therefore, if you have any doubt about the appropriateness of a word or phrase, you might want to avoid using it, and choose words about which you feel more confident.

Excess words are as much a problem as inexact words. When people don't know what to write, they often try to pad the paragraphs with sentences that say the same thing in slightly different words or fill up the sentences with empty phrases. Superfluous words and sentences may bore, frustrate, or even confuse your reader. You will be spared these problems if you practice brainstorming for relevant and interesting details before you compose your essay. Here are some examples of padded writing:

Wordy: Education faces a crisis today. At the present time, a number of problems are troubling concerned citizens. Not a day goes by that you do not hear about one problem or another.

To the Point: Many problems in education call for our attention.

Wordy: Due to the fact that a problem arose concerning the time our committee should meet, we decided in the final analysis that it would be best to postpone our decision until the new chairperson took over.

To the Point: Unable to agree on a meeting time, our committee postponed the decision until the new chairperson took over.

EXERCISE H

1. Find places in your own writing where you could eliminate words without losing meaning.

2. Trim unnecessary words from the following sentences and rewrite.

   a. The aspects of teaching that I imagine I will most enjoy are the diversity of students and the freedom to organize my own classes.

   b. The problem that I foresee causing the most difficulty in the future is that a few years from now we are going to have even more non-native English speaking students than we do now and people don't understand the need for bilingual education.

   c. In conclusion, the final point that I want to make is to say that the productivity of our economic system will decline unless we do something to tackle the problem of illiteracy among the many people who can't read at all or who can barely read.

EXERCISE I

There are a number of commonly confused words. Use a dictionary or handbook to check the correct choice for each of the sentences that follow.

1. I _____ your invitation to the party. (accept, except, expect)
2. I _____ to do well on my math exam. (accept, except, expect)
3. Everyone is going _____ Susan. (accept, except, expect)
4. I went to my guidance teacher for some good _____. (advise, advice)
5. I always _____ my students to take French literature. (advise, advice)
6. The _____ of the hurricane was horrendous. (affect, effect)
7. Does this test _____ my grade? (affect, effect)
8. _____ never too late to try. (Its, It's)
9. The committee reported _____ decision. (its, it's)
10. Please place the books over _____. (there, they're, their)
11. _____ my brother's friends. (There, They're, Their)
12. The boys have lost _____ shoes. (there, they're, their)

13. Most of the students could not choose _____ the four answers. (between, among)
14. Mary is trying to decide _____ two majors: History and French. (between, among)
15. John arrived at the game, _____. (to, too, two)
16. Please place _____ books on this corner. (to, two, too)
17. David gave the ball _____ Mark. (to, two, too)
18. Peter ran the mile _____. (bad, badly)
19. I feel _____ when it rains. (bad, badly)
20. Teachers often have to _____ packaged materials to the special needs of their students. (adopt, adapt)
21. Our school would like to _____ a dress code for all students. (adopt, adapt)
22. This corner will be the _____ for the reading materials. (site, cite)
23. Students must learn how to _____ source materials in a research paper. (site, cite)
24. Individualized activities are needed to _____ group activities. (compliment, complement)
25. Teachers should _____ children often on the work that they successfully complete. (compliment, complement)

GRAMMAR AND MECHANICS

An occasional error in grammar or mechanics in an essay written without access to a dictionary will not result in failing the writing portion of the exam. However, frequent errors will detract from the effectiveness of your message and can cause failure. There are so many possible errors, that they cannot be covered in this brief guide. A discussion of the most serious errors will be followed by a set of sentences you can use to test your proofreading skills.

1. <u>Sentence Boundaries</u>: Running two or more independent clauses together without linking words or proper punctuation violates basic rules. A grammatically incomplete sentence is equally distracting.

    a. Run-on, fused sentence, or comma splice: Teaching is not an easy field, the rewards aren't always there. (A comma is not sufficient to separate two independent clauses. Substitute a period, a semi-colon, or a linking word, such as *because* for the comma.)

    b. Fragment: The best example being the difference between the way we see a character on TV and the way we visualize a character in a story. (The *ing* form of the verb creates a fragment. Substitute *is* for *being* to correct the sentence.)

2. <u>Agreement of Sentence Elements</u>: Verbs must agree with their subjects; pronouns with the nouns to which they refer. Similar elements must have parallel structure. Parts of the sentence must fit together grammatically.

    a. Lack of subject-verb agreement: The problems that young readers have seems to come partly from the environment. (*problems* calls for the verb form *seem* not *seems*. In sentences where several words come between subject and verb, it is easy to lose track of the elements.)

b. Lack of pronoun agreement: Everyone wants to achieve their potential. (*Everyone* is singular and calls for *his/her*, not *their*.)

c. Lack of parallel structure: I learned to operate the computer, write some simple programs, and the fundamentals of word processing. (*Operate* and *write* set up a pattern which calls for a similar word. Therefore, the last part of the sentence should be rephrased to include a verb; for example, *...and use the fundamentals of word processing.*)

d. Lack of grammatical fit: While taking an elective course in design my freshman year sparked my interest in art. (The introductory phrase, *While taking an elective course*, calls for a subject to come before the verb. This sentence could be revised in at least two ways:
While taking an elective course in design my freshman year, I became interested in art.
Taking an elective course in design my freshman year sparked my interest in art.

SELECTED CAPITALIZATION RULES

A few of the rules governing capitalization are reviewed below. Consult a dictionary or handbook for more complete coverage of this topic.

1. Capitalize proper nouns and adjectives.
   Example: Capitalize: *Judy Blume* and *Southington High School*.
   Do not capitalize *the author* or *my high school*.

2. Capitalize titles when they precede proper names, but not when they follow proper names or are used alone.
   Example: Professor Kent Curtis
   Kent Curtis, professor of history
   the history professor

3. Do not capitalize the names of academic years or terms.
   Example: spring semester
   my sophomore year

4. Capitalize the names of specific courses, but not fields of study unless they are languages.
   Example: Capitalize *English, Spanish,* and *Math 101*
   Do not capitalize *math, physics,* or *education*.

5. Capitalize the important words in titles of books and underline the titles.
   Example: <u>Catcher in the Rye</u>
   <u>Grapes of Wrath</u>

PUNCTUATION

Punctuation is another area that you should review with the help of a good handbook or dictionary. One simple rule to remember is: Do not use the dash as a substitute for the proper punctuation. Example of a punctuation error: Although I took up swimming—the doctors said it would be good exercise—but I found that I did not have the ability to make the team

(The problem with relying on dashes is that, as in the example, dependence can lead to sloppy sentence construction. The sentence above should be revised: I took up swimming because the doctors said it would be good exercise, but I found that I did not have the ability to make the team.)

EXERCISE J

1. Proofread the following essay to identify errors in grammar, mechanics, and word use. Underline or cross out all errors.

2. Rewrite the essay, using correct grammar, mechanics, and wording.

The extent of illiteracy in the Country is documented in Illiterate America—a book by Jonathan Kozol. When I read this book and realized the extent of illiteracy gave me a shock. Kozol claims that 25 million people can not red warning labels or a simple news story, another 35 million do not read well enough to survive in the Modern Age—Like being able to follow printed instructions. For someone who can't read and has to support himself or a family could be a real disadvantage.

The problem of illiteracy will be difficult to solve. There being many causes that go deep into our society. Schools have failed to halt the problem and may be contributing to it. My parents say that the problem with schools today are a lack of respect for authority. Years ago, everyone know what would happen if they disobeyed a teacher. Today, teachers must contend with students who are often bored, rarely prepared and frequently they defy the teacher. Some respect and discipline is needed to create a learning environment.

Another problem with the schools is poorly prepare teachers. Students graduating from college without being able to read or write well. During the 1960s was the decline of strict academic standards. Students failed to learn what they should of learned. The decline may be ending, new tests and requirements are in place. For example, the college of arts and sciences at Northeastern State University changed their requirements because entering students were so poorly prepared. Some of them unable to identify Sophocles or locate spain on a map.

Kozol's book interested me in the larger issues of literacy—it is more than learning the ABCs. Literacy is when you can read and write well enough to survive in a complex technology and making informed opinions about government policies. Teachers can help to create a literate America. After reading about the problems of illiteracy facing this country, I want to become one,

19

PUTTING IT ALL TOGETHER

PRACTICE TOPICS

You will not know in advance the topic on which you will be asked to write an essay for the examination. However, the topic is likely to involve your education, education in general, or your choice of a career.

The best way to prepare for the writing subtest is to practice the skills presented in this book and to write whole essays under conditions similar to those found in examinations. Below are several topics you may use for practice.

Practice Prompt 1

The Academic Standards Committee of your college is considering changes in the current grading system and they have asked you to write a statement about the impact of the letter grade system (ABCDF) on learning. You may want to consider how the letter grade system affects certain types of students, how it is viewed by students, teachers, or prospective employers, whether there is a practical alternative, or whether modifications should be made. Write a statement of your opinion of the letter grade system and the reasons for your opinion.

Practice Prompt 2

A screening committee is reviewing your application for a teaching position and has asked you to submit a statement of your strengths and weaknesses for the position. Imagine a specific teaching position for which you might apply and write a statement about how well you qualify for that particular job. You might want to consider how your educational background, work experiences, internships, or special interests make you a suitable candidate. You might also want to consider whether there is anything about the position, the type of students you might face, the location, or the responsibilities that might be a challenge to you. Describe the teaching position for which you are applying and explain why you would be a good candidate for the position.

Practice Prompt 3

The committee considering your application to enter a teacher training program wants to learn about your awareness of students' non-academic needs. They have pointed out that a teacher must often do more than teach subject matter. Consider the psychological, physical, social, and economic problems that affect a student's ability to learn. Describe your understanding of the ways in which the role of a teacher goes beyond teaching academic subjects.

Practice Prompt 4

Your college is hosting a conference for state high school teachers to address the problem of the inadequate preparation of the average student for college work. The conference is focusing on the average student because college teachers are concerned about the many students entering freshman courses who are unable to meet the demands of college. You might want to describe how serious the problem is, whose problem it is, and to what extent high schools should consider changing what they are doing. Use your experience, observations, and knowledge to write a statement which gives your perspective on the gap between the academic requirements in high school and those in college.

POST-TEST

Writing Subtest Directions

This part of the examination consists of one writing exercise. You should allow approximately 60 minutes to complete this assignment. You may NOT use a dictionary during the subtest. Make sure you have time to plan, write, review, and revise what you have written.

Before you begin to write, read the topic carefully and take some time to think about how you will organize what you plan to say. Your writing exercise will be evaluated on the basis of how effectively it communicates a whole message to the intended audience for the stated purpose. Your writing exercise will be judged on the success of its total impression by a panel of language arts experts. When evaluating your ability to communicate a whole message effectively, the scorers will also consider your ability to:

1. state and stay on the topic;
2. address all specified parts of the writing assignment;
3. present your ideas in an organized fashion;
4. include sufficient detail and elaboration to statements;
5. choose effective words;
6. employ correct grammar and usage; and
7. use correct mechanics (spelling, capitalization, paragraph form).

PROMPT

The screening committee considering your application for a teaching position is concerned about teacher stress and burn-out. They would like to learn about your awareness of this problem and your susceptibility to it. You might want to discuss how you have handled stressful situations in the past and any techniques that you use to cope with stress. Describe in writing how you would confront the problem of stress and burn-out in the teaching profession.

NOTES/OUTLINE

21

KEY (CORRECT ANSWERS)

In some cases where there is no one right answer, possible answers are given. If your answer is significantly different, discuss it with a teacher or tutor.

EXERCISE B

1. I must describe an activity and tell the committee why it is important to me.

2. I must explain to the superintendent why I want to teach and how an experience or subject helped me make this decision.

3. I have to select three courses or activities and justify why they would be worthwhile.

4. I have to write a letter to the director of admissions at the college of my choice and explain why I want to go there.

5. I have to describe to the committee a significant book and concentrate on what I got out of it.

EXERCISE C

Answers will vary.

EXERCISE D

Answers will vary.

EXERCISE E

1. Answers will vary.

2. A. An ideal wheel:

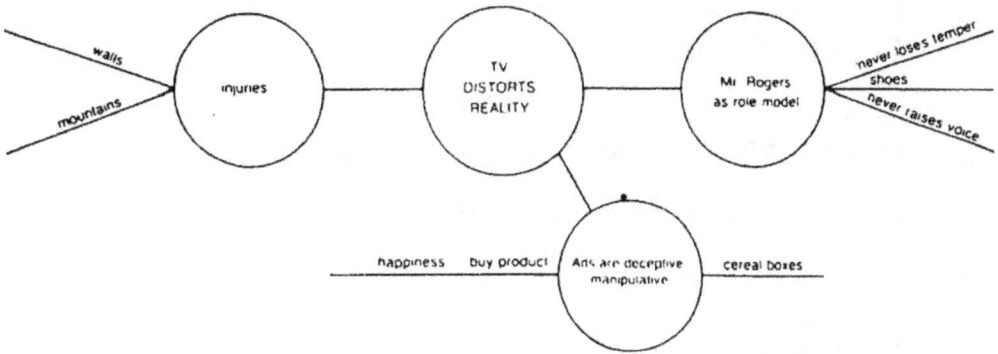

233

B. A flow chart:

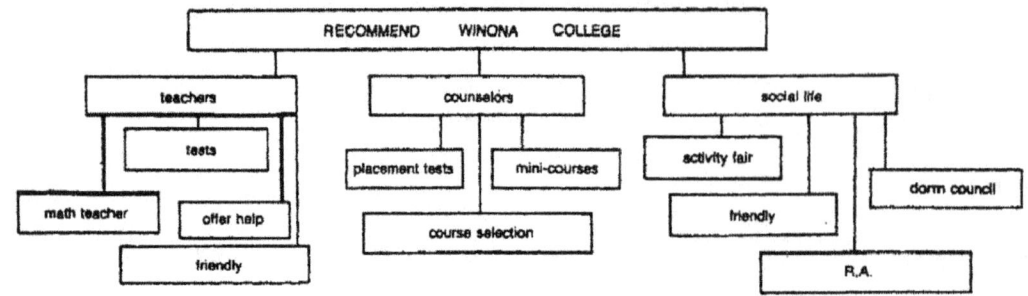

C. Using an outline:

Thesis: My job as a clerk has taught me about the reality of work and how to get along with supervisors.

    I.   I don't have time for special activities.
        A. School
        B. Need job
        C. Friends

    II.   Work is not like school because if you don't work, you don't get paid.

    III.   Boss is not always fair.
        A. No respect for clerks
        B. Gets impatient
        C. Got annoyed about lines

    IV.   I'm trying to get on top of the situation rather than just reacting.
        A. Boss is part of pecking order
        B. Make small talk
        C. Anticipate orders

    V.   I am still frustrated.
        A. No recognition
        B. No incentive
        C. Easily replaced

D. Using a list:
Death of a Salesman – connections between the play and my life

    1.   Different readings – different reactions

    2.   Describe characters
        Willy: salesman
        Linda: wife
        Biff: good looking, football hero breaks with Willy, drifts around
        Happy: ordinary, shadowed by Biff

3. Identified with Happy
      My older brother
      Wanted parents' attention
      School troubles
      Realized I was hurting myself
      Attention hurt Biff

   4. Sympathy for Willy
      No respect from boss
      My job as a clerk, dime a dozen
      Want more than a paycheck

   5. TV version – admiration for Linda
      Held family together
      Loyal to Willy
      Want someone like her

E. Another list:
   Choices: integrate courses and experiences

   1. Reading Methods Required – would choose it
      What I'll learn; assessment, skills

   2. Activity – literacy volunteer
      Why don't people learn
      How to teach skills
      Effect on a person's life
      Failure of system

   3. Course or individual study in writing
      Keep journal
      Make connections
      Write feature stories for newspaper

EXERCISE F

1. Answers will vary.

2. A. One benefit of teaching is personal satisfaction.
   B. Mr. McGrath ran a tightly structured class.
   C. Many teachers work harder than people realize.

EXERCISE G

1. Example: furthermore, for example, also, like, but
   A. but
   B. then, after, finally
   C. in addition, also, another

2. Answers will vary.

EXERCISE H

1. Answers will vary.

2. A. I will enjoy the diversity of students and the freedom to organize my own classes.

   B. The failure of people to understand the need to provide bilingual education to the increasing numbers of non-native English speaking students will be our biggest problem.

   C. Finally, failure to tackle the various forms of illiteracy will cause a decline in our economic productivity.

EXERCISE I

1. accept
2. expect
3. except
4. advice
5. advise
6. effect
7. affect
8. It's
9. its
10. there
11. they're
12. their
13. among
14. between
15. too
16. two
17. to
18. badly
19. bad
20. adapt
21. adopt
22. site
23. cite
24. complement
225. compliment

EXERCISE J

The extent of illiteracy in this country is documented in *Illiterate America*, a book by Jonathan Kozol. When I read this book and realized the extent of illiteracy, I was shocked. Kozol claims that 25 million people cannot read warning labels or a simple news story; because they are unable to another 35 million do not read well enough to survive in the Modern Age, being able to follow printed instructions. Someone who can't read and has to support himself or her or a family is at a real disadvantage.

The problem of illiteracy will be difficult to solve. Its causes go deep into our society. Schools have failed to halt the problem and may be contributing to it. My parents say that the problem with schools today is a lack of respect for authority. Years ago, students knew what would happen if they disobeyed a teacher. Today, teachers must contend with students who are often bored, rarely prepared, and frequently defiant of the teacher. Respect and discipline are needed to create a learning environment.

Another problem with the schools is poorly prepared teachers. Students graduating from college without being able to read or write well. During the 1960s strict academic standards declined. Students failed to learn what they should have learned. The decline may be ending because new tests and requirements are in place. For example, the College of Arts and Sciences at Northeastern State University changed its requirements because entering students were so poorly prepared. Some of them were unable to identify Sophocles or locate Spain on a map.

26

Kozol's book interested me in the larger issues of literacy. Literacy means more than learning the ABCs. It means reading and writing well enough to survive in a complex society, and making informed opinions about government policies. Teachers can help to create a literate America. After reading about the problems of illiteracy facing this country, I want to become a teacher.

BASIC FUNDAMENTALS OF INTERVIEWING

TABLE OF CONTENTS

	Page
INSTRUCTIONAL OBJECTIVES	1
CONTENT	1
INTRODUCTION	1
1. Before the Interview Starts	1
Reasons for Interviews	1
Completing Applications or Forms	2
2. Conducting Interviews	2
Starting the Interview	2
Importance of Understanding People	3
Guiding the Body of the Interview	3
Related Factors	3
Purpose of Interview	3
Closing the Interview	4
Remembering Key Points	4
Problems in Interviewing	4
3. After the Interview	6
Evaluating the Interview	6
Checking References	7
Obtaining Information from References	7
STUDENT LEARNING ACTIVITIES	8
TEACHER MANAGEMENT ACTIVITIES	8
EVALUATION QUESTIONS	9
Answer Key	11

BASIC FUNDAMENTALS OF INTERVIEWING

INSTRUCTIONAL OBJECTIVES

1. Ability of the public-service employee to work toward becoming a good interviewer or interviewee on his job and in his life
2. Ability to conduct referral or other interviews to obtain and verify information
3. Ability to observe interviewees skillfully
4. Ability to evaluate the effectiveness of an interview
5. Ability to cope with problems that come up during an interview
6. Ability to check an applicant's references

CONTENT

INTRODUCTION

This unit is designed to develop the student's ability to interview people, and to obtain and verify information. It will also give trainees practice in special-purpose interviews, such as making referrals, classifying prohibited behavior, protective intervention, employment, financial eligibility, etc.

Public-service workers will be required to give different kinds of interviews on various occasions. They may be required to interview other professional personnel in their major occupational group and to grant interviews to official personnel. They will certainly be interviewed at some time for such things as jobs, raises, credit ratings, and opening bank accounts. Certain public-service workers will also be required to interview clients, patients, pupils, families, etc.

For the majority of the students, the role of an interviewer will be a new one. In the past, some of them have been the unwilling, nervous, perhaps hostile recipients of interviews by welfare workers, police, and employers. Practice interviews, relative to their future jobs, can serve as a base for proficiency in interviewing skills.

Students should acquire necessary theory and skills to become aware of the various kinds of interviews and the people who conduct them. Various types of interviews include: employment, counseling, newspaper reporting and police interrogation. Interviews are performed by a wide variety of people: psychologists, social-service workers, lawyers, salesmen, policemen, tax inspectors, immigration officers, journalists, and many more.

1. BEFORE THE INTERVIEW STARTS

Reasons for Interviews: The kind of interview depends basically on its reason – some give advice, some seek information, some give information. Here are some of the major reasons for conducting an interview:
- To obtain information
- To evaluate a person's background
- To evaluate the interviewee's character and/or personality

- To provide information
- To maintain good public or employee relations

<u>Completing Applications or Forms:</u> Another major reason for conducting an interview is to help the public or coworkers in filling out applications or forms. In this kind of interview one needs to assist the interviewee in clarifying needed information or in filling in the form correctly. Since needed information can easily be omitted, the forms must be checked for completeness.

If a form is to be used for a later interview, the interviewer may want to prepare questions from the information furnished. Areas to look for in this case include:
- Identifying factors needing elaboration
- Identifying factors that will bring out more information
- Identifying factors that are not clear

In reviewing applications or forms, there are certain critical areas to watch for, such as an interviewee's work experience. The applicant's work experience should contain sufficient details in these areas:

- Amounts of time
- Types of work experience
- Financial levels of compensation

These three factors are usually given great weight in evaluating the applicant. Other important areas to watch include the applicant's financial ability, and his prior credit references. Age should be taken into account when checking credit references. A young man or woman, for example, should not be expected to have established an extensive credit rating.

2. CONDUCTING INTERVIEWS

An interview is essentially an interaction between people through words and acts. During this process, knowledge is acquired by both interviewer and interviewee.

It is important to note that the information sought should be purposeful and related to the reason for the interview. A license interviewer should not be primarily concerned with attempting to classify whether the interviewee's behavior requires intervention from the law enforcement agencies. Common sense should dictate that the kinds of questions asked should be determined by the "role" of the agency, and the immediate concerns of the person being interviewed.

<u>Starting the Interview</u>: One of the first tasks in the beginning of an interview is the establishment of rapport, or mutual liking or respect. After a friendly atmosphere has been created by putting the applicant at ease, the interviewer can ask the first question. If the interview has to do with a specific application, the interviewer should pick non-controversial matter from the form to discuss first. Use of these techniques is designed to get the applicant talking. An atmosphere should be created that will encourage the interviewee to discuss freely what is on his mind.

Importance of Understanding People: The interviewer should have a good knowledge of human behavior and interpersonal relationships. He should realize that people often behave in an inconsistent way. They may give themselves away in an interview by saying one thing orally, and by expressing the opposite meaning in body movements.

The interviewer should be able to observe applicants skillfully. The responsibility of utilizing all the senses to obtain and mentally verify information received during the interview occurs daily on the job. The successful social-service worker, for example, must master these techniques quickly in order to improve his effectiveness.

Guiding the Body of the Interview: Ask questions to get information. There are basically two kinds of questions: *directive* and *nondirective*.

The *directive question,* as its name implies, guides or directs the interviewee in a specific area. Directive questions can usually be answered with a few words, such as "yes" or "no." A typical directive question might be, "How long have you worked at the XYZ Company?"

Nondirective questions, on the other hand, give the interviewee a chance to say what is on his mind. Words such as *what, how,* and *why* are often used in nondirective questioning. A typical nondirective question might be, "Why did you leave the XYZ Company, Mr. Rean?"

A good technique to use to encourage the applicant to talk is to begin with a nondirective question. If the applicant does not respond appropriately to a nondirective question, then use a more directive question. An example of this technique could be:

Interviewer: *What did you dislike most about your last job?*
Interviewee: *Oh, not much.*
Interviewer: *Did you feel as though your supervisor treated you fairly?*
Interviewee: *My supervisor! That guy was definitely not fair – let me tell you...*

In the above simplified example one can see how the interviewer began with a general question about the job, and when he felt that the applicant didn't respond appropriately, he used a more specific directive question, which in this case triggered a response from the applicant. By alternating between directive and nondirective questions, an interviewer can skillfully guide the discussion and obtain the necessary information from the interviewee.

Related Factors: Factors that will affect the relationship in the interview can either help or hinder the process. These will strengthen the relationship: interest, demonstrated concern, attentiveness, willingness to listen, and questioning for fuller understanding of issues at hand. On the other hand, there are some factors which obstruct relationships, such as indifference, judgmental attitudes, insensitivity, being aloof, inactivity, or being late for appointments.

Purpose of Interview: If the purpose of the interview is to help the interviewee, the interviewer should be *supportive,* and exhibit a positive and active understanding of feelings which are given expression by his behavior. However, if the interview is designed to be an interrogation of a prisoner, the method of its conduct is determined by many factors: suspect, crime, time element, and location (field, home, or headquarters).

Techniques and methods of police interrogation have had to change in recent years, and the police must now be more aware of protecting each citizen's private rights. Each suspect should be advised of his rights before his statement will be considered admissible for evidence. Citizens must not be arbitrarily subjected to interrogation; the officer must have more than just a hunch, and must be able to substantiate his reason for an interrogation. However, if an officer has good reason to be suspicious, whatever the reasons may be, he has a duty to make the inquiry or interrogation.

As can be seen, the purpose of the interview can have a drastic effect on guiding the body of the interview.

Closing the Interview: In terminating the interview, the interviewee should be told when he can expect a decision or obtain the necessary information he needs. If possible, the interviewer should answer any final questions the applicant may have.

If the applicant has to be rejected, the interviewer should accomplish this diplomatically. Courtesy and tact are especially important at this point in the interview, if a good image of the interviewer's agency is to be projected to the public.

If the interview had definite time limits, it is a good idea to remind the applicant at the beginning of this fact, and once again a few minutes before the time is up, to give the interviewee a chance to conclude his discourse.

Remembering Key Points: An effective technique for the interviewer to use during the interview is to take notes. This will help him to remember the main points of the conversation. On some occasions, however, taking notes during the course of an interview can be distracting to the applicant, or can sometimes inhibit the interviewee's responsiveness. In such cases, the interviewer should write his notes immediately after the interview. The applicant will not then be distracted, and the interviewer can remember the key points of the discussion while they are still fresh in his mind.

Problems in Interviewing: A major difficulty in interviewing involves dealing with *ambivalence* (feelings of simultaneous attraction and repulsion) and sometimes, open conflict. The interviewer should become aware of these types of applicant behavior:

- The person asks for advice, but doesn't use it
- The person agrees to a plan, but doesn't carry it out
- The person says one thing, and does another

Does this ambivalence exist in only the interviewee, or does it also exist in the interviewer? In fact, the degree to which the interviewer understands himself and is aware of his own feelings has a direct effect on the conduct of the interview. Problem areas to explore include:

- *The feelings of the Interviewer* – Do they interfere in an interview? What forms of expression do they take? Is control of one's own feelings important? Why?
- *Over-involvement by the Interviewer* – Is this helpful or harmful? What kinds of behavior might result from a non-professional approach to interviewing?

Prejudice: If the interviewer is rigid and inflexible in his thinking, this could have a harmful impact on the interview. The goal of the interviewer should be to become aware of his personal biases, and honestly try to control them, so that the interview can be conducted in a fair and honest way.

Confidentiality: A public office is, in many ways, a public trust. As an interviewer, one should become familiar with the extent to which confidential information is shared by other people in his agency. The procedures for sharing confidential information should be known, and a clear definition should be given at each agency as to what constitutes confidential information. Whenever information of a confidential nature must be shared with others, it should be on a need-to-know basis, and its confidentiality should be carefully explained to the person receiving the information.

Dependence, Interdependence and Independence:

- How are the qualities of dependence, interdependence and independence manifested in the interview? To some extent, these characteristics exist in all people.
- Are these qualities good or bad, or does it depend upon the circumstances?

For example, a positive aspect of dependence is the ability to trust and form deep personal relationships. A negative aspect of being overly dependent is the resultant lack of self-reliance and initiative. People who are independent are usually self-confident; however, too much independence could be a problem in the interviewing process. Interdependence among individuals can be seen in marriages, working relationships, and in interviewing. Examples of group interdependences include:

- Between agencies
- Between agencies and the community, and
- Between local, state and federal governmental agencies

Undue Hurry When Questioning Applicants:

- Don't anticipate what the interviewee is going to say. It's easy to jump to conclusions; much harder to hold one's judgment.
- Another habit to avoid is putting words in the applicant's mouth.
- Don't let the applicant lead you astray in the interview.
- Get the interviewee back on the track by acknowledging his remark, and asking a directive question back on the main point of the discussion.

Controlling the Interview: The extent to which the interviewer feels a need to control the interview will, of course, be determined by the purpose of the interview. Much less control would be exerted on an interviewee in a social-service agency than in a law enforcement agency while interrogating a suspect.

Shy applicants should be encouraged to open up by asking them non-directive or open-ended questions. An overly talkative applicant can be controlled by asking more directive questions, and by watching for digressions during the discussion.

Common Weaknesses of Interviewers: Here are some of the more common faults of interviewers:

- *Talking too much* – especially in those interviews that are designed to get information from the interviewee.
- *Guiding applicant too much* – particularly in those interviews that are designed to allow the interviewee to express whatever is troubling him.
- *Dominating the interview* – it should be a process of give and take.
- *Talking down to the applicant* – this condescending attitude can usually be spotted pretty easily.
- *Failing to listen* – a common fault, however, inexcusable for an interviewer.

3. AFTER THE INTERVIEW

Evaluating the Interview

- What information was learned about the applicant?
- Was it sufficient?
- What was not learned that should have been?
- If problems came up in the interview, who made the decisions?
- What was the role of the interviewer and interviewee?

Some of the factors involved in decision-making are:

- Facts involved – how are they maintained?
- Availability of acceptable alternatives
- Readiness to take action

There are definite dangers to be aware of when making decisions or evaluating an interviewee. One such danger is irrational prejudice. Each of us is biased to a certain extent, either for or against certain ethnic, racial, or religious groups. The better the interviewer understands himself, and In particular the more he is aware of his personal beliefs towards certain individuals and groups, the better off he will be for having recognized them. He can then compensate for any prejudicial bias.

This bias could work in the opposite manner. For example, an interviewer could be so blinded by an applicant's good traits, that he would not see his faults because of this *halo effect*.

Checking References: A part of the process of many interviews involves the actual checking of personal references for these purposes:

- To verify information obtained from the application and interview
- To obtain an evaluation by people who know the interviewee's work history
- To obtain additional information not disclosed on the application or during the interview

Additional verifying information may be obtained from letters of reference supplied by the applicant. There are some disadvantages to letters of reference. They may be vague or even dishonest. Sometimes, such letters may not contain the information sought. Quite often, information supplied directly by the applicant's past employers is the best source to use. When evaluating replies, consider these factors:

- They may not be complete
- They may be vague to cover negative factors
- They may contain information taken from records which may not tell the complete story

Obtaining Information from References: Letter writing is a standard way of obtaining information about an individual. However since a letter may take too much time, or cost too much, it is recommended that the telephone should be used whenever possible. One reason for the telephone's effectiveness is that a direct contact with the reference is possible. This makes for better communication, since specific questions and follow-up answers can be obtained. In addition, doubts and omissions can be picked up from the person's voice.

Before making a telephone call to a reference, a checklist of questions should first be prepared. In talking to the reference, the following guidelines should be utilized.

- Establish rapport
- Be businesslike
- Let reference talk freely
- Don't put words in respondent's mouth
- Probe for strengths and weaknesses

A personal visit is sometimes advantageous, and can often be more effective in bringing out more information about the applicant. In such cases, arrange to meet the reference and use the same principles as in the telephone checks.

Finally, information may be obtained concerning references by the hiring of outside investigators. This method has the advantages of getting more personal and more objective information. There are, however certain disadvantages: the outside investigator may not obtain the best available information, and there may be considerable expense involved.

STUDENT LEARNING ACTIVITIES

- Participate in role-playing exercises after being given a brief introduction to the basic techniques of interviewing.
- Role-play in a wide variety of interviews, such as employment, welfare eligibility, and license application, and gain experience as both an interviewer and interviewee.
- Observe interviews during role-playing exercises, evaluating what the interviewee is communicating.
- Listen to examples of interviews on tape, and be prepared to discuss the techniques used to overcome problems that developed during the interview.
- Interview public-service workers in your community about their jobs to learn more about careers, and practice newly acquired interviewing skills.
- Write a short essay on how to conduct an interview. Include the start, guidance, conclusion, and evaluation of the results.
- Talk to public-service employees who do a great deal of interviewing in their jobs. Be prepared to discuss questions with them.
- Talk to your school guidance counselor or psychologist about interviewing skills.

TEACHER MANAGEMENT ACTIVITIES

- Plan on utilizing role-playing exercises to practice knowledge learned.
- Have students play both the interviewer and interviewee in various types of interviews, such as eligibility, employment, license interviews, etc.
- Prepare tapes of different types of interviews, and play them for the class to discuss and evaluate.
- Encourage students to use all their senses as interviewers to carefully observe what is being communicated by the interviewee.
- Encourage individual practice of interviewing skills whenever possible, such as with local public-service employees.
- Assign short essays on the process of interviewing: starting, guiding, concluding, and evaluating.
- Obtain specialized interviewing materials, such as public-safety techniques from neighboring police departments.
- Arrange to have public service workers come into the class to talk about interviewing techniques.
- Provide opportunities for the school guidance counselor or psychologist to discuss interviewing skills.
- Approach the theory of interviewing through practice situations whenever possible.
- Borrow interviewing films from the local library or educational resource center.

Evaluation Questions
Interviewing Skills

1. The purpose of an interview could be:
    A. To obtain information
    B. To give information
    C. To evaluate a person's background
    D. All of the above

    1._____

2. The first job of the interview is to:
    A. Get to the subject quickly
    B. Put the applicant at ease
    C. Tell the applicant about the boss
    D. Tell the applicant about the job that is open

    2._____

3. A skillful interview will:
    A. Watch the applicant's body language
    B. Listen to the applicant
    C. Ask questions to get information
    D. All of the above

    3._____

4. Questions that are specific and can be answered "yes" or "no" are:
    A. Directive
    B. Non-directive
    C. Indirective
    D. None of the above

    4._____

5. If the applicant cannot be hired, the interview should:
    A. Avoid telling the applicant
    B. Tell the applicant as bluntly as possible
    C. Tell the applicant tactfully
    D. Give the applicant another chance

    5._____

6. Taking notes during an interview can:
    A. Help the interviewer remember the main points
    B. Be distracting to the interviewee
    C. Make the interviewee reluctant to talk
    D. All of the above

    6._____

7. An interviewer with personal likes and dislikes should:
    A. Try to control them in order to be flexible
    B. Try to find people with the same likes and dislikes
    C. Try to get rid of all personal likes and dislikes
    D. None of the above

    7._____

8. The telephone is an effective way of finding information because   8._____
    A. Doubts can be picked up from a person's voice
    B. The person called can talk freely
    C. It doesn't take much time
    D. All of the above

9. Interviewers should: 9._____
    A. Reach conclusions about the applicant as soon as possible
    B. Keep applicants on track by asking directive questions
    C. Let applicants talk on any subject comfortable to them
    D. Help with words when the applicant is unable to think

10. Shy applicants may talk more if the interviewer: 10._____
    A. Looks bored
    B. Asks open-ended questions
    C. Asks directive questions
    D. Does most of the talking

11. Interviewers should: 11._____
    A. Talk down to the applicant
    B. Make sure they dominate the interview
    C. Listen as well as talk
    D. Guide the applicant's words

12. After interviews, interviewers should ask themselves: 12._____
    A. What was learned about the applicant?
    B. What was not learned?
    C. What problems came up and if they were solved?
    D. All of the above

13. Which one is not a reason for asking for personal references?   13._____
    A. To find out information about the applicant's family
    B. To find what people who know the applicant think of their work
    C. To find out if the information on the application is true
    D. To get more information

14. Letters of reference may be: 14._____
    A. Incomplete
    B. Vague
    C. Dishonest
    D. All of the above

15. Information told in confidence should: 15._____
    A. Not be kept from all office personnel
    B. Not be told to anyone
    C. Be told to those who need-to-know
    D. None of the above

KEY (CORRECT ANSWERS)

1. D	6. D	11. C
2. B	7. A	12. D
3. D	8. D	13. A
4. A	9. B	14. D
5. C	10. B	15. C

www.ingramcontent.com/pod-product-compliance
Lightning Source LLC
Chambersburg PA
CBHW082033300426
44117CB00015B/2460